ILLEGAL DRUGS AND GOVERNMENTAL POLICIES

ILLEGAL DRUGS AND GOVERNMENTAL POLICIES

LEE V. BARTON
EDITOR

Nova Science Publishers, Inc.

New York

NOTICE TO THE READER

The Publisher has taken reasonable care in the preparation of this book, but makes no expressed or implied warranty of any kind and assumes no responsibility for any errors or omissions. No liability is assumed for incidental or consequential damages in connection with or arising out of information contained in this book. The Publisher shall not be liable for any special, consequential, or exemplary damages resulting, in whole or in part, from the readers' use of, or reliance upon, this material.

Independent verification should be sought for any data, advice or recommendations contained in this book. In addition, no responsibility is assumed by the publisher for any injury and/or damage to persons or property arising from any methods, products, instructions, ideas or otherwise contained in this publication.

This publication is designed to provide accurate and authoritative information with regard to the subject matter cover herein. It is sold with the clear understanding that the Publisher is not engaged in rendering legal or any other professional services. If legal, medical or any other expert assistance is required, the services of a competent person should be sought. FROM A DECLARATION OF PARTICIPANTS JOINTLY ADOPTED BY A COMMITTEE OF THE AMERICAN BAR ASSOCIATION AND A COMMITTEE OF PUBLISHERS.

Library of Congress Cataloging-in-Publication Data

Illegal drugs and governmental policies / Lee V. Barton (editor).
    p. cm.
Includes index.
ISBN 13 978-1-60021-351-9
ISBN 10 1-60021-351-0
1. Drug traffic--Prevention--Government policy--United States. 2. Drug control--United States.
3. Transnational crime. I. Barton, Lee V.
HV8079.N3I47   2006
363.45--dc22   2006022749

Published by Nova Science Publishers, Inc. ✦*New York*

CONTENTS

Preface   vii

Chapter 1   Drug Trafficking and North Korea: Issues for U.S. Policy   1
                 Raphael F. Perl

Chapter 2   Drug Control: International Policy and Approaches   17
                 Raphael Perl

Chapter 3   Drug Crop Eradication and Alternative Development in the Andes   35
                 Connie Veillette and Carolina Navarrete-Frías

Chapter 4   Medical Marijuana: Review and Analysis of Federal and State   59
                 Policies
                 Mark Eddy

Chapter 5   Afghanistan: Narcotics and U.S. Policy   97
                 Christopher M. Blanchard

Chapter 6   Methamphetamine: Legislation and Issues in the 109th Congress   137
                 Celinda Franco

Index   143

PREFACE

This book deals with the rising epidemic of illegal drug use and its relation to governmental policies. Drug trafficking in the United States has become a significant problem, both within the country and from foreign sources. The development of international drug policies can prove difficult, as other countries exhibit different national policies, goals and concerns. Terrorist funding is yet another threat resulting from drug trafficking activity.

Chapter 1 - At least 50 documented incidents in more than 20 countries around the world, many involving arrest or detention of North Korean diplomats, link North Korea to drug trafficking. Such events, in the context of credible, but unproven, allegations of large scale state sponsorship of drug production and trafficking, raise important issues for the United States and its allies in combating international drug trafficking. The challenge to policy makers is how to pursue an effective counter drug policy and comply with U.S. law which may require cutting off aid to North Korea while pursuing other high-priority U.S. foreign policy objectives including (1) limiting possession and production of weapons of mass destruction; (2) limiting ballistic missile production and export; (3) curbing terrorism, counterfeiting, and international crime; and (4) addressing humanitarian needs.

Reports that the Democratic People's Republic of North Korea (DPRK) may be limiting some of its food crop production in favor of drug crop production are particularly disturbing given the country's chronic food shortages, though the acreage in question is comparatively small. Another issue of rising concern is the degree to which profits from any North Korean drug trafficking, counterfeiting, and other crime-for-profit enterprises may be used to underwrite the costs of maintaining or expanding North Korean nuclear and missile programs. As the DPRK's drug trade becomes increasingly entrenched, and arguably decentralized, analysts question whether the Pyongyang regime (or any subsequent government) would have the ability to restrain such activity, should it so desire. While recent seizures of North Korean-linked methamphetamine and heroin appear down, indications are that both the scope and scale of North Korean criminal activity may be expanding, with the income from such activity playing a pivotal role in overall DPRK finances.

Chapter 2 - Efforts to significantly reduce the flow of illicit drugs from abroad into the United States have so far not succeeded. Moreover, over the past decade, worldwide production of illicit drugs has risen dramatically: opium and marijuana production has roughly doubled and coca production tripled. Street prices of cocaine and heroin have fallen significantly in the past 20 years, reflecting increased availability. The effectiveness of international narcotics control programs in reducing consumption is a matter of ongoing concern. Despite apparent national political resolve to deal with the drug problem, inherent contradictions regularly appear between U.S. anti-drug policy and other national policy goals and concerns. Pursuit of drug control policies can sometimes affect foreign policy interests and bring political instability and economic dislocation to countries where narcotics production has become entrenched economically and socially. Drug supply interdiction programs and U.S. systems to facilitate the international movement of goods, people, and wealth are often at odds. U.S. international narcotics policy requires cooperative efforts by many nations which may have domestic and foreign policy goals that compete with the requirements of drug control. The mix of competing domestic and international pressures and priorities has produced an ongoing series of disputes within and between the legislative and executive branches concerning U.S. international drug policy. One contentious issue has been the Congressionally-mandated certification process, an instrument designed to induce specified drug-exporting countries to prioritize or pay more attention to the fight against narcotics businesses. Current law requires the President, with certain exceptions, to designate and withhold assistance from countries that have failed demonstrably to meet their counternarcotics obligations. P.L. 106-246, "Plan Colombia," a $1.3 billion military assistance-focused initiative to provide emergency supplemental narcotics assistance to Colombia, was signed into law July 13, 2000. Recently, U.S. policy toward Colombia has focused increasingly on containing the terror- ist threat to that country's security. The Bush Administration's FY2005 budget request continues a policy, begun in FY2002, to request authority for the State and Defense Departments to supply assistance to Colombia for counterterrorism purposes. For instance, U.S.-supplied helicopters and intelligence could be used to support military operations against guerrillas financed by drugs as well as against drug traffickers themselves. See CRS Report RL32337, *Andean Counterdrug Initia- tive (ACI) and Related Funding Programs: FY2005 Assistance.*

An issue likely to achieve increased attention in the 109th Congress is that of sky-rocketing opium poppy cultivation in Afghani- stan and whether to press for aerial crop eradi- cation against the wishes of the local Afghan leadership. See CRS Report RL32686, *Afghanistan: Narcotics and U.S. Policy.*

Drug control approaches addressed in this issue brief include:

— Expansion of efforts to reduce foreign production at the source.
— Expansion of interdiction and enforcement activities to disrupt supply lines.
— Expansion of efforts to reduce worldwide demand.
— Expansion of economic disincentives for international drug trafficking.

Chapter 3 - The United States has supported drug crop eradication and alternative development programs in the Andes for decades. Colombia, Bolivia, and Peru collectively produce nearly the entire global supply of cocaine. In addition, Colombia has become a producer of high quality heroin, most of it destined for the United States and Europe. The United States provides counternarcotics assistance through the Andean Counterdrug Initiative (ACI). The program supports a number of missions, including interdiction of drug trafficking, illicit crop eradication, alternative development, and rule of law and democracy promotion. From FY2000 through FY2005, the United States has provided a total of about $4.3 billion in ACI funds.

Since 2001, coca cultivation in the Andes has been reduced by 22%, with the largest decrease occurring in Colombia, according to the State Department. Opium poppy crops, grown mainly in Colombia and from which heroin is made, have been reduced by 67%. However, the region was still capable of producing 640 metric tons of cocaine, and 3.8 metric tons of heroin in 2004, according to the White House Office of National Drug Control Policy.

Congress has expressed a number of concerns with regard to eradication, especially the health and environmental effects of aerial spraying, its sustainability and social consequences, and the reliability of drug crop estimates. With regard to alternative development, Congress has expressed interest in its effectiveness, its relationship to eradication, and the long-term sustainability of programs once they are started.

Drug crops are eradicated either manually or by aerial spraying of a herbicide mixture, the main ingredient being glyphosate, used commercially in the United States under the brand name of Roundup®. Eradication can be conducted with the voluntary agreement of growers, or involuntarily. Peru and Bolivia do not allow aerial eradication, which has proven to be controversial. Critics believe it poses risks to the environment and the health of inhabitants living in sprayed regions. Proponents believe it is the most effective and safe means to defoliate large areas being used for drug crop cultivation, thereby removing a lucrative source of income from the illegally armed Colombian groups.

Providing alternatives to drug crops is believed to be crucial to achieve effective eradication. This often includes technical support for farmers, marketing assistance, and strengthening the transportation infrastructure in order to get crops to market. The U.S. approach to alternative development (AD) is to link it to eradication. Growers who agree to eradicate are eligible for assistance.

Chapter 4 - The issue before Congress is whether to continue to support the executive branch's prosecution of medical marijuana patients and their providers, in accordance with marijuana's status as a Schedule I drug under the Controlled Substances Act, or whether to relax federal marijuana prohibition enough to permit the medical use of botanical cannabis products by seriously ill persons, especially in states that have created medical marijuana programs under state law.

Bills have been introduced in recent Congresses to allow patients who appear to benefit from medical cannabis to use it in accordance with the various regulatory schemes that have been approved, since 1996, by the voters and legislatures of 11 states. In the current Congress, the States' Rights to Medical Marijuana Act (H.R. 2087, Frank) would move marijuana from Schedule I to Schedule II of the Controlled Substances Act and make it available under federal law for medical use in states with medical marijuana programs. The Steve McWilliams Truth in Trials Act (H.R. 4272, Farr) would make it possible for defendants in federal court to reveal to juries that their marijuana activity was medically related and legal under state law.

In June 2005, the House defeated, for the third time, the Hinchey-Rohrabacher amendment to prevent federal enforcement of the Controlled Substances Act against medical marijuana patients in states that have approved such use. The amendment is expected to be offered again in the 2nd session of the 109th Congress.

Eleven states, mostly in the West, have enacted laws allowing the use of marijuana for medical purposes, and many thousands of patients, having registered in their state programs, are seeking relief from a variety of serious illnesses by smoking marijuana or using other herbal cannabis preparations. Meanwhile, the federal Drug Enforcement Administration

(DEA) continues to investigate and arrest medical marijuana providers in those states as elsewhere.

Claims and counterclaims about medical marijuana — much debated by journalists and academics, policymakers at all levels of government, and interested citizens — include the following: Marijuana is harmful and has no medical value; marijuana effectively treats the symptoms of certain diseases; smoking is an improper route of drug administration; marijuana should be rescheduled to permit medical use; state medical marijuana laws send the wrong message and lead to increased illicit drug use; the medical marijuana movement undermines the war on drugs; patients should not be arrested for using medical marijuana; the federal government should allow the states to experiment and should not interfere with state medical marijuana programs; medical marijuana laws harm the drug approval process; the medical cannabis movement is a cynical ploy to legalize marijuana and other drugs. With strong opinions being expressed on all sides of these complex issues, the debate over medical marijuana does not appear to be approaching resolution.

Chapter 5 - Opium poppy cultivation and drug trafficking have become significant factors in Afghanistan's fragile political and economic order over the last 25 years. In 2005, Afghanistan remained the source of 87% of the world's illicit opium, in spite of ongoing efforts by the Afghan government, the United States, and their international partners to combat poppy cultivation and drug trafficking. U.N. officials estimate that in-country illicit profits from the 2005 opium poppy crop were equivalent in value to 50% of the country's legitimate GDP, sustaining fears that Afghanistan's economic recovery continues to be underwritten by drug profits.

Across Afghanistan, regional militia commanders, criminal organizations, and corrupt government officials have exploited opium production and drug trafficking as reliable sources of revenue and patronage, which has perpetuated the threat these groups pose to the country's fragile internal security and the legitimacy of its embryonic democratic government. The trafficking of Afghan drugs also appears to provide financial and logistical support to a range of extremist groups that continue to operate in and around Afghanistan, including remnants of the Taliban regime and some Al Qaeda operatives. Although coalition forces may be less frequently relying on figures involved with narcotics for intelligence and security support, many observers have warned that drug related corruption among appointed and newly elected Afghan officials may create new political obstacles to further progress.

The initial failure of U.S. and international counternarcotics efforts to disrupt the Afghan opium trade or sever its links to warlordism and corruption after the fall of the Taliban led some observers to warn that without redoubled multilateral action, Afghanistan would succumb to a state of lawlessness and reemerge as a sanctuary for terrorists. Following his election in late 2004, Afghan president Hamid Karzai identified counternarcotics as the top priority for his administration and since has stated his belief that "the fight against drugs is the fight for Afghanistan." In 2005, U.S. and Afghan officials implemented a new strategy to provide viable economic alternatives to poppy cultivation and to disrupt corruption and narco-terrorist linkages. According to a U.N. survey, these new initiatives contributed to a 21% decrease in the amount of opium poppy cultivation across Afghanistan in the 2004-2005 growing season. However, better weather and higher crop yields ensured that overall opium output remained nearly static at 4,100 metric tons. Survey results and official opinions suggest output may rise again in 2006.

In addition to describing the structure and development of the Afghan narcotics trade, this report provides current statistical information, profiles the trade's various participants, explores alleged narco-terrorist linkages, and reviews U.S. and international policy responses since late 2001. The report also considers current policy debates regarding the role of the U.S. military in counternarcotics operations,

Chapter 6 - Illicit methamphetamine (MA) production and use are longstanding and severe problems in some states. In recent years they have spread increasingly widely, emerging as an object of heightened federal concern. During the 109th Congress, over twenty-five bills have been introduced to address the MA problem. MA abuse has implications for public health, child welfare, crime and public safety, border security, and international relations. This report provides a brief overview of MA abuse, production, trafficking, and of the federal methamphetamine-specific programs, and legislation that is being actively considered by the 109th Congress.

In: Illegal Drugs and Governmental Policies
Editor: Lee V. Barton, pp. 1-15

ISBN 978-1-60021-351-9
© 2007 Nova Science Publishers, Inc.

Chapter 1

DRUG TRAFFICKING AND NORTH KOREA: ISSUES FOR U.S. POLICY[*]

Raphael F. Perl

SUMMARY

At least 50 documented incidents in more than 20 countries around the world, many involving arrest or detention of North Korean diplomats, link North Korea to drug trafficking. Such events, in the context of credible, but unproven, allegations of large scale state sponsorship of drug production and trafficking, raise important issues for the United States and its allies in combating international drug trafficking. The challenge to policy makers is how to pursue an effective counter drug policy and comply with U.S. law which may require cutting off aid to North Korea while pursuing other high-priority U.S. foreign policy objectives including (1) limiting possession and production of weapons of mass destruction; (2) limiting ballistic missile production and export; (3) curbing terrorism, counterfeiting, and international crime; and (4) addressing humanitarian needs.

Reports that the Democratic People's Republic of North Korea (DPRK) may be limiting some of its food crop production in favor of drug crop production are particularly disturbing given the country's chronic food shortages, though the acreage in question is comparatively small. Another issue of rising concern is the degree to which profits from any North Korean drug trafficking, counterfeiting, and other crime-for-profit enterprises may be used to underwrite the costs of maintaining or expanding North Korean nuclear and missile programs. As the DPRK's drug trade becomes increasingly entrenched, and arguably decentralized, analysts question whether the Pyongyang regime (or any subsequent government) would have the ability to restrain such activity, should it so desire. While recent seizures of North Korean-linked methamphetamine and heroin appear down, indications are that both the scope and scale of North Korean criminal activity may be expanding, with the income from such activity playing a pivotal role in overall DPRK finances.

---

[*] Excerpted from CRS Report RL32167, Updated March 4, 2005

BACKGROUND

Allegations of North Korean drug production, trafficking, and crime- for- profit activity have become the focus of rising attention in Congress, the press, and diplomatic and public policy fora. As early as October 28, 1997, Senators Charles Grassley and Jessie Helms sent a letter to Secretary of State, Madeleine Albright, questioning why North Korea was not included in the State Department's March 1, 1997, annual International Narcotics Control Strategy Report (INCSR) as a country involved in illicit drug production and trafficking. The Senators noted that according to press reports, North Korea's opium production in 1995 was 40 metric tons (mt) (roughly comparable to Mexico's) and that they believed that this figure "clearly represents a figure of over 1,000 hectares," the threshold cropland figure for inclusion in the report and designation as a major drug producing country.[1]

The Department of State's response of December 12, 1997, cited an inability to obtain data to substantiate North Korean production levels. Subsequently, in October 1998, the conferees for the Fiscal Year 1999 Omnibus Appropriations Act directed the President to include in the (March 1, 1999) INCSR "...information regarding the cultivation, production, and transhipment of opium by North Korea. The report shall be based upon all available information."[2] A Senate Bill (S. 5), Section 1209 of the Drug Free Century Act, introduced January 19, 1999, proposed a statement of congressional concern that the Department of State had "evaded its obligations with respect to North Korea" under the Foreign Assistance Act and encouraged the President to submit any required reports. It was not acted upon by the Senate.

The Department of State has consistently been cautious not to pin an ironclad label of "state sponsorship"on North Korean drug trafficking activity. To do so would arguably require the imposition of foreign aid sanctions on the Pyongyang regime, a move seen by many as (1) over prioritizing drugs vis-à-vis more pressing issues (i.e., nuclear proliferation) and (2) unwisely restricting the portfolio of Administration options for dealing with what has been called a rogue state.

Moreover, if the amount of North Korean illicit poppy cultivation cannot be verified, the 1,000 hectare threshold potentially triggering foreign aid cutoff under the Foreign Assistance Act of 1961 will not be met. Consistent with such policy concerns, the Department of State has maintained that although allegations of illicit drug activity "remain profoundly troubling. ... the United States has not been able to determine the extent to which the North Korean Government is involved in manufacturing and trafficking in illegal drugs."[3]

The provisions of the Foreign Assistance Act of 1961 referred to above require that countries cultivating 1,000 hectares or more of illicit opium poppy be subject to annual (March 1st) drug reporting and certification procedures. Current law on International Drug Control Certification Procedures (P.L.107-228, Section 706) requires the President to submit to Congress, not later than September 15 of the preceding fiscal year, a report identifying each country determined to be a major drug transit or drug producing country as defined in section 481(e) of the Foreign Assistance Act of 1961. In the report the President must designate each country that has "failed demonstrably" to meet its counternarcotics obligations. Designated countries are ineligible for foreign assistance unless the President determines that assistance is vital to the U.S. national interest or that the country had made "substantial efforts" to improve its counternarcotics performance.[4] International disaster assistance (such as the food aid received by North Korea) is specifically exempted from all limitations on providing assistance under the act.[5] Previous certification requirements had established a 30- calendar day review process during which the Congress could override the President's determinations and stop U.S. foreign aid from going to specific countries, but this process is no longer extant.[6]

U.S. foreign aid to North Korea is severely restricted because of North Korea's designation by the U.S. Secretary of State as a country that has "repeatedly provided support for acts of international terrorism."[7] Assistance is currently limited to humanitarian assistance (food). In December 2002, the Bush Administration suspended petroleum assistance, i.e. heavy fuel oil shipments to North Korea for electrical generating capabilities as an alternative to nuclear generation of electrical power because North Korea has not lived up to its agreement to suspend its nuclear weapons program. As negotiated in the October 1994 US-DPRK Agreed Framework, the U.S. committed to provide 500,000 tons of oil annually until completion of two lightwater nuclear reactors that are less susceptible to proliferation than facilities that North Korea has previously operated, but "frozen" under the agreement. In Fiscal Year 2004, North Korea received 110,000 metric tons of wheat from the United States valued roughly at $52.8 million.[8]

For the year 2003, North Korea's legal exports were estimated by the Korean Trade Promotion Investment Agency (KOTRA) to amount to $1.1 billion in goods — most of which were to its neighbors China, Japan and South Korea.[9] During the same period, imports (mostly from the same three nations) totaled roughly $2 billion, leaving an estimated shortfall of $999 million.[10] North Korea's need for hard currency is exacerbated by ongoing dismal economic conditions — an estimated per capita gross domestic product in the lower range of $750 to $1000 — and an ongoing nuclear program the costs of which may have exceeded $200 million per year in 1998 and which North Korea accelerated from 1999 on.[11]

ALLEGATIONS OF DRUG TRAFFICKING

President George W. Bush, in his annual determination for 2004 of major illicit drug trafficking and transit countries, registered his growing concern over heroin and methamphetamine trafficking linked to North Korea, and expressed his intent for the United States to intensify its efforts to stop North Korean involvement in narcotics production and trafficking. In the words of his memorandum for the Secretary of State:

> We are deeply concerned about heroin and methamphetamine linked to North Korea being trafficked to East Asian countries, and are increasingly convinced that state agents and enterprises in the DPRK are involved in the narcotics trade. While we suspect opium poppy is cultivated in the DPRK, reliable information confirming the extent of opium production is currently lacking. There are also clear indications that North Koreans traffic in, and probably manufacture, methamphetamine. In recent years, authorities in the region have routinely seized shipments of methamphetamine and/or heroin that had been transferred to traffickers ships from North Korean vessels. The April 2003 seizure of 125 kilograms of heroin smuggled to Australia aboard the North Korean-owned vessel "Pong Su" is the latest and largest seizure of heroin pointing to North Korean complicity in the drug trade. Although there is no evidence that narcotics originating in or transiting North Korea reach the United States, the United States is intensifying its efforts to stop North Korean involvement in illicit

narcotics production and trafficking and to enhance law-enforcement cooperation with affected countries in the region to achieve that objective.[12]

President Bush's concern over the probable scale of North Korean drug trafficking activity is mirrored in earlier testimony before the U.S. Congress on May 20, 2003, by William Bach, of the Department of State's Bureau of International Narcotics and Law Enforcement Affairs:

> For some 30 years, officials of the DPRK and other North Koreans have been apprehended for trafficking in narcotics and other criminal activity, including passing counterfeit U.S. notes. Since 1976, there have been at least 50 arrests and drug seizures involving North Koreans in more than 20 countries around the world. More recently, there have been very clear indications especially from the series of methamphetamine seizures in Japan that North Koreans traffic in and probably manufacture methamphetamine drugs.[13]

The Department of State's March , 2005 International Narcotics Control Strategy Report (INCSR) notes longstanding DPRK links to drug trafficking as well:

> For decades, North Koreans have been apprehended trafficking in narcotics and engaged in other forms of criminal behavior, including passing counterfeit U.S. currency and trade in copyright products. Numerous instances of North Korean drug trafficking and trade in copyright products, and other criminal behavior by North Korean officials, in many cases using valuable state assets, such as military-type patrol boats, has caused many observers and the Department to come to the view that it is likely, though not certain that the North Korean Government sponsors such illegal behavior as a way to earn foreign currency for the state and for its leaders.

Similarly, the Department of State's March 1, 2003 International Narcotics Control Strategy Report (INCSR) states:

> For years during the 1970s and 1980s and into the 1990s, citizens of the Democratic People's Republic of (North) Korea (DPRK), many of them diplomatic employees of the government, were apprehended abroad while trafficking in narcotics and breaking other laws. More recently, police investigation of suspects apprehended while making large illicit shipments of heroin and methamphetamine to Taiwan and Japan have revealed a North Korean connection to the drugs. Police interrogation of suspects apprehended while trafficking in illicit drugs developed credible reports of North Korean boats engaged in transporting heroin and uniformed North Korean personnel transferring drugs from North Korean vessels to traffickers' boats. These reports raise the question whether the North Korean government cultivates opium illicitly, refines opium into heroin, and manufactures methamphetamine drugs in North Korea as a state-organized and directed activity, with the objective of trafficking in these drugs to earn foreign exchange.[14]

The March 2003 INCSR includes little information on North Korea in its money laundering section, but notes reports that Pyongyong has used Macau to launder counterfeit $100 bills and used Macau's banks as a repository for the proceeds of North Korea's growing trade in illegal drugs.[15] More detail on DPRK criminal activity is included in the 1998 INCSR's money laundering section which reads in part as follows: "The most profitable lines of state-supported illegal businesses remain drug trafficking, gold smuggling, illegal sale and distribution of endangered species, trafficking of counterfeit U.S. currency, and rare earth metals.......North Korean officials appear to be increasing their involvement in financial crimes as a means to generate operational funds and support their country's anemic economy."[16]

Concerns over North Korea's role in international drug trafficking were echoed in the December 2000 United States Government International Crime Threat Assessment which states:

A large share of the methamphetamine consumed in Japan comes from North Korea, according to media reports; more than 40 percent of the methamphetamine seized in Japan in 1999 came from North Korea. There have been regular reports from many official and unofficial sources that impoverished North Korea has engaged in drug trafficking — mostly to Japan, Russia, and China — as a criminal state enterprise to raise badly needed revenue. Over the years, customs and police officials of many countries have apprehended North Korean persons employed as diplomats or in quasi-official capacities at North Korean state trading companies trying to smuggle drugs produced elsewhere.[17]

Concerns over North Korean drug production and trafficking were also expressed in the 1997 Report of the International Narcotics Control Board (INCB). The report, in circumspect language common to such U.N. documents, notes that "The Board has received disquieting reports on the drug control situation in the Democratic People's Republic of Korea. Therefore, the Board expresses its concern that the Government of the Democratic People's Republic of Korea has not yet accepted its proposal, originally made in 1995, to send a mission to that country to study and clarify drug control issues."[18] In June 2002, the Board sent a mission to the DPRK to review the Government's compliance with the international drug control treaties, and reported in its 2002 annual report that the DPRK authorities "have expressed their willingness to cooperate at the regional and international levels in order to address drug control issues in a concerted manner."[19]

In addition, U.S. Drug Enforcement Administration (DEA) data compiled from foreign media services in 1999,[20] Department of Defense analysis[21] dated 2000, and a plethora of domestic and foreign press reports portray an ongoing pattern of drug trafficking, trafficking of counterfeit U.S. currency,[22] and other smuggling-for- profit activities by North Korean diplomats over the past 27 years. Since 1976, North Korea has been linked to over 50 verifiable incidents involving drug seizures in at least 20 countries. A significant number of these cases has involved arrest or detention of North Korean diplomats or officials. All but four of these incidents have transpired since the early 1990s.[23]

Press reports citing North Korean defectors and South Korean intelligence sources as well as U.S. government investigative agency source material, paint a grim picture of an anemic economy in North Korea, held back by disproportionate military spending, dysfunctional economic policies and the consequences of a broad economic and trade embargo led by the United States since the Korean War. Pressed for cash, and perceiving its vital national security at stake, the regime reportedly created an office to bring in foreign currency: "Bureau No. 39," under the ruling North Korean Communist Party which is headed by North Korean Leader Kim Jong Il.[24] This office is reported to be in charge of drug trafficking and according to some reports all crime-for-profit activity including (1) opium production and trafficking; (2) methamphetamine production and trafficking; (3) counterfeiting; and (4) smuggling. Drugs are reportedly exported through China and Russia to Asia and Europe via government trading companies, diplomatic pouches, and concealed in legitimate commercial cargo. Foreign exchange earned by Bureau 39 is reportedly used to: (1)

buy loyalty from Party elites and military leaders to Leader Kim Jong Il; (2) fund costs of overseas diplomatic missions; (3) finance national security activity — especially technology and electronic purchases for the intelligence and military services, and (4) procure overseas components for North Korea's weapons of mass destruction programs.[25] Bureau 39 activities, according to interviews conducted by the *Wall Street Journal* with Asian intelligence officials, have generated a cash hoard, of which an amount in the range of $5 billion is believed to be currently stashed away by the Pyongyang regime.[26]

Farmers in certain areas reportedly are ordered to grow opium poppies[27], with cultivation estimates of 4,000 hectares for the early 1990s and 7,000 hectares for 1995. Subsequent production, however, is believed to be below 1995 figures, initially because of heavy rains, but also as part of a broad decline of agricultural output as a consequence of poor policies, and insufficient fertilizer and insecticides. Looking at all available estimates, a cultivation estimate of 3000-4,000 hectares for 1998 would appear reasonable, but nevertheless based on indirect and fragmented information. U.S. government investigative agency sources in 1998 estimated North Korean raw opium production capacity at 50 tons annually, with 40 tons reportedly produced in 1995. The March 2000, INCSR states that estimates of the area under opium cultivation range from 4,200 hectares to 7,000 hectares which would yield from about 30 metric tons to 44 metric tons of opium annually.[28] North Korean government pharmaceutical labs reportedly have the capacity to process 100 tons of raw opium per year.[29] U.S. government production estimates, to the extent that they may be available, would likely be classified, but clearly would not be expected to be below 1998 levels as Pyongyang's need for foreign exchange appears to have grown more pressing to accelerate foreign purchases of components for North Korea's secret uranium enrichment program.

Methamphetamine production in North Korea is reported to have started in 1996 after heavy rains decreased income from poppy production. This coincides with reports that markets for methamphetamine at that time began dramatically expanding in Asia, especially in Thailand, Japan, and the Philippines.[30] For example, in 2002, North Korea was the source of approximately 1/3 of the methamphetamine seized by Japanese authorities.[31] North Korea's maximum methamphetamine production capacity is estimated by some South Korean officials to be 10-15 tons per year of the highest quality product for export. According to the INCB, North Korean legitimate pharmaceutical needs for ephedrine (a traditional precursor for methamphetamine) are 2.5 tons per year, one ton higher than U.S. investigative agency source estimates. INCB officials confirm receipt of reports of North Korean involvement in an alleged diversion of 20 tons of ephedrine.[32] Moreover, U.S. and foreign investigative agency personnel have in the past noted concerns that North Korea may be bypassing the highly regulated market for ephedrine in favor of an alternate technology for a benzine based product, raising speculation that U.S. and allied petroleum assistance to North Korea may be being used to sustain illicit drug production.

Conservative estimates suggest North Korean criminal activity, carefully targeted to meet specific needs, generated about $85 million in 1997: $71 million from drugs and $15 million from counterfeiting.[33] Some recent estimates of Pyongyang's clandestine drug income, however, are substantially higher with the *Wall Street Journal* citing U.S. military estimates that North Korea's annual drug exports have risen to at least $500 million from about $100 million a few years ago.[34] Figures widely encountered in the U.S. policy community throughout 2004 are roughly $200 million in profit from the combined illicit methamphetamine and heroin trade and $500 million in profit from additional aggregate criminal activity. Income from counterfeiting of U.S. bills is unclear, with U.S. military sources reportedly estimating such income at $15-20 million for the year 2001.[35]

If credence is to be given to U.N., Department of State reporting, and DEA shared information, as well as press reports citing foreign law enforcement activity, North Korean defectors and South Korean intelligence sources, a pattern of activity emerges which indicates that (1) in the 1970s, North Korean officials bought and sold foreign source illicit drugs; (2) in the mid-1970s, North Korea began cultivating opium poppy as a matter of state policy; (3) in the mid 1980s, North Korea began refining opium poppy for export and exporting refined opium products; (4) and in the mid-1990s, after heavy rains reduced opium production in 1995 and 1996, North Korea, began manufacturing and exporting methamphetamine to expanding markets in Southeast Asia — increasingly enlisting the help of foreign criminal groups in its smuggling operations. If this pattern reflects reality, an important question is the degree to which the Government of North Korea may respond to increased financial pressures and expanding methamphetamine markets in Southeast Asia by dramatically increasing already record levels of reported drug trafficking activity.

Some analysts, however, question the reliability of information reported in the press attributed to North Korean defectors and South Korean government sources. They note that in a closed state such as North Korea "hard"data is difficult to obtain, thus what is obtained is fragmentary and indirect at best. North Korea continues to dismiss media reports and speculation on government involvement in drug trafficking activities as anti-North Korean slander based on politically motivated adversary propaganda sources. North Korean officials are known to stress privately that corruption, drug use, trafficking, and criminal activity in general are maladies to which individuals in all societies may fall prey, and that any involvement by North Korean individuals in such activity is in no way state-connected or state sanctioned. Further, officials have stressed that in instances where such activity has come to the attention of authorities, individuals involved have been duly punished. Finally, North Korean officials maintain that issues such as drug trafficking and production are matters that should be handled, and are best handled, by their government as an internal matter. U.N. officials also point to the politically charged milieu of allegations of drug trafficking by North Korea and point out that drug smuggling by individuals in the diplomatic community is not limited to North Korea.[36]

ISSUES FOR DECISIONMAKERS

At least fifty documented drug trafficking incidents coupled with allegations of large scale North Korean state sponsorship of opium poppy cultivation, and heroin and methamphetamine production and trafficking, raise significant issues for the United States and America's allies in combating international drug trafficking. The challenge to policy makers, is how to pursue sound counter-drug policy and comply with U.S. law which may require cutting off aid to North Korea while effectively pursuing other high priority U.S. foreign policy objectives including (1) limiting possession and production of weapons of mass destruction; (2) limiting ballistic missile production and export; (3) curbing terrorism, counterfeiting and international crime, and (4) addressing humanitarian needs.

As of March, 2005, U.S. aid to North Korea is limited to providing food and other humanitarian assistance. Reports that North Korea may be limiting some of its food crop production in favor of drug crop production are particularly disturbing, though the acreage in question is comparatively small. Another issue of rising concern is the use of profits from any North Korean drug trafficking, counterfeiting, and other crime-for-profit enterprises to underwrite the costs of maintaining or expanding North Korean nuclear and missile programs.

Central to the policy debate over the quantity of DPRK illicit poppy production is the need for hard data such as satellite imagery to confirm the extent of reported opium poppy cultivation in North Korea. If such data have been collected through remote sensing, they have not been publically disclosed.[37]

Enhanced policy focus and law enforcement intelligence cooperation on targeting, reporting, and tracking North Korean opium/heroin and methamphetamine trafficking and production in the late 1990s have made it significantly more difficult for North Korean entities to engage in illicit smuggling activities.[38] The apparent result has been a need for North Korean trafficking fronts to enter into joint venture arrangements with criminal organizations in neighboring nations, notably Russian, Chinese, and South Korean and Japanese criminal enterprises. As profits are generally shared (often as much as 50/50) in such ventures, the level of North Korean drug smuggling activity might need to more-or-less double to keep income levels for DPRK illicit drug enterprises constant with levels achieved in 1998.

The case of the "Pong Su," arguably, is demonstrative of such joint venture activity — reportedly Southeast Asian non-DPRK origin heroin carried by a North Korean crew on a North Korean vessel. The April 20, 2003 "Pong Su" case, however, presents an interesting twist of events.[39] Traditionally, it was assumed that any such joint ventures were established to facilitate the smuggling and distribution of DPRK source drugs. In contrast, reported information in the "Pong Su" case can be interpreted as a sign that such joint venture relationships — to the degree they may exist- have become a "two-way street" with North Korean enterprises smuggling drugs for partner groups as well. A growing area of international concern is escalating ties between those in the DPRK who engage in criminal activity and foreign transnational criminal groups.

Notwithstanding, some attach significance to the fact that there have been few documented instances of DPRK drug trafficking activity being detected recently. They note that the scale of North Korean linked drug trafficking activities that has been detected in 2004 is small relative to seizures linked to the DPRK in previous years. They cite as well the fact that although, in 2004, two incidents were publically reported involving DPRK officials stationed abroad at embassies, these two incidents are the first to come to light in several years.[40]

In addition, the March 2005 *INCSR* notes that there were no seizures of methamphetamines in Japan in 2004 linked to the DPRK. Traditionally as much as 30% to 40% of methamphetamine seizures in Japan have been linked to the DPRK. Likewise, the 2005 *INCSR* notes that the origin of heroin and methamphetamine seized in Taiwan during 2004 was generally ascribed to domestic manufacture; whereas in past years, DPRK origin illicit drugs have been among those seized. Arguably however, fewer seizures may simply be the result of changes in patterns of shipments designed to conceal any direct DPRK role in the process —countermeasures spurred by increased international scrutiny of North Korean trading activities. Most suggest, however, since levels of enforcement success against DPRK linked trafficking in illicit drugs often vary dramatically, it is not possible at this time to reach a definitive consensus about any changes in trends underlying such enterprise.

In contrast, the aggregate portfolio of North Korean criminal activity over the past decade paints a different picture. Information available points to an expansion in both the scale and scope of North Korean cash generating criminal activity.[41] In addition to production and trafficking in heroin and methamphetamines, major sources of revenue from criminal activity for the DPRK now include (1) counterfeit cigarettes; (2) counterfeit pharmaceuticals (for example "USA" manufactured viagra; (3) counterfeit currency (e.g. U.S. $100 bill "supernotes"); and (4) indiscriminate sales of small arms, i.e. "gun running."[42] The result is a situation in which criminal activity is seen as playing an increasingly pivotal role in supporting North Korea's fragile economy.

Best U.S. available source estimates suggest that the DPRK earns at least $500 million per year in profit from combined criminal activity, and gross revenues are suggested by some to total $1 billion or more. Regardless, however, of the current dollar amount such ventures generate, it appears that the scale and scope of North Korean criminal activities are on the rise. Increasingly, analysts view this as a global and not just as a regional concern.

Another question, yet unresolved, is the degree to which Pyongyang will be able to maintain control over drug smuggling — and other foreign currency generating —activities if they become more decentralized with more foreign criminal organizations and gangs participating. Deteriorating economic conditions and rising corruption among mid-level DPRK party functionaries threatened with declining lifestyles gives rise to speculation in the intelligence community that rogue operations constitute an increasing proportion of DPRK drug smuggling activity.[43]

A final and daunting challenge facing policymakers both in the DPRK and beyond, is the degree to which the North Korea regime would be able to curtail its illicit drug activity — and other foreign currency generating criminal enterprises —should it desire to do so. Policy analysts in the past have suggested that North Korean drug trafficking activity has been carefully controlled and limited to fill specific foreign exchange shortfalls. However, increasingly concern exists that North Korean crime-for-profit activity may become a "runaway train," gaining momentum, but out of control. Experience suggests that those engaged in the drug trade and other continuing criminal enterprises often find themselves "addicted" to the income generated and are unlikely to cease such activity, absent draconian disincentives. Moreover, over time, such illicit activity is often seen as becoming "institutionalized" — taking on a life on its own, a phenomenon which does not bode well for those who would seek to curb drug trafficking and other revenue generating international criminal activity based in North Korea.

REFERENCES

[1]   North Korean climate and soil are relatively inhospitable to poppy cultivation and fertilizer is reportedly in short supply. Rough calculations suggest that perhaps such conditions might yield roughly the equivalent of 10 kilograms of opium gum per hectare. Under such a formula, 40 metric tons of raw opium production would be roughly indicative of 3,000 to 4,000 hectares of poppy cultivation. Note also that the DPRK produces some licit opium. According to the International Narcotics Control

Board (INCB), the DPRK reported cultivating 91 hectares of opium poppy in 1991 which produced 415 kg. of opium.

[2]   H.R. 4328, P.L. 105-277, 112 Stat. 2681, signed into law October 21, 1998. For conference report language see *Congressional Record*, October 19, 1998, H11365.

[3]   U.S. Department of State, *International Narcotics Control Strategy Report* [INCSR], March 2003, p. VIII-45. See also Bach congressional testimony, note 14, below. Note also that experience from the trial by the U.S. of Panamanian leader Manuel Noriega on drug trafficking related charges has heightened concerns in the U.S. criminal justice community that U.S. government released information on drug trafficking activities of foreign leaders may not have the degree of reliability to qualify as evidence in a court of law.

[4]   Id., Sec. 614 "Special Authorities".

[5]   Id. Sec. 491 (b).

[6]   P.L. 87-195 as amended, Sections 481(e)(2), 489, and 490. See CRS Report RL32038, *Drug Certification/Designation Procedures for Illicit Narcotics Producing and Transit Nations*.

[7]   See CRS Issue Brief IB10119, *Terrorism and National Security*, by Raphael Perl (updated regularly).

[8]   See CRS Report RS21832, *U.S. Assistance to North Korea*, by Mark Manyin. Prior to Oct. 1998, humanitarian assistance was allocated under Title II of P.L. 480; subsequent food assistance falls under sec. 416 of the Agricultural Act of 1949, P.L. 81-439. Fuel assistance for FY2003 and earlier years is authorized by the corresponding Foreign Operations Appropriations Legislation with some restrictions lifted pursuant to a presidential waiver under Section 614 (a) (1) of the Foreign Assistance Act of 1961. See Presidential Determination 97-21, 62 F.R. 23939.

[9]   Contrast this amount with $1.7 billion in exports in 1990 according to South Korea's central bank. According to *Agence France Presse* (October 23, 2003) since the mid-1980s, North Korea has exported some 400 SCUD missiles along with missile- related parts to the Middle East valued at approximately $110 million. Estimates by U.S. Military Forces Command in Korea are reportedly substantially higher: $580 million from missile exports to the Middle East for the year 2001 alone. See *Yomiuri Shimbum*, "Risky Business Leading North Korea to Ruin," August 22, 2003 and "New N. Korea Food Aid Pledges Only a Beginning," *Reuters*, March 4, 2003 dispatch from Seoul. Chosen Soren (ethnic North Korean) overseas remittances to the DPRK are estimated at some $200-$600 million annually. See *Yomiuri Shimbum* (file No. 555), May 18, 2003.

[10] Source: KOTRA (Korea Trade Investment Promotion Agency) and Korean Ministry of Unification, 2004. See also, May 20, 2003 congressional testimony by Nicholas Eberstadt of the American Enterprise Institute placed North Korea's overall merchandise trade deficit at about $1,200 million a year. See note 13 for hearing citation details. See also: *U.S. Assistance to North Korea*, CRS Report RL31785, by Mark E. Manyin, and "Threats and Responses: The Asian Arena," by James Brooke, *New York Times*, December 30, 2002. p.A8. For a detailed analysis of shortfalls and trends in the DPRK's illicit activity and the importance of such activity for North Korea's economic survival, see the May 20,2003 congressional testimony of Nicholas Eberstadt (hearing citation found in note 13).

[11] The 1998 figure cited on cost of nuclear programs is relatively low because of minimal labor costs. Not included here, but arguably also a motivation for DPRK criminal activity, is the amount of hard currency North Korea needs to support its missile development and production program.

[12] Presidential Determination No. 2003-38, September 15, 2003, *Presidential Determination on Major Drug Transit or Major Illicit Drug Producing Countries for 2004*, p. 5.

[13] Testimony of William Bach, Director, Office of Asia, Africa, and Europe, Bureau of International Narcotics and Law Enforcement Affairs, Department of State, before the Financial Management, Budget, and International Security Subcommittee of the Senate Governmental Affairs Committee, May 20, 2003.

[14] U.S. Department of State, *International Narcotics Control Strategy Report* [INCSR], March 2003, p. VIII-43.

[15] Id., p. XII-200. Note that one press reports cites the existence of a videotape of Kim Jong Il's son, Kim Jong Nam, using counterfeit supernotes at a Macao casino. See The Far East Soprano*s*, by David E. Kaplan, *U.S. News & World Report*, January 27, 2003.

[16] *INCSR*, March 1998, p. 623.

[17] *International Crime Threat Assessment*, December 2000. The assessment is the product of a government interagency working group led by the CIA.

[18] *INCB Report for 1997*, p. 17.

[19] *INCB Report for 2002*, p. 55. U.N. Document E/INCB/2002/1.

[20] See Major Incidents of Drug Trafficking by North Koreans, prepared by the Europe/Asia/Africa Unit Strategic Intelligence Section, DEA, reproduced in *North Korea Advisory Group Report to the Speaker,* U.S. House of Representatives, November 1999, pp. 43-48.

[21] See *North Korean Drug Trafficking,* Department of Defense Joint Interagency Task Force West Assessment (unclassified), May 2000. Appendix "A" to the report cites 52 incidents linking the DPRK to drug trafficking activity through the month of February 2000.

[22] For example, the 1998 *INCSR*, p. 623, cites a February 1997 *Izvestia* article on the arrest of a third secretary of the North Korean Embassy who was apprehended attempting to exchange counterfeit U.S. dollars. Russian officials tied him to a smuggling operation designed to sell more than $100,000 in counterfeit U.S. bills which they believe was his main function at the embassy.

[23] For example, May 1976, 400 kg hashish seized from a North Korean (DPRK) diplomat in Egypt; July 1994, Chinese officials arrested a Chinese national on charges of smuggling 6 kg. of North Korean produced heroin through the DPRK Embassy in China; August 1994, a DPRK intelligence agent arrested by Russian authorities for trying to sell heroin to Russian mafia group; January 1995, Chinese officials in Shanghai seize 6 kg. of heroin and arrest two DPRK nationals, one with a diplomatic passport; July, 1998, DPRK. diplomat arrested in Egypt with 500,000 tablets of rohypnol — the so called "date rape" drug; January 1998, Russian officials arrest two DPRK diplomats in Moscow with 35 kg. of cocaine smuggled through Mexico; and October 1998, German officials arrested a DPRK diplomat in Berlin seizing heroin believed made in North Korea. On February 12, 1999, an employee of the DPRK consulate in Shenyang, China was caught attempting to illicitly sell 9 kilograms of

opium. On April 3, 1999, Japanese police caught Yakuza gang members attempting to smuggle 100 kilograms of methamphetamine into Japan on a Chinese ship. In April 1999, authorities at the Prague airport detained a DPRK diplomat stationed in Bulgaria attempting to smuggle 55 kilograms of the "date rape" drug rohypnol from Bulgaria. On May 3, 1999, Taiwanese police apprehended four members of a Taiwanese drug organization attempting to smuggle 157 kilograms of DPRK source methamphetamine. On October 3, 1999, Japanese authorities seized 564 kilograms of DPRK methamphetamine from the Taiwanese ship "Xin Sheng Ho"; 250 kilograms of DPRK made methamphetamine were also seized by Japanese authorities on February 5, 2000 leading to arrests of members of a Japanese Crime group and members of a Chosen Soren run trading company. During October through November 2001, Filipino authorities detained a ship twice in their territorial waters which had received first 500 kilograms and then 300 kilograms of methamphetamine from a North Korean ship. On December 22, 2001, Japanese patrol boats, in a skirmish, sank a North Korean vessel believed to be carrying drugs to Japan —the same vessel had been photographed in 1998 smuggling drugs into Japan. On January 6, 2002, Japanese authorities seized 150 kilograms of DPRK source methamphetamine from a Chinese ship in Japanese territorial waters that had earlier rendezvoused with a DPRK vessel for the drug transfer. In July 2002, Taiwanese authorities confiscated 79 kilograms of heroin which a local crime group had received from a North Korean battleship. In November and December 2002, packages containing 500 pounds of methamphetamine believed to be of DPRK origin floated ashore in Japan. On April 20, 2003, Australian police seized the DPRK ship, the "Pong Su", which had attempted to smuggle 125 kilograms of heroin through Singapore into the territorial waters of Australia. In June 2004, two North Korean diplomats working at the North Korean Embassy in Egypt were detained for smuggling 150,000 tablets of Clonazipam, an anti-anxiety drug. In December 2004, Turkish authorities arrested two North Korean diplomats suspected of smuggling the synthetic drug captagon to Arab markets. The diplomats, assigned to North Korea's Embassy in Bulgaria, were found to be carrying over half a million captagon tablets, with an estimated street value of over $7 million.

[24] Note that in April 1998 Russian police reported arresting Kil Chae Kyong [believed to be personal secretary in charge of secret funds for Kim Jong Il] on charges of trying to sell $30,000 in counterfeit U.S. currency.

[25] For a well researched discussion of DPRK crime for profit activity, see "Money Trail," by Jay Solomon, *The Wall Street Journal*, July 14, 2003, p.A1. See also: "The Wiseguy Regime," by David E. Kaplan, *U.S. News & World Report*, February 15, 1999, p.36-39. See also, "N. Korea Said To Be in Drug Business," *Washington Times*, February 26, 1995, A-1; "Drug Trafficking by North Korean Service," *Moscow-Interfaks*, June 22, 1997; "Kim Chong-il's Fund Manager Commits Suicide," *Tokyo Sankei Shimbum*, December 29, 1998; "North Korean Business: Drugs, Diplomats and Fake Dollars," AP, May 24, 1998; "Seoul Says N. Korea Increasing Opium Output for Export," *Kyodo*, June 8, 1993; "DPRK Officially Involved in Drugs, Counterfeiting," *Digital Chosun Ilbo* [South Korea], November 12, 1996; "DPRK Defectors Attest to Realities of DPRK System," *Seoul Tong-A Ilbo*, February 14, 96, p.5; "N.Korea Accused of Promoting Opium Farms," *Seoul Choson Ilbo*, August 7, 1994, p. 5. Bureau 39 reportedly directs the expenditure of North Korea's foreign exchange resources with

two priorities: (1) procurement of luxury products from abroad that Kim Jong-Il distributes to a broad swath of North Korean military, party, and government officials to secure their loyalty — Mercedes Benz automobiles, food, wines, stereos, deluxe beds, Rolex watches, televisions, etc., estimated at $100 million annually by U.S. military officials in Seoul, according to a *Reuters* report of March 4, 2003; and (2) procurement overseas of components and materials for North Korea's WMDs and missiles. See also: CRS Issue Brief IB98045, *Korea: U.S. Korean Relations — Issues for Congress* by Larry A. Niksch, updated regularly).

[26] See "Money Trail," by Jay Solomon, *The Wall Street Journal*, July 14, 2003, p.A1.

[27] See North Korea and Narcotics Trafficking: A View from the Inside, by Kim Young Il, *North Korea Review,* Vol 1, Issue 1, Feb. 27, 2005.

[28] *INCSR*, March 2000, p. VIII-39

[29] *See "U.S. says North Korea Sponsors Drug Smuggling," Kyodo News Service* (Japan), December 13, 1998. Total arable land in the DPRK is estimated to exceed 1.3 million hectares.

[30] In August 1998, Japanese authorities arrested members of a Japanese criminal organization and seized 200 kg of a 300 kg shipment of methamphetamine believed manufactured in North Korea. Earlier, in April, 58.6 kg of the same drug, thought to have been manufactured in China, was seized by Japanese authorities in the cargo of a North Korean freighter. See "Police Say Seized Drugs Originated in North Korea, " *Yomiuri Shimbun* (Japan), Jan. 8, 1999.

[31] Between 1999 and 2001, Japanese authorities reportedly seized 1,113 kilograms of methamphetamine en route from North Korea — some 34% of Japanese seizures. For China during the same period the percentage reportedly constitutes 38% (some 1,780 kg). See "Trying a Quick Fix: North Korea Tied to the Drug Trade," by Jay Solomon and Jason Dean, *Asian Wall Street Journal*, April 23, 2003, p.1.

[32] For example, in January 1998, Thai police reportedly seized, but later released, 2.5 tons of ephedrine en route from India to North Korea. This was reportedly part of an 8 ton shipment North Korea had attempted to purchase which the INCB reportedly limited to two 2.5 ton shipments over a two year period. However, INCB officials staunchly deny that such an arrangement transpired. Pyongyang, at the time, reportedly argued for the right to buy 30 tons from India — enough for a 135 year supply of cold tablets (see *Bangkok Times*, 6/13/99, p.6).

[33] The $71 million for drugs is broken down as $59 million from opium/heroin and $12 million from amphetamines, although one, admittedly speculative, U.S. law enforcement agency source estimate for "world" market price of heroin produced by the DPRK in 1995 was $600 million. For the $15 million figure on counterfeiting, see *Korea Herald*, Nov.16, 1998. See also, "Is Your Money Real?", *Newsweek*, June 10, 1996, p. 10. According to some sources, income from counterfeiting is considerably higher, i.e. $100 million. (See May 20, 2003 congressional testimony of Larry Wortzel of the Heritage Foundation, citation details in note no. 14.) Note also that data on amounts of U.S. dollars counterfeited are not widely publicized (and arguably publicly downplayed) so as not to undermine confidence in the U.S. dollar. North Korean counterfeit U.S. $100 notes have been detected in at least 14 countries including the United States since the 1970's. On June 20, 2004, the BBC aired a "Superdollar" special which traced counterfeit $100 bills from North Korea to an official IRA source

in the U.K. Reportedly millions of fake $100 bills were laundered through a bureaux de change in Britain. In July, 1996, a former member of the Japanese Red Army, traveling on a DPRK diplomatic passport was arrested in Thailand while trying to pass counterfeit U.S. $100 bills. See "Japanese Fake Bill Suspect Had N. Korean Passport," *Kyodo News*, July 5, 1996. For data on other forms of DPRK criminal/smuggling activity, see *Avoiding the Apocalypse: The Future of the Two Koreas* by Marcus Noland, Institute for International Economics, Washington, D.C., June 2000, p.119.

[34] See Money trail, by Jay Solomon, The *Wall Street Journal*, July 14, 2003, p.A1. For another income estimate of "as much as $500 million" see The Far East Sopranos, by David E. Kaplan, *U.S. News & World Report*, January 27, 2003. Given that drug trafficking is by very nature a clandestine activity and that North Korea is a closed society, any overall estimates of DPRK income from illicit drug sources are based on fragmented data and are speculative at best. However, arguably, what may be more important here than the exact dollar amount generated by such illicit activity, is the strategic significance of the income — whatever the dollar amount be — given speculation that it is being used to underwrite Pyongyang's nuclear weapons program. Clearly such data should be considered a "far cry" from anything that might be remotely considered as evidence in a U.S. court of law. Note also that the dollar amount the DPRK received in profit from drug sales to Japan in 2003 has been roughly and unofficially estimated at $100 million, according to non-U.S. sources.

[35] See "N.K. Exported $580 Million Worth of Missiles to Middle East," *Seoul Yonhap* (English), May 13, 2003, citing Japanese *Yomiuri Shimbum* report of May 12, 2003. Media reports suggest that when Assistant Secretary of State, James A. Kelly, visited North Korea in October 2002, he asked that printing of the counterfeit bills be suspended. Some of the bills are reportedly printed on machines stolen by the KGB from the U.S. mint after WWII and provided to North Korea by the USSR in the late 1980s (See "DPRK Prints Super K Dollar Bills on Machine Provided by Former USSR KGB," *Tokyo Forsight* (in Japanese) 15 March-18 April 2003.) Others are believed to be printed on equipment purchased by the DPRK in Europe in the 1990s. Quality control is reportedly exercised by use of state of the art equipment designed to detect counterfeiting, reportedly also purchased in Europe. Note that not only U.S. currency is reportedly counterfeited. DPRK payment for a typical purchase of goods or technology from the Middle East, for example, may well include a percentage of top quality Middle Eastern counterfeit bills.

[36] Conversations with North Korean and United Nations officials, September 1998.

[37] Some analysts have compared the alleged poppy cultivation situation in the DPRK with that of Colombia in the mid-1980s. Beginning about 1986, numerous reports were received from informants regarding poppy cultivation in Colombia. However, despite U-2 aircraft broad sweep imagery, it was not until the mid-1990s that such imagery was able to confirm cultivation which at that time approximated the 4,000-5,000 hectare range.

[38] See for example: "U.S. to Send Signal to North Koreans in Naval Exercise" by Steven R. Weisman, *New York Times*, August 18, 2003, p.1. which refers to the existence of a program known as the "D.P.R.K. Illicit Activities Initiative" characterized as a quiet crackdown by many nations against North Korea's narcotics trade, counterfeiting, moneylaundering, and other illicit smuggling activity.

[39] See text at end of note number 23. The DPRK government maintains that the "Pong Su" is a civilian trading ship and that its owner had no knowledge of the heroin. Heroin seized may have been of Burmese origin (and picked up in Myanmar or Thailand), raising speculation of a budding relationship between the DPRK and criminal enterprises in either Myanmar or Thailand. See, "Dangerous Bedfellows" by Bertil Lintner and Shawn W. Crispin, *Far Eastern Economic Review,* November 20, 2003. Myanmar (reportedly the world's largest opium cultivator in 2002) is often characterized as one of the most isolated nations in the world as well as a nation where rampant corruption prevails. See, "N. Korea's Growing Drug Trade Seen in Botched Heroin Delivery" by Richard Paddock and Barbara Demick, *Washington Post,* May 21, 2003 and Myanmar's Problems Are Thailand's Dilemma by Sorapong Buaroy, *Bankok Post,* 1/28/03.

[40] For details on the two incidents involving DPRK diplomats stationed in Bulgaria and Egypt, see the Department of State's March 2005, *INCSR* which states: "It is impossible to say with certainty that such individuals were acting under the instructions of their government...."

[41] For a discussion of U.S. response options reportedly under discussion see U.S. is Shaping Plan to Pressure North Korea, by David E. Sanger, *New York Times,* Feb. 14, 2005, A-1.

[42] In July 2004, for example, the U.S. Secret Service reportedly uncovered a network selling counterfeit North Korean made cigarettes, pharmaceuticals, and $100 bills. See Fakes by Frederik Balfour et al, *Business Week,* February 7, 2005.

[43] DPRK defectors maintain that North Korea's underground economy is controlled by some 1000 "big dealers" who regularly give bribes in U.S. dollars and valuable gifts to Kim Jong-il and party, administration and military elites, See "DPRK Defectors Say Underground Economy Spawning Influential 'Big Dealers,' *Seoul Chugan Chosen* (in Korean) June 19, 2003. Mr. Kim's personal assets in foreign countries have been estimated to be in $130 billion range, with as much as $4.3 billion reportedly in Swiss bank accounts. See "Kim Jong Ils Huge Secret Assets," *Tokyo Shukan Posuto,* June 16, 2003, citing, Chuck Downs, a former Pentagon official in the Bush I and Clinton Administrations. Press reports citing U.S. military sources in Seoul, state that Pyongyang spends about $100 million a year on imported luxury cars and liquor for its elite, see "New N. Korea Food Aid Pledges Only a Beginning," *Reuters,* March 4, 2003 dispatch from Seoul.

In: Illegal Drugs and Governmental Policies
Editor: Lee V. Barton, pp. 17-33

ISBN 978-1-60021-351-9
© 2007 Nova Science Publishers, Inc.

Chapter 2

DRUG CONTROL:
INTERNATIONAL POLICY AND APPROACHES[*]

Raphael Perl

SUMMARY

Efforts to significantly reduce the flow of illicit drugs from abroad into the United States have so far not succeeded. Moreover, over the past decade, worldwide production of illicit drugs has risen dramatically: opium and marijuana production has roughly doubled and coca production tripled. Street prices of cocaine and heroin have fallen significantly in the past 20 years, reflecting increased availability. The effectiveness of international narcotics control programs in reducing consumption is a matter of ongoing concern. Despite apparent national political resolve to deal with the drug problem, inherent contradictions regularly appear between U.S. anti-drug policy and other national policy goals and concerns. Pursuit of drug control policies can sometimes affect foreign policy interests and bring political instability and economic dislocation to countries where narcotics production has become entrenched economically and socially. Drug supply interdiction programs and U.S. systems to facilitate the international movement of goods, people, and wealth are often at odds. U.S. international narcotics policy requires cooperative efforts by many nations which may have domestic and foreign policy goals that compete with the requirements of drug control. The mix of competing domestic and international pressures and priorities has produced an ongoing series of disputes within and between the legislative and executive branches concerning U.S. international drug policy. One contentious issue has been the Congressionally-mandated certification process, an instrument designed to induce specified drug-exporting countries to prioritize or pay more attention to the fight against narcotics businesses. Current law requires the President, with certain exceptions, to designate and withhold assistance from countries that have failed demonstrably to meet their counternarcotics obligations. P.L. 106-246, "Plan Colombia," a $1.3 billion military assistance-focused initiative to provide emergency supplemental narcotics assistance to Colombia, was signed into law July 13, 2000. Recently, U.S. policy toward Colombia has focused increasingly on containing the terror- ist threat to that country's security. The Bush Administration's FY2005 budget request continues a policy, begun in FY2002, to request authority for the State and Defense Departments to supply assistance to Colombia for counterterrorism purposes. For instance, U.S.-supplied helicopters and intelligence could be used to support military operations against guerrillas financed by

---

[*] Excerpted from CRS Report IB88093, Updated February 2, 2006

drugs as well as against drug traffickers themselves. See CRS Report RL32337, *Andean Counterdrug Initia- tive (ACI) and Related Funding Programs: FY2005 Assistance.*

An issue likely to achieve increased attention in the 109th Congress is that of sky-rocketing opium poppy cultivation in Afghani- stan and whether to press for aerial crop eradi-cation against the wishes of the local Afghan leadership. See CRS Report RL32686, *Af-ghanistan: Narcotics and U.S. Policy.*

Drug control approaches addressed in this issue brief include:

— Expansion of efforts to reduce foreign production at the source.
— Expansion of interdiction and enforcement activities to disrupt supply lines.
— Expansion of efforts to reduce worldwide demand.
— Expansion of economic disincentives for international drug trafficking.

MOST RECENT DEVELOPMENTS

On January 28, 2006, President Evo Morales of Bolivia appointed Felipe Caceres, a coca leaf grower, to head his government's fight against drug trafficking — escalating concern in U.S. policy circles that Morales will follow through on his pre-election pledge to roll back U.S. efforts to curb coca production in Bolivia. U.S. counternarcotics programs in Bolivia were funded at $79.2 million in FY2006 (alternative development and law enforcement). The Administration's FY2007 request is expected to be somewhat less.

A report released by the Government Accountability Office (GAO-06-200) argues for the development of better counter-drug performance measures by government agencies and warns that the diversion of military assets to Iraq and Afghanistan is likely to hamper the ability of U.S. law enforcement to intercept drug shipments in the future. Proponents of strong drug interdiction policies have long been concerned that the nation's focus on anti-terror objectives will detract from resources and political will needed to combat foreign source illicit drug production and trafficking.

BACKGROUND AND ANALYSIS

Problem

More than 14 million Americans buy illicit drugs and use them at least once per month, spending by most conservative estimates over $60 billion annually in a diverse and fragmented criminal market. Such drugs are to varying degrees injurious to the health, judgment, productivity and general well-being of their users. The 2002 *National Drug Control Strategy* (hereafter *Strategy*) of the White House Office of National Drug Control Policy (ONDCP) estimates the total costs of drug abuse to American society to be approximately $160 billion. The major components of this total are health care costs ($14.9 billion), workplace productivity losses ($110.5 billion) and losses related to crime, the criminal justice system, and social welfare ($35 billion). According to the *Strategy* more than 60% of the inmates in the federal prison system are drug law violators; moreover, the addictive nature and high price of most illegal drugs contribute significantly to the incidence of violent crime and property crime in the United States. Additionally, the U.S. illicit drug market generates billions of dollars in profits. Such profits provide international drug trafficking organizations with the resources to effectively evade and compete with law enforcement agencies, to penetrate legitimate economic structures, and, in some instances, to challenge the authority of national governments.

Calculated in dollar value terms, at least four-fifths of all the illicit drugs consumed in the United States are of foreign origin, including virtually all the cocaine and heroin and most of the marijuana, according to the ONDCP *Strategy* and the U.S. Drug Enforcement Administration (DEA) 2002 report, *Drug Trafficking in the United States*. According to DEA, the methamphetamine market is supplied predominantly from laboratories in both the United States and Mexico while most of the hallucinogens and illegally marketed psychotheraputic drugs and "designer" drugs are of domestic U.S. origin.

Drugs are a lucrative business and a mainspring of global criminal activity. According to a 2002 estimate by the State Department's Bureau of International Narcotics and Law Enforcement Affairs (INL), as much as 930 tons of cocaine could have been produced from coca leaf grown in South America in 2001. If sold internationally at an average U.S. street price per gram of $100, the drug would yield a gross value of $93 billion, a figure exceeding the Gross National Income of three-quarters of the world's nations. A November 2002 study by the United Nations Office on Drugs and Crime estimated the net regional earnings of the illicit drug industry in the Caribbean at $3.3 billion, or about half the Gross National Income of Jamaica or Trinidad. Little is known about the distribution of revenues from illicit drug sales, but foreign supply cartels exercise considerable control over wholesale distribution in the United States and illicit proceeds are often laundered and invested through foreign banks and financial institutions.

In December 2002, the Chief of Operations of the U.S. Drug Enforcement Administration (DEA) told a Congressional panel that the number of hard-core heroin users in the United States had increased to "almost a million" from an estimated 630,000 in 1992. The DEA Heroin Signature Program, which identifies the sources of that drug seized by U.S. federal authorities, found that 56% of the seized heroin was of Colombian origin.

The federal anti-drug initiative has two major elements: (1) reduction of demand and (2) reduction of supply. Reduction of demand is sought through education to prevent dependence, through treatment to cure addiction and through measures to increase prices and risk of apprehension at the consumer level. Reduction of supply (which currently accounts for about 53% of the federal anti-drug control budget, according to the *Strategy*) is sought by programs aimed at destabilizing the operations of illicit drug cartels at all levels and severing their links to political power, and by seizing their products, businesses, and financial assets. As most illicit drugs are imported, a major interdiction campaign is being conducted on the U.S. borders, at ports of entry, on the high seas, and along major foreign transshipment routes and at production sites. An international program of source crop eradication is also being pursued. As reported in the *Strategy*, approximately 18% of the requested federal drug control budget of $11.7 billion for FY2004 is for interdiction and 9.2% is for international assistance programs. These ratios continue to remain relatively constant. The major international components of federal policies for the reduction of illicit supply are discussed below.

On or about March 7, 2005, the State Department released its annual International Narcotics Control Strategy Report (INCSR), a comprehensive assessment of the efforts of foreign nations to combat the illicit drug trade and drug related money laundering.

Current International Narcotics Control Policy

The primary goal of U.S. international narcotics policy is to reduce the supply of illicit narcotics flowing into the United States. A second and supporting goal is to reduce the amount of illicit narcotics cultivated, processed, and consumed worldwide. U.S. international narcotics control policy is implemented by a multifaceted strategy that includes the following elements: (1) eradication of narcotic crops, (2) interdiction and law enforcement activities in drug-producing and drug-transiting countries, (3) international cooperation, (4) sanctions/economic assistance, and (5) institution development. The U.S. State Department's Bureau of International Narcotics and Law Enforcement (INL) has the lead role coordinating U.S. international drug intervention and suppression activities.

In April 2001, the President requested $882 million in economic and counternarcotics assistance for Colombia and regional neighbors as part of an Andean Regional Initiative (ARI). The ARI proposal differed from the Plan Colombia program in two key areas: (1) spending on economic and social programs would be roughly equal to the drug control and interdiction components that had been the primary focus of Plan Colombia; and (2) more than half of the assistance was targeted to neighboring countries experiencing spillover effects from Colombia's civil conflict and from narcotrafficking activities in that country. The enacted appropriations bill (P.L. 107-115) cleared by Congress on December 20, 2001, provided $783 million for the Initiative, a cut of $99 million from the President's request. Of the appropriation, not less than $215 million was to be apportioned directly to the Agency for International Development (AID) for economic and social programs. The enacted bill included conditions on the use of funds for purchase of chemicals for the aerial spraying program in Colombia, limited the number of U.S. civilian and military personnel involved in Colombia to 800, and blocked funding for restoration of flights in support of the Peruvian air interdiction program until a system of enhanced safeguards is in place. The State Department's request for its Andean Drug Counter Drug Initiative (ACI) for FY2003 and FY2004 totaled $731 million for each year respectively. The Administration requested $731 million for the Andean Counterdrug Initiative for FY2005, and $114 million for economic assistance programs. Congress also raised from 400 to 800 the level of U.S. military personnel and from 400 to 600 the level of civilian contractor personnel allowed to be deployed in Colombia, in response to an Administration request.

Eradication of Narcotic Crops

A long-standing U.S. policy regarding international narcotics control is to reduce cultivation and production of illicit narcotics through eradication. The United States supports programs to eradicate coca, opium, and marijuana in a number of countries. These efforts are conducted by a number of U.S. government agencies administering several types of programs. The United States supports eradication by providing producer countries with chemical herbicides, technical assistance and specialized equipment, and spray aircraft. The U.S. Agency for International Development (AID) funds programs designed to promote economic growth and to provide alternative sources of employment for the people currently growing, producing, or processing illicit drugs. AID also provides balance of payments support (especially to the Andean countries) to help offset the loss of foreign exchange (from diminished drug exports) occurring as a result of U.S.-supported anti-drug programs. U.S. eradication policy receives informational support from the State Department's Office of Public Diplomacy and Public Affairs (formerly the U.S. Information Agency (USIA)) which publicizes the dangers of drug abuse and trafficker violence. In addition, AID sponsors drug education and awareness programs in 33 Latin American, Asian, and East European countries.

The eradication program in the Andes resulted in the elimination of an estimated 110,000 hectares of coca in Peru and Bolivia between 1995 and 2001, or almost 70% of the combined cultivated area in those countries. Nevertheless, cultivation in Colombia increased by 119,000 hectares or 234% over the same period.[1] The shift in cultivation has had implications for Colombia's civil conflict, putting more "taxable" resources into the hands of Colombia's leftist guerrillas. The State Department's International Strategy report for 2001 notes that "The Colombian syndicates, witnessing the vulnerability of Peruvian and Bolivian coca supply to joint interdiction operations in the late 1990s, decided to move most of the cultivation to Colombia's southwest corner, an area controlled by the FARC, the country's oldest insurgent group." This trend continues in Colombia today.

On January 2, 2005, the *Los Angeles Times* reported that the Bush Administration is split over how to respond to Afghanistan's skyrocketing opium poppy production. The debate reportedly centers over whether to push for large scale aerial eradication, or to leave the issue to the discretion of local officials. Central to the debate is what some view as potentially competing U.S. policy objectives in the war-torn nation, i.e., counterterrorism, counter-narcotics, and political stability.

Interdiction and Law Enforcement

A second element of U.S. international narcotics control strategy is to help host governments seize illicit narcotics before they reach America's borders. A related imperative is to attack and disrupt large aggregates of criminal power, to immobilize their top leaders and to sever drug traffickers' ties to the economy and to the political hierarchy. Training of foreign law enforcement personnel constitutes a major part of such endeavors. The Department of State funds anti-narcotics law enforcement training programs for foreign personnel from more than 70 countries. In addition, the Department of State provides host country anti-narcotics personnel with a wide range of equipment, and U.S. Drug Enforcement Administration (DEA) agents regularly assist foreign police forces in their efforts to destabilize trafficking networks. U.S. efforts to promote effective law enforcement against narcotics traffickers also include suggestions to nations on means to strengthen their legal and judicial systems. Finally, an important judicial tool against drug dealers is extradition. Since 1997, the U.S. government has successfully extradited at least 14 major traffickers from Colombia to face justice in the United States.

International Cooperation

Essentially all elements of U.S. international narcotics control strategy require international cooperation. By use of diplomatic initiatives, both bilateral and multilateral, the

Department of State encourages and assists nations to reduce cultivation, production, and trafficking in illicit drugs. These bilateral agreements and international conventions have thus far been largely ineffective in reversing the growth of international narcotics trafficking, in part because they lack strong enforcement mechanisms and are not uniformly interpreted by member nations.

U.S. international narcotics control strategy also requires cooperation among governments to coordinate their border operations to interdict traffickers. To this end, the U.S. government has provided technical assistance for anti-drug programs in other countries. For FY2005, the State Department's international narcotics control budget request totaled $1.05 billion to assist programs globally, including $90.2 million for Bolivia, $115.4 million for Peru, $462.8 million for Colombia, and $25.8 million for Ecuador. Also requested was $69.4 million for interregional aviation support, to provide aircraft for anti-drug programs in other countries. The United States also participates in multilateral assistance programs through the U.N. International Drug Control Program and actively enlists the aid and support of other governments for narcotics control projects. The U.N. currently assists 67 developing countries through development, law enforcement, education, treatment, and rehabilitation programs. For FY2005, the Bush Administration requested $15 million for general anticrime/anticorruption programs and $5 million for narcotics control-related contributions to international organizations; the majority of the latter constituted the U.S. voluntary contribution to the U.N. drug control program.

Sanctions/Economic Assistance

A fourth element of U.S. international narcotics control strategy involves the threat of, or application of, sanctions against drug producer or trafficker nations. These range from suspension of U.S. foreign assistance to curtailment of air transportation. Current law on International Drug Control Certification Procedures (P.L.107-228, Section 706) requires the President to submit to Congress not later than September 15 of the preceding fiscal year a report identifying each country determined to be a major drug transit or drug producing country as defined in section 481(e) of the Foreign Assistance Act of 1961. In the report the President must designate each country that has "failed demonstrably" to meet its counternarcotics obligations. Designated countries would be ineligible for foreign assistance unless the President determined that that assistance was vital to the U.S. national interest or that the country had made "substantial efforts" to improve its counternarcotics performance. Previous certification requirements had established a 30- calendar day review process in which the Congress could override the President's determinations and stop U.S. foreign aid from going to specific countries, but this process is no longer extant.

A multilateral [drug performance] evaluation mechanism (MEM) has also been established under the auspices of the Organization of American States (OAS). This mechanism is seen by many as a vehicle to undermine and facilitate abolishment of the existing U.S. sanctions-oriented unilateral certification process which is often viewed as an irritant to major illicit drug-producing countries, and which, opponents argue, does little to promote anti-drug cooperation.

U.S. sanctions policy has been augmented with programs of economic assistance to major coca producing countries (see "Use of Sanctions or Positive Incentives" and "Bush

Administration Anti-Drug Strategy," below). For FY2005 the State Department requested for drug related alternative development: approximately $124.7 million for Colombia, $53.9 million for Peru, $41.7 million for Bolivia and $14.9 million for Ecuador.

On June 2, 2003, President Bush submitted to Congress a list of foreign narcotics kingpins subject to U.S. legislative efforts to deny such individuals and entities access to U.S. financial systems and to prohibit U.S. individuals and companies from doing business with these kingpins. For the first time, foreign "entities" such as the Colombia's FARC and United Self-Defense Forces (AUC) are included in the list.

Institution Development

A fifth element of U.S. international narcotics control strategy increasingly involves institution development, such as strengthening judicial and law enforcement institutions, boosting governing capacity, and assisting in developing host nation administrative infrastructures conducive to combating the illicit drug trade. Institution development includes such programs as corruption prevention, training to support the administration of justice, and financial crimes enforcement assistance.

POLICY APPROACHES

Overview

The primary goal of U.S. international narcotics control policy is to stem the flow of foreign drugs into the United States. A number of approaches have been proposed to reshape U.S. international narcotics control policy and implement it more effectively. Whatever ideas are ultimately selected will have to consider the scope of the drug problem. It is estimated that the illicit drug trade generates as much as half of the approximately $750 billion in illegal funds laundered internationally each year. Policymakers face the challenge of deciding the appropriate level of funding required for the nation's international narcotics control efforts within the context of competing budgetary priorities.

Another challenge facing the U.S. international narcotics control efforts concerns how to implement policy most effectively. Some observers argue that current U.S. policy is fragmented and overly bilateral in nature. These analysts suggest that to achieve success, policy options must be pursued within the context of a comprehensive plan with a multilateral emphasis on implementation. For example, they point out that some studies indicate that interdiction can actually increase the economic rewards to drug traffickers by raising prices for the products they sell. They agree, however, that interdiction as part of a coordinated plan can have a strong disrupting and destabilizing effect on trafficker operations. Some analysts suggest that bilateral or unilateral U.S. policies are ill-suited for solving what is in effect a multilateral problem. They cite the need for enhancing the United Nations' ability to deal effectively with the narcotics problem and for more international and regional cooperation and consultation on international narcotics issues. Proponents of bilateral policy do not necessarily reject a more multilateral approach. They point out, however, that such multinational endeavors are intrinsically difficult to arrange, coordinate, and implement effectively.

Between 1981 and 2001 The United States spent $8.57 billion on international narcotics control, mostly in Latin America. Yet estimated potential production of South American cocaine over the period increased from 140 to 170 tons to almost 870 tons, according to State Department and other U.S. government figures. According to ONDCP's *Strategy* the average price per pure gram of cocaine in 2000 was $212, approximately half what it was in 1981, and the average purity of a gram of street cocaine was 69% higher. For heroin the price and purity respectively were 77% lower and 147% higher in 2000 than in 1981. Some analysts believe, viewing such trends, that current efforts to reduce the flow of illicit drugs into the United States have essentially failed and that other objectives, policies, programs, and priorities are needed. Four major approaches which have been suggested, in various combinations as part of an overall effort, are set out below.

Expansion of Efforts to Reduce Production at the Source

This option involves expanding efforts to reduce the volume of narcotic plants and crops produced in foreign countries before the crops' conversion into processed drugs. Illicit crops may either be eradicated or purchased (and then destroyed). Eradication of illicit crops may be accomplished by physically uprooting the plants, or by chemical or biological control agents. Development of alternative sources of income to replace peasant income lost by nonproduction of narcotic crops may be an important element of this option.

Proponents of expanded efforts to stop the production of narcotic crops and substances at the source believe that reduction of the foreign supply of drugs available is an effective means to lower levels of drug use in the United States. They argue that reduction of the supply of cocaine — the nation's top narcotics control priority — is a realistically achievable option.

Proponents of vastly expanded supply reduction options, and specifically of herbicidal crop eradication, argue that this method is the most cost-effective and efficient means of eliminating narcotic crops. They maintain that, coupled with intensified law enforcement, such programs will succeed since it is easier to locate and destroy crops in the field than to locate subsequently processed drugs on smuggling routes or on the streets of U.S. cities. Put differently, a kilogram of cocaine hydrochloride is far more difficult to detect than the 300 to 500 kilograms of coca leaf that are required to make that same kilogram. Also, because crops constitute the cheapest link in the narcotics chain, producers will devote fewer economic resources to prevent their detection than to concealing more expensive and refined forms of the product.

In addition, eradication successes have been recorded in individual countries. According to INL's *International Narcotics Control Strategy Report* of 2002, for example, Pakistan has reduced opium cultivation by more than 95% since 1995 and Taliban-controlled Afghanistan accomplished a similar feat in a single year, eliminating more than 62,000 hectares or 97% of the opium crop between 2000 and 2001. However, INL reports that cultivation surged beginning in 2002 under the relatively weak Afghan political authority that succeeded the Taliban, suggesting that an effective central government presence in drug crop areas is critical to the success of eradication projects.

Opponents of expanded supply reduction policy generally question whether reduction of the foreign supply of narcotic drugs is achievable and whether it would have a meaningful impact on levels of illicit drug use in the United States. They argue that aerial spraying in Colombia has failed to contain the spread of coca cultivation and point to drug syndicates' moving into opium poppy cultivation in Colombia and (more recently) Peru. Total Andean cultivation, in fact, has remained relatively stable in the past decade despite U.S. efforts, and because farmers are finding ways to increase productivity per unit of land according to INL figures. Critics also suggest that even if the supply of foreign drugs destined for the U.S. market could be dramatically reduced, U.S. consumers would simply switch to consumption of domestically-grown or synthetic drug substitutes. Thus, they maintain, the ultimate solution to the U.S. drug problem is wiping out the domestic market for illicit drugs, not trying to eliminate the supply in source countries.

Some also fear that environmental damage will result from herbicides. As an alternative, they urge development, research, and funding of programs designed to develop and employ biological control agents such as coca-destroying insects and fungi that do not harm other plants. Others argue that intensified eradication will push the drug crop frontier and the attendant polluting affects of narcotics industries farther into ecologically sensitive jungle areas, with little or no decrease in net cultivation. In addition, reports have surfaced in Colombia of toxic effects of herbicides on legal crops and on the health of animals and humans, although the veracity of such accounts is debated.

Others question whether a global policy of simultaneous crop control is politically feasible since many areas in the world will always be beyond U.S. control and influence. Such critics refer to continuously shifting sources of supply, or the so-called "balloon syndrome": when squeezed in one place, it pops up in another. Nevertheless, many point out that the number of large suitable growth areas is finite, and by focusing simultaneously at major production areas, substantial reductions can be achieved if adequate funding is provided.

Some also question the value of supply reduction measures since world production and supply of illicit drugs vastly exceeds world demand, making it unlikely that the supply surplus could be reduced sufficiently to affect the ready availability of illicit narcotics in the U.S. market. Such analysts also suggest that even if worldwide supply were reduced dramatically, the effects would be felt primarily in other nation's drug markets. The U.S. market, they argue, would be the last to experience supply shortfalls, because U.S. consumers pay higher prices and because U.S. dollars are a preferred narco-currency.

Political and Economic Tradeoffs. Some suggest that expanded and effective efforts to reduce production of illicit narcotics at the source will be met by active and violent opposition from a combination of trafficker, political, and economic groups. In some nations, such as Colombia, traffickers have achieved a status comparable to "a state within a state." In others, allegations of drug-related corruption have focused on high-level officials in the military and federal police, as well as heads of state; In Mexico, according to a *Washington Times* report, smugglers often are protected by heavily-armed Mexican military troops and police who "have been paid handsomely to escort the drug traffickers and their illicit shipments across the border and into the United States." In addition, some traffickers have aligned themselves with terrorist and insurgent groups, and have reportedly funded political candidates and parties, pro-narcotic peasant workers and trade union groups, and high visibility popular public works projects to cultivate public support through a "Robin Hood" image. Because some constituencies that benefit economically from coca are well armed, if the United States were successful in urging foreign governments to institute widespread use of chemical/biological control agents, cooperating host governments could well face strong domestic political challenge and violent opposition from affected groups. Heavy military protection, at a minimum, would be required for those spraying or otherwise eradicating drug crops.

Some critics have argued, with respect to Colombia, that eradication campaigns can have the unintended effect of aggravating the country's ongoing civil conflict. Since Colombia's guerrilla groups pose as advocates of growers, spraying may broaden support for such groups, thereby contradicting the objectives of the government's counterinsurgency efforts in the affected zones. Such observers believe that Colombia's enforcement priorities should shift to targeting critical nodes in transportation and refining and, to the extent possible, sealing off traffic routes to and from the main coca producing zones. The argument is made that interdiction can disrupt internal markets for coca derivatives and that, compared to eradication, it imposes fewer direct costs on peasant producers and generates less political unrest.

For some countries, production of illicit narcotics and the narcotics trade has become an economic way of life that provides a subsistence level of income to large numbers of people from whom those who rule draw their legitimacy. Crop reduction campaigns seek to displace such income and those workers engaged in its production. In this regard, these campaigns may threaten real economic and political dangers for the governments of nations with marginal economic growth. Consequently, some analysts argue that the governments of such low-income countries cannot be expected to launch major crop reduction programs without the substitute income to sustain those whose income depends on drug production.

Use of Sanctions or Positive Incentives. Those promoting expansion of efforts to reduce production at the source face the challenge of instituting programs that effectively reduce production of narcotic crops and production of refined narcotics without creating unmanageable economic and political crises for target countries. A major area of concern of such policymakers is to achieve an effective balance between the "carrot" and the "stick" approach in U.S. relations with major illicit narcotics-producing and transit countries.

Proponents of a sanctions policy linking foreign aid and trade benefits to U.S. international narcotics objectives argue against "business as usual" with countries that permit illicit drug trafficking, production, or laundering of drug profits. They assert that this policy includes a moral dimension and that drug production and trafficking is wrong, and that the United States should not associate with countries involved in it. Such analysts maintain that U.S. aid and trade sanctions can provide the needed leverage for nations to reduce production of illicit crops and their involvement in other drug related activities. They argue that both the moral stigma of being branded as uncooperative and the threat of economic sanctions prod many otherwise uncooperative nations into action. They further stress that trade sanctions would be likely to provide a highly effective lever as most developing countries depend on access to U.S. markets.

Opponents of a sanctions policy linking aid and trade to U.S. international narcotics objectives argue that sanctions may have an undesirable effect on the political and economic stability of target countries, making them all the more dependent on the drug trade for income; that sanctions have little impact because many countries are not dependant on U.S. aid; that sanctions historically have little effect unless they are multilaterally imposed; and that sanctions are arbitrary in nature, hurt national pride in the foreign country, and are seen in many countries as an ugly manifestation of "Yankee imperialism." Finally, an increasing number of analysts suggest that if sanctions are to be fully effective, they should be used in conjunction with additional positive incentives (subject perhaps to an expanded certification/approval process) to foster anti-drug cooperation.

Alternatively, some suggest positive incentives instead of sanctions. They believe that narcotics-producing countries must be motivated either to refrain from growing illicit crops, or to permit the purchase or destruction of these crops by government authorities. Many argue that since short term economic stability of nations supplying illegal drugs may depend upon the production and sale of illicit narcotics, it is unrealistic to expect such nations to limit their drug-related activities meaningfully without an alternative source of income. The House Appropriations Committee report on the 1993 foreign operations appropriations bill suggested that when it comes to narcotics related economic development "there is too little emphasis in either actual funding or policy."

It has been suggested by some analysts that a massive foreign aid effort — a so-called "mini-Marshall Plan" — is the only feasible method of persuading developing nations to curb their production of narcotic crops. Such a plan would involve a multilateral effort with the participation of the United States, Europe, Japan, Australia, other industrialized nations susceptible to the drug problem, and the rich oil producing nations. The thrust of such a plan would be to promote economic development, replacing illicit cash crops with other marketable alternatives. Within the framework of such a plan, crops could be purchased or else destroyed by herbicidal spraying or biological control agents while substitute crops and markets are developed and assured.

Any such program would be coupled with rigid domestic law enforcement and penalties for non-compliance. Thus, it could require a U.S. commitment of substantially increased enforcement assets to be used against both growers and traffickers, and some observers assert it might require direct U.S. military involvement at the request of the host country. Significant coercion might be required, since drug crops typically produce a better cash flow than licit crops grown in the same region. For example, in Afghanistan a hectare of opium earns 30 to 45 times as much as a hectare of wheat at prevailing prices ($13,000 compared to $300 to $400). Even if the international community bought up the entire Afghan opium crop, the temptation to plant new opium could prove irresistible to farmers.

Critics have concerns regarding positive incentive concepts. They warn of the precedent of appearing to pay "protection" compensation, that is, providing an incentive for economically disadvantaged countries to go into the drug export business. They also warn of the open-ended cost of agricultural development programs and of extraterritorial police intervention. Finding markets for viable alternative crops is yet another major constraint. Some experts argue that typical conditions of drug crop zones, such as geographical remoteness, marginal soils and, in certain countries, extreme insecurity, tend to limit prospects for legal commercial agriculture. According to one report, the soils in Colombia's Putumayo Department, an important center of coca cultivation, are simply too poor to support the number of people currently farming in the province if all converted to growing legal crops. Such observers believe that a more promising strategy is to foster development of the legal economy in other locales, including urban settings, in order to attract people away from areas that have a comparative advantage in coca or opium production. In the view of these analysts, the best "substitute crop" for coca or opium could well be an assembly plant producing electronic goods or automobiles for the international market.

Expansion of Interdiction and Enforcement Activities to Disrupt Supply Lines/Expanding the Role of the Military

Drug supply line interdiction is both a foreign and domestic issue. Many argue that the United States should intensify law enforcement activities designed to disrupt the transit of illicit narcotics as early in the production/transit chain as possible — well before the drugs reach the streets of the United States. This task is conceded to be very difficult because the United States is the world's greatest trading nation with vast volumes of imports daily flowing in through hundreds of sea, air, and land entry facilities, and its systems have been designed to facilitate human and materials exchange. This has led some analysts to suggest that the military should assume a more active role in anti-drug activities.

Some in Congress, in the late 1980s and prior to appropriations for FY1994, had urged an expanded role for the military in the "war on drugs." The idea of using the military is not novel. Outside the United States, U.S. military personnel have been involved in training and transporting foreign anti-narcotics personnel since 1983. Periodically, there have also been calls for multilateral military strikes against trafficking operations, as well as increased use of U.S. elite forces in preemptive strikes against drug fields and trafficker enclaves overseas.

The military's role in narcotics interdiction was expanded by the FY1990-1991 National Defense Authorization Act. The conference report (H.Rept. 100-989) concluded that the Department of Defense (DOD) can and should play a major role in narcotics interdiction. Congress, in FY1989 and FY1990-1991 authorization acts, required DOD to promptly provide civilian law enforcement agencies with relevant drug-related intelligence; charged the President to direct that command, control, communications, and intelligence networks dedicated to drug control be integrated by DOD into an effective network; restricted direct participation by military personnel in civilian law enforcement activities to those authorized by law; permitted the military to transport civilian law enforcement personnel outside the U.S. land area; expanded the National Guard's role in drug interdiction activities; and authorized additional $300 million for DOD and National Guard drug interdiction activities.

DOD's requested drug budget total for FY2005 was 852.7 million as compared to $908.6 million for FY2004 and as compared to $905.9 million for FY2003.

Despite the military's obvious ability to support drug law enforcement organizations, questions remain as to the overall effectiveness of a major military role in narcotics interdiction. Proponents of substantially increasing the military's role in supporting civilian law enforcement narcotics interdiction activity argue that narcotics trafficking poses a national security threat to the United States; that only the military is equipped and has the resources to counter powerful trafficking organizations; and that counter drug support provides the military with beneficial, realistic training.

In contrast, opponents argue that drug interdiction is a law enforcement mission, it is not a military mission; that drug enforcement is an unconventional war which the military is ill-equipped to fight; that a drug enforcement role detracts from readiness; that a drug enforcement role exposes the military to corruption; that it is unwise public policy to require the U.S. military to operate against U.S. citizens; and that the use of the military may have serious political and diplomatic repercussions overseas. Moreover, some in the military remain concerned about an expanded role, seeing themselves as possible scapegoats for policies that have failed, or are likely to fail.

Expansion of Efforts to Reduce Worldwide Demand

Another commonly proposed option is to increase policy emphasis on development and implementation of programs worldwide that aim at increasing public intolerance for illicit drug use. Such programs, through information, technical assistance, and training in prevention and treatment, would emphasize the health dangers of drug use, as well as the danger to regional and national stability. The State Department's Office of Public Diplomacy and Public Affairs and AID currently support modest efforts in this area. Some believe these programs should be increased and call for a more active role for the United Nations and other international agencies in development and implementation of such demand reduction programs.

Expansion of Economic Disincentives for Illicit Drug Trafficking

Proponents of this approach say that the major factor in the international drug market is not the product, but the profit. Thus, they stress, international efforts to reduce the flow of drugs into the United States must identify means to seize and otherwise reduce assets and profits generated by the drug trade. Some critics point out the challenges of tracking, separating out and confiscating criminal assets. These include the huge volume of all international electronic transfers — more than $2 trillion each day — and the movement of much illegal money outside of formal banking channels (through hawala-type chains of money brokers).

Policymakers pursuing this option must decide whether laws in countries where they exert influence are too lenient on financial institutions, such as banks and brokerage houses, which knowingly facilitate financial transactions of traffickers. If the answer is "yes," national leaders might then take concerted action to promote harsher criminal sanctions penalizing the movement of money generated by drug sales, including revocation of licenses of institutions regularly engaging in such practices. Finally, those supporting this option favor increased efforts to secure greater international cooperation on financial investigations related to money laundering of narcotics profits, including negotiation of mutual legal assistance treaties (MLATs).

THE GEORGE W. BUSH ADMINISTRATION'S ANTI-DRUG STRATEGY

The direction of drug policy under President George W. Bush does not appear to be an immediate top foreign policy priority for the Administration. To date, issues of international terrorism and homeland security appear to command more attention. However, Bush administration officials are beginning to portray Colombia's counter-insurgency campaign as part of the broader worldwide campaign against terrorism. While Congress has stipulated that U.S. military aid to Colombia be dedicated to fighting drugs, support is reportedly growing in

Congress and the Administration for providing direct support to Colombia's efforts to rein in the rebel groups. The extent of any such support — and whether it might involve the use of American combat forces — remains to be determined.

On or about February 23, 2005, the White House released its annual National Drug Control Strategy, [http://www.whitehousedrugpolicy.gov/publications/policy/ndcs05/]. Central to the international component of the strategy is disrupting the operations of drug traffickers "including destroying the economic basis of the cocaine production business in South America by fumigating the coca crop, seizing enormous and unsustainable amounts of cocaine from transporters, and selectively targeting major [drug] organization heads for law enforcement action and, ultimately, extradition and prosecution in the United States."

Possible issues of concern to Congress relating to international drug control policy include the following:

(1) Can the Plan Colombia and the Andean Regional Initiative as currently envisioned have a meaningful impact on reducing drug shipments to the U.S. or in reducing the current level of violence and instability in Colombia? To what degree can a counter-drug plan which does not aim to deal a decisive blow to insurgent operations in Colombia be expected to meaningfully curb drug production and violence there?

(2) To what degree might a more regional approach to the drug problem in Colombia prove more effective and how might such an expanded initiative be funded?

(3) How does U.S. involvement in anti-drug efforts in the Andean nations affect other aspects of American foreign policy in the region, and in Latin America generally? Does a concentration on drug-related issues obscure more fundamental issues of stability, governance, poverty , and democracy (i.e., to what degree are drugs a major cause, or result, of the internal problems of certain Latin American countries)? Might U.S. pursuit of drug control objectives conflict in certain ways with efforts to resolve Colombia's ongoing civil conflict, for instance by alienating large rural constituencies in contested regions of the country?

(4) In the case of Colombia and other nations where insurgents are heavily involved in the drug trade, how can the United States ensure that U.S. military aid and equipment is in fact used to combat drug traffickers and cartels, rather than diverted for use against domestic political opposition or used as an instrument of human rights violations? How great is the risk that such diversions could take place, and is the degree of risk worth the possible gains to be made against drug production and trafficking?

(5) How extensive is drug-related corruption in the armed forces and police of the Andean nations? What impact might such corruption have on the effectiveness of U.S. training and assistance to these forces?

(6) Will an active role for the military in counter-narcotics support to foreign nations (i.e. Colombia) result in U.S. casualties? If so, is there an exit strategy and at what point, if at all, might presidential actions fall within the scope of the War Powers Resolution; that is, does the dispatch of military advisers to help other governments combat drug traffickers constitute the introduction of armed forces "into hostilities or into situations where imminent involvement in hostilities is clearly indicated by the circumstances"? (The War Powers Resolution requires the President to report such an introduction to Congress, and to withdraw the forces within 60 to 90 days unless authorized to remain by Congress.)

(7) Will the evolving strategy under the Bush Administration produce better results than previous strategies in reducing illicit drug use in the United States and in supporting U.S. narcotics and other foreign policy goals overseas? Is a proper balance of resources being devoted to domestic (the demand side) vs. foreign (the supply side) components of an overall national anti-drug strategy? Are efforts to reduce the foreign supply level futile while domestic U.S. demand remains high? Are efforts to reduce domestic demand fruitless as long as foreign supplies can enter the country with relative impunity?

(8) To what extent will the Administration's current priority in fighting terrorism affect implementation of antidrug policy? Has repositioning of equipment and resources to improve U.S. defenses against acts of terrorism, for example the shift of Coast Guard vessels from the eastern Pacific and the Caribbean to perform coastal patrols and port security functions, lowered defenses with respect to curbing drug flows? On the flip side of the issue, to what degree has committing anti-drug resources to support anti-terrorism objectives significantly enhanced the effectiveness of counterterrorism efforts?

(9) To what extent should U.S. military assistance programs in Colombia target groups that use narcotics operations to finance terrorist activities (including leftist guerrillas and paramilitaries), as opposed to the narcotics trafficking infrastructure itself?

CERTIFICATION STATUS

In December 2001, legislation on "Modifications to the Annual Drug Certification Procedures" in the Foreign Operations, Export Financing and Related Programs Appropriations Act (P.L. 107-115, Section 591) was enacted that effectively waived the drug certification requirements for FY2002. It required the President to withhold assistance from the countries most remiss in meeting their international drug-fighting obligations, but permitted the President to determine what countries to put in the "worst offending" category and (under specified conditions) to provide U.S. foreign assistance to a designated country. Legislation on "International Drug Control Certification Procedures" in the Foreign Relations Authorization Act of September 2002 (P.L. 107-228) extended the waiver to FY2003, and subsequently provided for a *de facto* ongoing waiver. Such changes may reflect the fact that spokesmen from many countries have complained for years about the unilateral and noncooperative nature of the drug certification requirements, and have urged the United States to end the process or at least to replace it with multilateral evaluation mechanisms. Acting under this legislation, President Bush made designations on a transitional basis for FY2002 and FY2003, and then made designations on the designated date for FY2004 and FY2005.

On February 23, 2002, the President designated Afghanistan, Burma and Haiti as having "failed demonstrably" in counter-narcotics efforts, but granted national interest waivers to Haiti and Afghanistan under the new government.

On January 31, 2003, he designated Burma, Guatemala, and Haiti, but granted national interest waivers to Guatemala and Haiti.

On September 15, 2003, he designated Burma and Haiti, but granted a national interest waiver to Haiti.

On September 15, 2004, he removed Thailand from the list of major illicit drug transit or producing countries, and designated Burma as having "failed demonstrably" in counter-narcotics efforts.

On September 15, 2005, President Bush issued the annual determination that lists major illicit drug producing or drug transit countries. The President identified 20 countries to be included on the so-called "majors list": Afghanistan, The Bahamas, Bolivia, Brazil, Burma, Colombia, Dominican Republic, Ecuador, Guatemala, Haiti, India, Jamaica, Laos, Mexico, Nigeria, Pakistan, Panama, Paraguay, Peru, and Venezuela. Burma was again singled out a county which had "failed demonstrably" to adhere to its obligations under international counternarcotics agreements. Venezuela was singled out as well as having failed demonstrably, but was granted a national interests waiver exempting it from U.S. aid and trade sanctions and possible access to loans from international financial institutions. China and Vietnam were removed from the list.

PLAN COLOMBIA

On July 13, 2000, U.S. support for Plan Colombia was signed into law (P.L. 106-246). Included was $1.3 billion in emergency supplemental appropriations in equipment, supplies, and other counter narcotics aid primarily for the Colombian military. The plan aimed to curb trafficking activity and reduce coca cultivation in Colombia by 50% over five years. Though focused on military and law enforcement initiatives, Plan components included helping the Colombian Government control its territory; strengthening democratic institutions; promoting economic development; protecting human rights; and providing humanitarian assistance. Included as well was $148 million for Andean regional drug interdiction and alternative development programs. Supporters of the Plan argued that without enhanced U.S. aid, Colombia risks disintegration into smaller autonomous political units — some controlled by leftist or rightist guerrilla groups that are heavily involved in drug trafficking and violent crime -for- profit activity. Other observers cautioned that narcotics-related assistance to Colombia can, at best, produce serious reductions in illicit drug production only within a multi-year timeframe. They warn against enhanced U.S. involvement in a conflict where clear- cut victory is elusive and to a large degree dependent on reduction of the so far intractable U.S. domestic appetite for illicit drugs. Still others warned of the so-called "spillover" effect of Plan Colombia on neighboring nations such as Ecuador where narco-linked insurgents and paramilitaries increasingly operate. For additional data on issues relating to Plan Colombia see CRS Report RL32774, *Plan Colombia, a Progress Report*, CRS Report RL30541, *Colombia: Plan Colombia Legislation and Assistance (FY2000-FY2001)*, and CRS Report RS20494, *Ecuador: International Narcotics Control Issues.*

ANDEAN REGIONAL INITIATIVE

In April 2001, the Bush Administration unveiled an Andean Regional Initiative (ARI) as a successor to Plan Colombia, requesting $882 million for the program. Of these funds approximately 45% percent were intended for Colombia and the remainder for six regional neighbors of Colombia (Bolivia, Brazil, Ecuador, Panama, Peru, and Venezuela) affected by drug trafficking and drug- related violence. By contrast, Colombia received two-thirds of the funds allocated under Plan Colombia. In December 2001, Congress passed the Foreign Operations Appropriations bill for FY2002, allocating $783 million to the ARI. Of the $783 million, 49% were provided to Colombia and the rest to the other six countries. Of the Colombia funds, 36% were earmarked for economic and social and governance purposes and 64% for counternarcotics and security, a ratio largely reflecting the enforcement orientation of Plan Colombia. In the case of Peru and Bolivia, the economic and social share was significantly higher — 61% in both countries. For FY2003, the Bush Administration requested $980 million in ARI funding, of which 55% was for Colombia. The ARI request for FY2004 totaled $990.7 million of which $463 million was for State Department Andean Counterdrug Initiative (ACI) programs for Colombia. For FY2005, Congress appropriated $731 million for the ACI (of which $466.5 was for Colombia) and an additional $106.5 million for Foreign Military Financing (FMF) funding.

REFERENCES

[1] Note, however, that in Congressional testimony on July 10, 2003, Acting State Department INL Assistant Secretary Paul E. Simons announced that coca cultivation in Colombia during the year 2002 had declined overall by more than 15%, a development he characterized as a "direct result of the robust U.S.-assisted aerial eradication program."

In: Illegal Drugs and Governmental Policies
Editor: Lee V. Barton, pp. 35-58

ISBN 978-1-60021-351-9
© 2007 Nova Science Publishers, Inc.

Chapter 3

DRUG CROP ERADICATION AND ALTERNATIVE DEVELOPMENT IN THE ANDES[*]

Connie Veillette and Carolina Navarrete-Frías

SUMMARY

The United States has supported drug crop eradication and alternative development programs in the Andes for decades. Colombia, Bolivia, and Peru collectively produce nearly the entire global supply of cocaine. In addition, Colombia has become a producer of high quality heroin, most of it destined for the United States and Europe. The United States provides counternarcotics assistance through the Andean Counterdrug Initiative (ACI). The program supports a number of missions, including interdiction of drug trafficking, illicit crop eradication, alternative development, and rule of law and democracy promotion. From FY2000 through FY2005, the United States has provided a total of about $4.3 billion in ACI funds.

Since 2001, coca cultivation in the Andes has been reduced by 22%, with the largest decrease occurring in Colombia, according to the State Department. Opium poppy crops, grown mainly in Colombia and from which heroin is made, have been reduced by 67%. However, the region was still capable of producing 640 metric tons of cocaine, and 3.8 metric tons of heroin in 2004, according to the White House Office of National Drug Control Policy.

Congress has expressed a number of concerns with regard to eradication, especially the health and environmental effects of aerial spraying, its sustainability and social consequences, and the reliability of drug crop estimates. With regard to alternative development, Congress has expressed interest in its effectiveness, its relationship to eradication, and the long-term sustainability of programs once they are started.

Drug crops are eradicated either manually or by aerial spraying of a herbicide mixture, the main ingredient being glyphosate, used commercially in the United States under the brand name of Roundup®. Eradication can be conducted with the voluntary agreement of growers, or involuntarily. Peru and Bolivia do not allow aerial eradication, which has proven to be controversial. Critics believe it poses risks to the environment and the health of inhabitants living in sprayed regions. Proponents believe it is the most effective and safe means to defoliate large areas being used for drug crop cultivation, thereby removing a lucrative source of income from the illegally armed Colombian groups.

---

[*] Excerpted from CRS Report RL33163, Updated November 18, 2005

Providing alternatives to drug crops is believed to be crucial to achieve effective eradication. This often includes technical support for farmers, marketing assistance, and strengthening the transportation infrastructure in order to get crops to market. The U.S. approach to alternative development (AD) is to link it to eradication. Growers who agree to eradicate are eligible for assistance.

BACKGROUND

The United States has provided support to drug crop eradication programs in the Andes since the 1980s and for alternative development (AD) since at least the 1970s. Since 2000, the centerpiece of the U.S. counternarcotics policy has been the Andean Counterdrug Initiative (ACI), with Colombia the major recipient. The ACI program is the centerpiece of U.S. support for Plan Colombia, a six-year plan developed by Colombian President Pastrana in 1999. ACI supports a number of missions, including interdiction of drug trafficking, illicit crop eradication, alternative development, and rule of law and democracy promotion in the Andes.

The three main producers of cocaine — Colombia, Bolivia and Peru —collectively produce nearly the entire global supply. In addition, Colombia has become a producer of high quality heroin, most of it destined for the United States. Colombia became the main producer of coca and cocaine in the Andean region in 1997, according to the U.N. Office on Drugs and Crime's (UNODC) *World Drug Report 2005*. Peru was the leading producer of coca and coca paste until that time, which its growers shipped to Colombia for processing into cocaine. Bolivia is the third largest producer of coca.

The United States has made a significant commitment of funds and material support to help the Andean region fight drug trafficking since 2000. (See **Table 1**.) Congress passed legislation providing $1.3 billion in assistance for FY2000 (P.L. 106-246) for Colombia and its neighbors. From FY2000 through FY2005, the United States has provided a total of about $4.3 billion from the Andean Counterdrug Initiative account. For FY2006, the Administration requested, and Congress approved, $734.5 million in ACI funding (P.L. 109-102). The Department of Defense has spent approximately $1.2 billion from FY2000 through FY2005 from its counternarcotics account, managed by the U.S. Army Southern Command. The State Department's International Narcotics Control and Law Enforcement (INL) bureau is responsible for managing the ACI account. The countries considered part of the ACI include Bolivia, Brazil, Colombia, Ecuador, Panama, Peru, and Venezuela,[1] with most funding allocated for Colombia, Peru and Bolivia.

Additional funding for the Andean region is provided through the Foreign Military Financing (FMF) program and the International Military Education and Training (IMET) program, both managed by the State Department. FMF provides grants to foreign nations to purchase U.S. defense equipment, services, and training. FMF assistance to Colombia, Peru, and Bolivia has the objective of establishing and strengthening national authority in remote areas that are prone to drug trafficking, and related activities of illegally armed groups. Some FMF funding has been used for infrastructure protection of oil pipelines in Colombia. The IMET program provides training for foreign militaries. Its objectives are to improve defense capabilities, develop professional and personal relationships between U.S. and foreign militaries, and influence these forces in support of democratic governance. Training focuses on the manner in which military organizations function under civilian control, civil-military relations, military justice systems, military doctrine, strategic planning, and operational procedures.

Table 1. U.S. Drug - Related Foreign Assistance to the Andean Region, FY2000-FY2006 (in millions U.S. $)

FY	ACI	FMF	IMET	Total
FY2000	1,174.8	—	2.4	1,177.2
FY2001	154.8	—	2.8	157.6
FY2002	651.0	3.5	3.0	657.5
FY2003	842.5	21.1	3.2	866.8
FY2004	726.7	102.5	2.3	831.5
FY2005	725.0	103.2	3.1	831.3
FY2006	734.5	94.0	3.5	832.0
Total	5,009.3	324.3	20.3	5,353.9

Source: Congressional Budget Justifications, Foreign Operations FY2002-FY2006; U.S. Department of State's Washington File, "U.S. Support for Plan Colombia, FY2000 Emergency Supplemental Appropriations," July 5, 2000.

Note: ACI figures reflect funding for all nations considered a part of the Andean Counterdrug Initiative. FMF and IMET figures are for Bolivia, Colombia, Ecuador, and Peru. FY2006 figures for FMF and IMET are amounts proposed by the Administration in its budget request.

Table 2. ACI Funding Eradication versus Alternative Development, FY2000-FY2006 (in millions U.S. $)

FY	Colombia		Peru		Bolivia	
	Eradic.	AD	Eradic.	AD	Eradic.	AD
FY2000	686.4	208.0	55.0	25.0	57.0	101.0
FY2001	48.0	—	21.0	27.0	32.0	20.0
FY2002	243.5	136.4	75.0	67.5	48.0	39.6
FY2003	412.0	168.2	59.5	68.6	49.0	41.7
FY2004	324.6	159.3	66.3	49.7	49.2	41.8
FY2005	310.7	152.1	61.5	53.9	48.6	41.7
FY2006	310.9	158.6	59.0	49.0	43.0	37.0
Totals	2,336.1	982.6	397.3	340.7	326.8	322.8

Note: Eradication figures include interdiction programs; AD figures include institution building programs. The FY2006 figures are the amounts provided in the FY2006 Foreign Operations Appropriations Act, P.L. 109-102. Other figures are drawn from Foreign Operations annual congressional budget justifications, FY2002 through FY2006.

ACI funds are divided between programs that support eradication and interdiction efforts, as well as those focused on alternative development and democratic institution building. On the interdiction side, programs train and support national police and military forces, provide communications and intelligence systems, support the maintenance and operations of host country aerial eradication aircraft, and improve infrastructure related to counternarcotics activities. On the alternative development side, funds support development programs in drug crop growing areas, including infrastructure, and marketing and technical support for alternative crops. It also includes assistance for internally displaced persons, promotion of the rule of law, and expansion of judicial capabilities.

Extent of Drug Crop Cultivation

The State Department reports that the area under coca cultivation in the Andes in 2003 was 428,595 acres, down from a high point of 552,763 acres in 2001, representing a 22% decline. The largest decrease has occurred in Colombia, with a 32% decline in coca cultivation since 2001, the year that Colombian production reached its peak.[2] For 2004, the Office of National Drug Control Policy (ONDCP) reported no decrease in Colombian coca cultivation.[3]

The eradication of opium poppies, grown mainly in Colombia, has resulted in crop decreases from about 16,000 acres in 2001 to nearly 5,200 acres in 2004, representing a 67% decrease. The largest portion of the decrease occurred from 2003 to 2004 when cultivation was cut in half.[4]

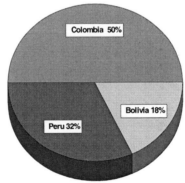

Source: United Nations Office on Drugs and Crime, Coca Cultivation in the Andean Region: A Survey of
     Bolivia, Colombia and Peru, June 2005.

Figure 1. Coca Cultivation 2004as Percent of Global Total

Both Peru and Bolivia allow a small level of legal cultivation for indigenous use. Coca leaf use is a deeply rooted cultural tradition in which the leaf is chewed or made into tea, and is used as a stimulant, appetite suppressant, and treatment for stomach ailments. It is also used to ease altitude sickness. When chewed or used as tea, coca does not have a hallucinogenic effect, and has been compared to the effects of coffee. Bolivia's Law 1008 allows nearly 30,000 acres of legal coca, while Peru's 1978 General Law on Drugs permits about 28,000 acres. In Bolivia, coca cultivation is legal in the Yungas region and some parts of Chapare. Growers may sell their product to intermediaries who are licensed by the government drug agency that also controls two legal coca markets. Peruvian law requires that growers are registered, and obligates its 14,463 registered growers to sell their coca leaf to the state-owned firm, National Coca Enterprise (ENACO). In neither country are there clear demarcations for which exact cultivation areas are legal versus illegal. For example, while

Bolivian law permits coca cultivation in the Yungas region, authorities have not identified which fields should be counted toward the 30,000 acre limit.[5]

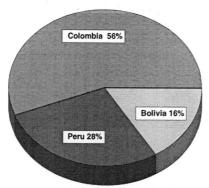

Source: United Nations Office on Drugs and Crime, Coca Cultivation in the Andean Region: A Survey of Bolivia, Colombia and Peru, June 2005.

Figure 2. Cocaine Production 2004 as Percent of Global Total

Eradication Programs

There are two types of eradication programs. Aerial eradication, often referred to as fumigation, involves dispersing the chemical glyphosate, an herbicide mixed with water and the surfactant Cosmo Flux 411F, from low-flying aircraft over illicit crops to kill or inhibit their growth. Drug crops can also be manually eradicated, often with the agreement of the grower, but also without his consent. Both aerial and manual eradication takes place in Colombia, while Bolivia and Peru allow only manual eradication. U.S. support for eradication programs is managed by the State Department's Bureau of International Narcotics and Law Enforcement Affairs (INL), and the Narcotics Affairs Section (NAS) of U.S. embassies. Spray missions are conducted by U.S.-hired contractors, through the State Department's Office of Interregional Aviation Support.

Colombia. Unlike Peru and Bolivia, Colombia has no legal market for coca leaf, with all of it destined for processing into cocaine. There are few indigenous communities that use coca leaf for traditional, cultural, or medicinal purposes. Putumayo has been the principal coca growing area, but cultivation has now spread to more than 20 of Colombia's 32 regions.[6] Opium poppy is grown mainly in the mountainous regions of Tolima, Huila, Cauca, and Nariño. Poppy is grown on very small plots of land and interspersed with other crops, making its detection and eradication difficult.

When Plan Colombia began in 2000, the aerial eradication of coca and poppy crops with a glyphosate herbicide mixture became a key component of the Colombian and U.S. efforts to reduce the supply of illegal drugs entering the U.S. market. Glyphosate had previously been used aerially in the successful eradication of marijuana in the 1980s in Colombia. Spray operations are conducted by the Colombian National Police with U.S. support through the State Department's Office of Interregional Aviation. The United States provides technical and scientific advice, herbicide, fuel, spray aircraft, and a limited number of escort helicopters. Spray aircraft are piloted by U.S. citizens, Colombian, or third-country national contractors, and are accompanied by escort helicopters that carry combined U.S. civilian contractors or third-country nationals, and Colombian National Police crews. Spray aircraft use global positioning computer systems to identify locations of crops, with areas for spraying chosen by the Colombian government. There are currently 17 fixed-wing and 26 helicopters devoted to spraying operations. Aircraft are flying missions from three forward operating locations (FOL) in Colombia.[7]

Reductions in coca and opium poppy cultivation began to be seen by 2003. Some areas where aerial eradication took place experienced marked decreases —Meta, Caquetá, and Putumayo. But, these successes have been accompanied by increases in other areas — Antioquia, Nariño, and Guaviare.[8] Areas that have been manually eradicated, Vichada, Bolívar, and Cauca, have had lower rates of reduction. While manual eradication does not carry as many risks as the aerial program, the rate of eradication is much slower and requires more manhours with operations in rugged, inaccessible, and often hostile territory. A 1988 Government Accountability Office (GAO) report concluded that manual eradication had been unable to keep pace with new plantings, and so had a minimal effect on cultivation.[9] The United States Agency for International Development (USAID) supports voluntary agreements with communities in coca growing regions, whereby the communities themselves eradicate their drug crops in exchange for development assistance. More recently, the government of Colombia has used demobilized right-wing paramilitary fighters, flying them to coca regions to manually eradicate crops.

Peru. Peru's support for eradication programs has varied historically, based on the political conditions in the country and the resolve of national governments. While once the largest producer of cocaine in the Andes, it is now second to Colombia. The traditional areas of coca cultivation are the Upper Huallaga/Monzon and the Apurimac/Ene Valleys, although the State Department has reported that dense cultivation is increasing in other areas. It also reports that there is an upward trend in opium poppy cultivation in northern Peru. Coca cultivation has decreased in Peru from its peak in 1995 and is considered an Andean success story. Some observers believe the reduction was due to several factors other than the eradication operations, including the following: the appearance of a soil fungus, Fusarium oxysporum in the Huallaga Valley; the decline of Colombia's dependence on Bolivian and Peruvian coca; and the successful dismantling of Colombia's drug cartels that were the principal buyers of Peruvian coca. This led to a collapse in coca prices in the early 1990s.[10] The government of Peru allows only the manual eradication of drug crops.

By the end of the 1980s, Peru was the world's leading producer of coca leaf, supplying 60% of world supply. Early in President Fujimori's government (1990-2000), he adopted an approach that emphasized alternative development and land titling, incorporating coca farmers into the formal economy, while de-emphasizing forced eradication. As his administration proceeded, Fujimori adopted policies that gave more authority to the military in drug matters, and combined counterinsurgency and drug control missions. Forced eradication was restarted in 1996 and increased in tempo toward the end of the 1990s. Eradication operations provoked the mobilization of coca growers, especially in light of unsubstantiated claims that spraying of crops was occurring. This led Fujimori to sign a decree prohibiting the use of chemical or biological defoliants in 2000. Under the Toledo government (2001 to present), alternative development programs using voluntary agreements have become again widely utilized, although forced eradication continues. Assistance for growers is provided, as long as they sign agreements to fully eradicate their crops. If an agreement is not signed, forced eradication occurs, and the grower reaps no assistance. The

State Department reports that in 2004, about 18,500 acres were forcefully eradicated, while another 6,000 acres were part of the alternative development/voluntary eradication program.

Bolivia.[11] Political instability in Bolivia has resulted in the uneven application of counternarcotics policy over the years. Despite this, Bolivia has seen some successes in reducing cultivation, but some observers would argue, at the expense of social unrest. The two main coca growing regions are Chapare and Yungas. Since the beginning of *Plan Dignidad* in 1998, the counternarcotics policy of former President Banzer (1997-2001) that focused on increasing forced eradication, cultivation in the Chapare has decreased. It has, however, dramatically increased in the Yungas. The State Department reports that the increase is far above the legal limit. As in Peru, indigenous Bolivians believe coca is a cultural right and use it for cultural, spiritual, and medical purposes.

Total coca cultivation in Bolivia decreased from its peak in the mid-1990s of 118,000 acres to around 36,000 acres in 2000, but in 2001, coca cultivation began to increase again and to expand to new areas. In 2004, the State Department estimates that there were nearly 61,000 acres of coca crops.[12] Bolivian law states that only manual and mechanical methods can be used to eradicate, and prohibits the use of "chemical means, herbicides, biological agents, and defoliants."[13] While interim presidents have reaffirmed their support for counternarcotics policy, continuing political instability and the mobilization of coca growers' organizations, especially in the context of an upcoming presidential election, have led some observers to question the resolve of the national government. Both the State Department and the UNODC reported increases in coca cultivation during 2004.

Alternative Development Programs

Providing alternatives to drug crop cultivation is believed to be a crucial component to achieve effective eradication. U.S. alternative development programs are managed by the U.S. Agency for International Development, and often include technical support for farmers agreeing to give up their drug crops, marketing assistance, and the strengthening of transportation infrastructure in order to get crops to market.

Alternative development began in the mid-1970s in Bolivia, (Chapare region) and in the early 1980s in Peru (Upper Huallaga Valley), as coca crop substitution. The United States was the principal donor, with UNODC involvement beginning in 1984. U.S. alternative development strategies played a modest role in Colombia until 2000, when the United States started investing in AD as part of its support for Plan Colombia. The legal framework for AD in Peru is Law 22095, which outlaws all coca cultivation except that grown by farmers registered with the government agency, National Coca Enterprise (ENACO). Bolivia's Law 1008 permits legal coca cultivation only in traditional coca-growing areas. Under these laws, alternative development programs benefit farmers growing illicit coca, while those cultivating legal coca for traditional purposes fail to receive assistance.

The main feature of U.S.-supported alternative development programs is that they are tied to agreements by farmers and communities to eradicate coca crops. USAID's objectives are to encourage farmers to grow alternative crops and become part of the legal economy. After farmers agree to eradicate illicit crops, they receive support for food crops, while plans for future cash crops are made. In a recognition that crop substitution is insufficient to realize sustainable development, projects are also undertaken to improve an affected area's infrastructure, such as road, water systems, schools and municipal buildings, which also provides employment opportunities for former coca farmers. Education, infrastructure, and health services are provided to make sure that coca and poppy growing regions would attract and support other economic activities.

Colombia. USAID works to strengthen Colombia's National Alternative Development Plan and the capabilities of local non-governmental organizations. By increasing licit economic opportunities, it is believed coca and poppy growers will be able to permanently give up illegal crops. Over the past five years, USAID reports that it established 62,964 hectares of legal crops, 31,461 hectares of forest land, and completed 918 social and productive infrastructure projects, benefitting over 54,780 families, in collaboration with local NGOs. In 2003, USAID started to support small- and medium-sized agribusiness and commercial forestry development activities. Projects cover areas such as wood projects, cocoa, coffee, rubber, oil palm, exotic fruits, medicinal herbs, and handcrafts in 30 of the 32 departments. Since 2000, the United States has allocated about $976 million for AD programs.

Peru. USAID describes its programs in Peru as a multi-sector approach that seeks to improve local governance, strengthen the rule of law, and increase the economic competitiveness of coca-growing areas. Its programs focus on generating temporary income to growers who voluntarily eradicate their crops, supporting basic services, and promoting community organization. USAID then seeks to promote sustainable economic and social development in and around primary coca-growing areas. This includes infrastructure projects, technical assistance and training to small farmers, private sector entrepreneurs, and government entities. The agency reports in its annual congressional budget justification for FY2006 that more than 27,000 families have voluntarily eradicated nearly 18,000 acres of coca since October 2002.

Since 2000, the United States has supported more than $330 million in AD programs. In 2004, USAID supported "legal productive activities" on about 49,000 acres, built or rehabilitated 134 schools, health facilities, and water systems, 205 kilometers of road, 12 bridges and irrigation projects, and brought electrification to six communities. Support for the rehabilitation and maintenance of a major highway out of the Huallaga Valley, a coca region, has eased the transportation of agricultural products to national markets. In 2004, USAID reports that 20,000 families made voluntary eradication agreements.

Bolivia. Bolivia has had the largest and longest running alternative development program in the Andes with USAID making major investments there. Since the start of the ACI, the United States has spent about $323 million on such programs. In the Chapare region, a coca growing area, USAID has focused on strengthening licit livelihoods, community development, legal land tenure, and access to justice. More recently, and in response to the decrease in cultivation there, USAID is adopting a more integrated approach that puts emphasis on sustainability and increased participation by municipalities to develop, implement, and monitor programs. In 2004, USAID assisted 28,290 rural families, and increased the number of licit jobs by 9,300 and licit cultivation by 21,000 acres in the region. Similar programs are conducted in the Yungas, along with assistance for coffee cultivation and rural electrification projects.[14]

ISSUES FOR CONGRESS

Congress has expressed a number of concerns with regard to eradication, including the following: the health and environmental effects of aerial spraying; the reliability of drug crop estimates; and the effectiveness and sustainability of eradication. With regard to alternative development, Congress has expressed interest in its effectiveness; its relationship with eradication; and the long-term sustainability of programs. Both eradication and alternative development face a number of challenges, some of which are general to the region, and others that are specific to the country in which they are conducted.

Health and Environmental Effects of Herbicides[15]

Since the inception of aerial coca crop eradication, Members of Congress have expressed concerns about the possible health and environmental effects of the herbicides used. There is also concern with the proposed use of aerial eradication in Colombia's national parks, which is currently prohibited by Colombian law. Congress has directed in annual Foreign Operations Appropriation legislation that the aerial spray program be certified by the U.S. State Department as causing no unreasonable risk to the environment or health of people living in sprayed areas. Congress has also directed that spraying in national parks can only occur if it is consistent with Colombian law, and no other viable alternatives exist.[16]

The program in Colombia uses a mixture of Roundup Ultra Herbicide®,[17] water, and Cosmo Flux 411F, which is a blend of two additives, whose identities are considered trade secrets.[18] The Roundup® product contains the active ingredient glyphosate, a surfactant — polyoxethylene alkylamine (POEA) — to aid penetration of foliage, and another unnamed additive.[19] The same herbicide mixture is used in Colombia for eradicating both coca plants and opium poppy, although because poppy is easier to eradicate, less glyphosate (relative to the amount of water) is needed in the formulation. Roundup Ultra Herbicide® (but not Cosmo Flux 411F) is registered, sold, and widely used in the United States, where it has generally been considered a relatively safe and environmentally friendly herbicide.[20]

Studies on Glyphosate. The State Department consulted with the U.S. Environmental Protection Agency (EPA) and reported in 2002 and 2003 that the EPA had found that "there is no evidence of significant human health or environmental risks from the spraying" in Colombia.[21] The State Department has certified four times since 2002 that the herbicide mixture poses no unreasonable risk to health or the environment, and that usage in Colombia is consistent with applications in the United States and with label recommendations.[22]

Both the EPA and the State Department have acknowledged that unintentional spraying of legal crops and natural vegetation, due to spray drift, is likely to kill plants downwind of coca fields.[23] But the State Department argues that such damage is reversible (that is, the forest re-grows and new crops may be planted) and not an unreasonable price to pay for drug eradication, given the severity of environmental and health impacts of coca production, processing, and distribution. Chemicals used by coca growers and processors include pesticides, herbicides (2,4-D and paraquat), kerosene, sulfuric acid, ammonia, and acetone.[24]

The State Department's 2005 certification is supported by a recent study by the Organization of American States (OAS).[25] The Inter-American Drug Abuse Control

Commission (CICAD), an OAS agency, undertook a "science-based risk assessment of the human health and environmental effects" of glyphosate in response to a request from the United States, United Kingdom, and Colombia. The report concluded that neither glyphosate nor Cosmo Flux 411F presents "a significant risk to human health." With regard to the environment, CICAD determined that risks were minimal in most circumstances, but that spray drift poses moderate risks to aquatic organisms in shallow or static water. (Risks to aquatic life are discussed below.) The probability and extent of such impacts is unknown. The report concluded that based on available data, glyphosate has less environmental impact than cocaine and poppy production and processing, which also cause deforestation, displacement of flora and fauna, and damage to non-target plants and animals. (The risks of certain additives are discussed below). However, the report also recommended testing of other additives that might pose less risk to aquatic life as well as further study to better understand the potential for adverse effects on human health or the environment.

The annual certifications by the State Department and the CICAD study have been criticized by environmental groups and some researchers.[26] Criticism often centers around the composition of the herbicide mixture used in Colombia, which is different from that applied in the United States.[27] However, EPA knows the identities of the ingredients in Cosmo Flux 411F and has stated that they are "approved for use in/on food by EPA."[28] The State Department's certification mentions that the application rate for Cosmo Flux 411F is within the manufacturer's recommended application rate. In addition, the State Department provided EPA with data from six acute toxicity studies conducted using the mixture used in Colombia, as well as information about health complaints. Of the 5,000 health complaints received through 2004, half were "rejected as invalid, because it was determined that spraying did not take place in the areas in question on the dates claimed."[29] Compensation for lost crops was paid in 12 cases. In no instance did the U.S. embassy or the Colombian government determine that spraying caused harm to human health or wildlife.[30] Based on this information, EPA concluded in its 2003 report that "there are no risks of concern from [sic] dietary, mixer/loader/ applicator or field workers, or bystanders (including children)."[31]

Others who disagree with the conclusions reached by the State Department and CICAD question the applicability of toxicity data gathered in the United States to a tropical environment and its ecosystems. Rather, it is argued, studies should be conducted to assess effects on the forests and wildlife of Colombia, and information should be gathered from Colombians. One such study, requested by the Colombian Ombudsman's Office, and conducted along the Ecuador-Colombian border, reported that blood samples taken from 22 women showed genetic damage. The incidence of damage was far greater (500% and 800%) than found in two control groups.[32] The State Department is cooperating with the Colombian government to collect data on health complaints in the areas where spraying occurs, but such information is difficult to collect and to interpret.

Toxicity of Additives. Several recent scientific studies have led to conclusions that apparently conflict with those of previous studies and raise the possibility that spraying might lead to adverse effects on human health or the environment. The weight of recent evidence seems to be pointing not to glyphosate, but rather to POEA, the surfactant in Roundup®, as a potential hazard.[33] One study, at the University of Caen, France, found that human placental cells are sensitive to Roundup® at concentrations lower than those found in agricultural use. This study found that the effects of Roundup® were greater than those of glyphosate alone, indicating that adjuvants had their own effect, either independently or in combination with glyphosate.[34] A Chinese study found that POEA was more toxic to aquatic creatures and algae than Roundup, which in turn was more toxic than glyphosate.[35] Another study, by a University of Pittsburgh biologist, reported that Roundup® may be "extremely lethal" to amphibians. The researcher's experiments with North American tadpoles produced high rates of mortality.[36] Similarly, experiments with young adult frogs and toads indicated a potential for significant toxicity.[37]

Spraying in National Parks. Because of the eradication program, some drug crop cultivation has moved to national parks. It is estimated that 28,000 acres of coca are being grown in Colombia's 49 national parks, a more than doubling of the 11,000 acres under cultivation three years ago. The Colombian government is now considering lifting its ban on spraying in the national parks. Critics fear that spraying will also kill many plant species in the jungles and mountains, and could also harm amphibians, mammals, and birds. Colombia's national parks contain a large number of diverse plant and animal species.[38]

Proponents of spraying in the national parks argue that coca cultivation does more harm to the environment than eradication. The processing of coca leaf into cocaine base is also harmful to the environment. Growers often clear forested land in order to plant crops, while traffickers do the same to build transportation routes and landing strips. The State Department reports that over the past 20 years, coca cultivation in the Andean region has resulted in the destruction of at least 5.9 million acres of rainforest. The processing of coca leaf into cocaine base involves the use of harsh precursor chemicals such as kerosene, ethyl ether, sulfuric acid, potassium permanganate, acetone, and thousands of tons of lime and carbide, which are allowed to seep into the water supply and soil, and contaminate the food chain. According to the Colombian government, traffickers have dumped more than one million tons of chemicals since the mid-1980s.

Alternative Methods. While the effects of coca and poppy production and processing may be more damaging to the environment and human health than crop eradication with glyphosate and Cosmo Flux 411F, eradication may motivate coca growers who lose their crops to start over in other, more remote parts of the forest, causing still more ecosystem destruction. If eradication is, nevertheless, the best option, then alternative methods of crop eradication might arguably be more benign.

Some alternatives, such as eradication by hand, might be impractical, due to the terrain and hostility of drug growers.

Other methods might hold more promise. Biological controls for drug crops were discussed in a 1993 report to Congress by the Office of Technology Assessment.[39] Biological controls use living things or their byproducts to reduce the target plant pest to a tolerable level. The living things may be native to an area and natural enemies of the target plant, or they might be imported. In either case, to be effective in controlling pests, they first must be identified and then established in sufficient numbers in proximity to the targeted plants. At the same time, it is important to ensure that such biological agents are controlled to keep them from attacking or competing with non-targeted, native plants and animals. It also would be necessary to consider the potential susceptibility of any live biological controls to pesticides that might be available to coca or poppy producers. In sum, development of potential biological controls could require significant investments in research and field testing.

A form of biological control that has received attention is the use of mycoherbicides, which are naturally occurring fungi that infect and kill plants. In the 109th Congress, the

Government Reform Subcommittee on Criminal Justice, Drugs and Human Resources approved an amendment to H.R. 2829, the Office of National Drug Control Policy Reauthorization Act of 2005, that authorizes a study on the health and environmental effects of mycoherbicides. The mycoherbicide *Fusarium oxysporum* (species *erythroxyli*, known as FoxyE) has received the most attention as a possible means of controlling drug crops. It was discovered on diseased coca plants in a research facility of the U.S. Department of Agriculture during the 1980s.[40] Some have advocated substitution of this fungus for glyphosate in aerial applications in Colombia, because, they argue, it is endemic to Andean countries, non-toxic to people and animals, does not attack non-target plants, and persists in the environment. However, other species of *fusarium* attack a wide range of plants and some fear that the coca-specific species might mutate.[41] The Colombian government has not approved its use.

Reliability of Drug Crop Estimates

Producing reliable estimates of illegal crop cultivation is difficult for several reasons relating to the methodologies used and the changing nature of cultivation. Several organizations monitor the cultivation levels of drug crops, often using different methodologies and producing different results. A 2003 Government Accountability Office (GAO) report examined the differences in methodology between the ONDCP and the State Department's Office of Aviation. In one area, the two organizations differed in the identification of drug crop fields by 79%. The discrepancy was largely based on differences in definition of what should be counted as a coca field. As a result, the report concluded that there are reliability problems with the both surveys. Neither had in place a statistically rigorous accuracy assessment, commonly known as an error rate, for their respective methodologies; and the technologies were insufficient for the purposes they were being used.[42]

The U.S. government data also often differs from that of the U.N. Office on Drugs and Crime (UNODC), which has consistently reported higher eradication rates. For example, the United States estimates that coca cultivation in Colombia decreased from 336,000 acres in 2000 to 282,000 in 2004, a 16% reduction. The United Nations reports that cultivation went from 403,000 acres to 198,000 in the same period, a 51% reduction. U.S. figures show that in 2004, Colombia cultivation remained stable, while UNODC reported a 7% decrease. Likewise, the United Nations reported increases in Bolivia (17%) and Peru (14%), while the United States reported decreases. ONDCP reports that estimates are made using survey-sampling techniques and satellite imagery, that it argues is similar to techniques used to estimate agricultural crops in the United States. The United Nations report interprets satellite images taken over a five month period, and verifies the results with aerial surveillance and on-the-ground observations. Margins of error can differ based on the resolution of satellite images, neglecting to include areas of new plantations, and missing areas where coca has been interspersed with licit crops. Opium poppy, grown in small plots and at high altitudes with nearly permanent cloud cover, are particularly difficult to survey.

The nature of cultivation is also changing as a result of eradication efforts. Growers are reducing the size of their crops and interspersing them among food crops in order to avoid detection. It is estimated that around half of Colombia's coca is grown on fields of less than

7.5 acres. Further, there is some evidence that farmers are increasing the density of plants per acre.[43]

Effectiveness and Sustainability of Aerial Eradication

Whether aerial eradication is an effective means to curb drug production has been a matter of intense debate. Even when eradication programs have been unable to reduce cultivation, as occurred in 2004 in Colombia, officials argue that drug production has still decreased because newer crops, planted to replace eradicated ones, are less productive. According to the Office of National Drug Control Policy, the eradication program in Colombia has resulted in potential cocaine production decreasing by 7% in 2004 to 430 metric tons of pure cocaine. This is down from its peak of 700 metric tons in 2001. The same report indicated that potential cocaine production throughout the Andes has fallen 5% in 2004. Total regional cocaine production is estimated at 640 metric tons, dropping nearly 30% from its peak of 900 metric tons in 2001. Potential heroin production in 2004 decreased by 51%.[44]

Some observers caution that the propensity of farmers to replant coca and poppy is a troubling indication with regard to the sustainability of eradication programs, demonstrating that no lasting change in preferences is being achieved. John Walters, the head of ONDCP, stated in 2004 during a trip to Colombia that 85% of crops sprayed are replanted very quickly. The Environmental Protection Agency (EPA) reports that the herbicide glyphosate has no residual effect; plants that would be susceptible to glyphosate can be planted shortly after its application.[45] Other observers believe that decreases in cultivation in one area will result in increases in other areas. For example, successful eradication programs in the Putumayo region, the traditional coca growing area of Colombia, have been accompanied by increases in other regions. While both the ONDCP and the State Department report that a balloon effect — coca cultivation moving from one area to another as eradication proceeds — has not been observed across borders, there is evidence that some cultivation has moved across borders, although not yet in size that would indicate a large shift in cultivation patterns.[46]

In Bolivia and Peru, cultivation has been sensitive to changes in price. When prices have been depressed, growers have abandoned their crops. When prices increase, abandoned crops have been reactivated.[47] In Peru, the head of its antidrug agency reported that the price of coca leaf had increased from 80 cents per dry ton in 1980 to around $4 in 2005. Part of the price increase was attributed to the aerial eradication campaign in Colombia which had forced traffickers to turn to Peruvian suppliers.[48] The price, purity, and availability of cocaine and heroin have generally remained stable since 2000. However, the ONDCP reported in November 2005 that cocaine prices were beginning to show increases across the country. This complements earlier data indicating a recent increase in heroin prices in some parts of the United States.[49] Some studies question the effect of eradication on drug prices. Even if increased eradication forced coca prices to double, the retail price of cocaine would likely be negligible. Since the mid-1990s, coca leaf prices in the Andes have increased, while the retail price of cocaine has not.[50] This may be due to the fact that coca leaf represents a very small fraction of the retail price. A 1994 study showed that coca leaf represents just 2% of the street price.[51]

Some Members of Congress have urged that the Colombian government take over the operation of the eradication program that is now provided by the United States. A 2003 GAO report found that neither the Colombian military nor the police are able to sustain the current program "without continued U.S. funding and contractor support for the foreseeable future."[52]

Eradication Challenges

Each country presents its own challenges to successful eradication. In Colombia, the armed conflict among illegally armed groups who profit from the drug trade and who control vast territory complicate eradication missions.[53] Other challenges there include difficulties with regard to the conduct of aerial eradication and criticism of the compensation system for accidental spraying of food crops. Peru and Bolivia face growing indigenous movements that are becoming formidable politically and are pushing for an end to eradication, and in some cases, for legalization of cultivation.

Spray Drift. Because Colombia allows aerial eradication of drug crops, there have been complaints about food crops, and even alternative development sites being sprayed. Supporters of the program contend that the targeted fields are identified with high precision, and the areas sprayed are electronically documented. Further, the spray drift is supposedly minimized by the use of large droplets, making the likelihood of accidental spraying from drift less than 1% of the total area sprayed.[54] While the State Department reports that "occasional errors are unavoidable," it argues that every effort is made to minimize human and mechanical mistakes.[55] Spray missions are not to be conducted when wind speed at the airport is above 10 m.p.h., relative humidity is below 75%, and the temperature is more than 90 degrees. Spray planes fly at low altitudes, generally less than 100 feet, when releasing the herbicide. According to the Colombian government, the Colombian National Police does not spray regions that are identified as present or future alternative development recipients.

However, there are numerous reports of spray drift affecting licit crops and forestland. The Colombian Ombudsman's Office reported that the Indigenous Organizations of Putumayo (OZIP) complained spraying had taken place in the Nasa Chamb community in Puerto Asis, and that the area has no coca cultivation. The office also reported complaints from other parts of Putumayo in 2001 and 2002 that areas with corn, fruit trees, and grasslands had been sprayed. The Comptroller's Office reported in 2004 that forests near targeted areas had been damaged by spray drift, and Ecuador has complained that spray drift has affected crops across its border with Colombia.[56]

Compensation for Accidental Spraying. The U.S. Congress has included provisions in the annual foreign operations appropriations legislation[57] requiring the evaluation of complaints of harm to licit crops, or human health caused by aerial eradication, and for fair compensation to be paid for "meritorious" claims. Colombian law also provides for compensation in such cases. Complaints of potential harm to licit crops are investigated by the Colombian government, with nearly 50% of cases eliminated after verifying that the specific places during the dates reported were not fumigated. The remaining complaints are verified by field visits, where it is often found that licit crops were planted near drug crops. Under Colombian law, illicit crops that are interspersed with licit crops are legitimate objects of aerial fumigation.

According to the State Department's March 2005 *International Narcotics Control Strategy Report*, the Colombian National Police Antinarcotics Directorate (DIRAN), the agency responsible for aerial eradication operations, has received approximately 5,500 complaints of accidental food crop and/or pastureland spraying since 2001. Of these, 12 received compensation, resulting in about $30,000 in compensation. DIRAN reported that as of June 2004, those filing reports were residents of remote rural areas. Almost two-thirds were rejected because they were filed late, or because coca plantings were found next to food crops, while one-third were still under consideration. DIRAN also reported that peasants had filed complaints in no spray zones, that some complaints of damaged food crops had coca interspersed (and therefore subject to spraying under Colombian law), and that health complaints were due to other unrelated factors.

Critics argue that the few claims for restitution that have been accepted do not indicate the extent of the problem. They cite the "substantial security risks, time, and expense involved in farmers traveling to town and filing claims."[58] Colombia's Ombudsman's Office has indicated that the long distances, lack of roads and the security situation constrain the registration of complaints as well as their verification within specified deadlines. That office, and the Comptroller General's Office (CGO), has questioned the advisability of having DIRAN review compensation claims when they are also responsible for eradication.[59]

Social Effects. Public opposition to eradication has contributed to the growth in indigenous political movements in Peru and Bolivia. These movements have in some cases undermined the political will of national governments to aggressively eradicate, and have spurred movements to legalize cultivation. In Colombia, the larger conflict, in which drug trafficking is a component, has produced a large internally displaced population as people flee drug zones.

Public opposition has been most evident in Bolivia where eradication has met with protests from coca growers (*cocaleros*) who have organized themselves in legally recognized labor unions. Coca growers have also formed their own political party, the Movement toward Socialism (MAS). The MAS presidential candidate, Evo Morales, came in a close second in the last presidential election in 2002, and is a candidate in the upcoming election scheduled for December 18, 2005. The continuing protests in Bolivia, orchestrated largely by coca growing unions and their supporters, have contributed to the resignations of two presidents, and continuing instability. Interim president, Eduardo Rodriguez, has made a commitment to not increase the pace of eradication until a study is completed to determine the current level of traditional coca leaf use. Cocaleros have also protested the use of combined military and police units for eradication; conflicts with growers resulted in 33 deaths of growers, and 27 police and military fatalities between 1998 and 2003.[60]

In Peru, there has been a growing movement to de-criminalize cultivation, above the government-sanctioned legal limits. The region of Cuzco passed an ordinance in June of 2005 to allow legal coca cultivation. This ordinance was accepted by the national government on the grounds that it applied to areas where cultivation is already legal. The Cuzco ordinance prompted two other regions to follow suit —Puno and Huánaco — although the national government has stated that these ordinances are incompatible with national law. With President Toledo's low popularity and growing discontent in coca growing regions, some observers believe the government is unwilling to take on the increasingly assertive coca growers.[61]

In 2004, the Peruvian drug agency, National Commission for Development and Life Without Drugs (DEVIDA), released a study on traditional uses of coca leaf. It found that approximately 2 million Peruvians use coca leaf either habitually or occasionally, with another two million using it for tea, or for traditional or ceremonial purposes, demand that can be satisfied with about 9,000 metric tons. About 24,700 acres are needed to produce this amount, a slightly smaller land area than what is allowed under current law. The study may form the basis for new legislation limiting cultivation to that needed to supply the licit domestic demand.

In Colombia, the conflict among leftist guerrilla groups, rightist paramilitaries, and the government has resulted in large numbers of displaced persons. Drug crop areas are some of the most contested regions as groups fight for their control for income generation. Some of the displaced relocate to other parts of the country, while others cross the border into neighboring countries. The Colombian Human Rights and Displacement Consulting Office (CODHES) and the Ombudsman's Office believe there is a direct link between eradication and the increase in internally displaced persons (IDPs). The U.S. and Colombian position is that the drug trade itself and the armed conflict that it continues to fuel are the causes of displacement for those living in conflictive areas. According to the two governments, eradicating drug crops and removing the availability of its profits for illegally armed groups will result in the end produce peace and stability.

Effectiveness and Sustainability of Alternative Development

Congress has expressed interest in the effectiveness of alternative development programs to promote general economic development, their level of funding in relation to eradication programs, and their general ability to accomplish the objective of sustainability in reducing or eliminating drug crop cultivation. It is difficult to assess the success of AD with regard to promoting economic development because we do not know what poverty levels would be in the absence of alternative development assistance. Even in the presence of such programs, it is difficult to ascertain if they are helping to reduce poverty when there are so many variables that can inhibit economic development. Many observers believe that without a sustained alternative development program, eradication efforts will ultimately fail as farmers will replant drug crops as their only viable means to support themselves.

With regard to achieving counternarcotics goals, USAID maintains that alternative development is essential because it can foster political support for eradication programs and provide incentives that, coupled with the eradication disincentive, ensure the permanent eradication of illicit crops. Some observers, however, contend that the value of alternative development lies in its conjunction with "intelligent law enforcement, interdiction and community-based voluntary eradication," and that these three components are rarely adequately combined.[62] Other observers believe that AD alone does not reduce cultivation, particularly when it is not funded sufficiently or carried on for a long enough period of time.[63]

On the issue of sustainability, many foreign aid policy analysts believe that alternative development programs need to be comprehensive with a long-term commitment by sponsors. U.S. programs target a number of related problems, from infrastructure development to basic health and education. Proponents of AD believe that for results to be sustainable, programs must be oriented toward poverty reduction with a focus on generating both agricultural and non-agricultural income. Toward that end, they recommend including education, basic health care, land titling, and conflict management.[64]

Alternative Development Challenges

Challenges to AD programs in the Andes include the isolation of sites of production, poor transportation infrastructure, and the lack of access to marketing opportunities. Critics maintain that the United States too closely links the receipt of AD assistance on voluntary eradication, and puts more resources into eradication rather than alternative development. With regard to AD programs in Colombia, the Government Accountability Office reported that obstacles included difficulty in marketing products, poor soil conditions, security constraints, lack of territorial control that impedes the development of infrastructure, and lack of established markets and private sector investment. In addition, GAO mentions that individual projects reach a small group of families, are rather localized and small, and may not be sustainable. While the report's focus was Colombia, many of its conclusions may be applicable to Peru and Bolivia.[65]

Linking Eradication and AD. In Colombia, the United States considers aerial spraying a prerequisite for alternative development. For example, USAID contends that growers in Putumayo showed little interest in participating in alternative development until after parts of the region were sprayed involuntarily at the end of 2000. This resulted in 37,000 families agreeing to sign up for voluntary eradication and alternative development support.[66] While the threat of forced eradication can act as an incentive to participate in alternative development programs, some observers argue that the two are contradictory, not complementary.[67] These observers believe that educating farmers on the negative impacts of illegal crop production is a more effective prevention tool. Some believe that coca farmers would prefer not to grow illicit crops because they understand the negative consequences for their communities — the social impact of coca production, a spiral of violence, and drug abuse — but feel compelled to do so in the absence of an alternative sustainable livelihood.

U.S. alternative development programs, however, require that growers eradicate all coca before being eligible for assistance. There have been complaints that AD has not kept pace with eradication, that it has been unable to provide adequate income for subsistence, and that poor soils and poor transportation infrastructure prevent getting agricultural or other income generating products to national markets. GAO has reported that USAID in Colombia is not sufficiently coordinating its efforts, with implementing partners cited as being unaware of each other's projects. The report concluded that successful continuation of projects requires better coordination between USAID and its contractors and grantees.[68]

In Bolivia's two main coca growing regions — Chapare and Yungas — growers have complained that they have not been able to benefit from alternatives to growing coca, citing a lack of coordination between existing community organizations and local governments, among other problems.[69] The Bolivian Law to Regulate Coca and Controlled Substances (Law 1008) authorizes forced eradication, but also requires simultaneous alternative development programs. Bolivia's 1998 *Plan Dignidad* stated that alternative development should accompany forced eradication.

Resources. Critics say that the resources devoted to alternative development programs are insufficient to provide a long-term alternative to illicit crops, and that the ratio between drug-related programs and development assistance is skewed toward the former. Since 2000, alternative development funding has been a little more than half that for eradication and interdiction programs. For Colombia, Peru, and Bolivia combined, spending on eradication has totaled about $3 billion, while total spending on alternative development is $1.6 billion. In Peru and Bolivia, the ratio between eradication and AD programs is approximately equal. In Colombia, eradication far outpaces AD programs. The cost of the aerial eradication program in Colombia may account for differences with Peru and Bolivia, where aerial spraying is not permitted. (See **Table 2**).

GAO reported in 2004 that funding constraints adversely affect nonmilitary assistance and complicate sustainability efforts. While USAID estimated in 2001 that a program for 136,600 families could cost up to $4 billion, the United States has allocated about $1.6 billion since 2000.[70] Both proponents and critics of AD programs believe that the continuation of financial and technical support is necessary for them to reach a sustainable momentum.

Appropriate Crop Substitution. Some observers have questioned the viability of crops recommended for alternative development programs. The head of Peru's antidrug agency, DEVIDA, has stated that crop substitution programs fail because the land is acidic and not conducive to other crops. The Peruvian agriculture minister also stated that programs to replace coca crops with alternative crops have been a failure, because the crops used, such as papayas and pineapples, are not profitable. While he proceeded to argue that AD would continue to be pursued, he recommended finding more profitable crops.[71] Similar complaints have been heard in Bolivia where some AD sites have been affected by falling global prices and a lack of assistance in exporting some commodities, such as hearts of palm and pineapples.

APPENDIX A. MAP OF THE ANDEAN REGION

Source: Map Resources. Adapted by CRS. (K.Yancey 10/13/05)

REFERENCES

[1]   Panama and Brazil are not considered Andean countries, but share borders with Colombia. Bolivia is an Andean country, but does not border Colombia.

[2]   Some analysts use 1999 as the pre-Plan Colombia baseline, which would show a 7.5% reduction instead of 32%. U.S. State Department, *International Narcotics Control Strategy Report, Volume I, Drug and Chemical Control*, March 2005.

[3]   White House Office of National Drug Control Policy, "2004 Coca and Opium Poppy Estimates for Colombia and the Andes," March 25, 2005.

[4]   Ibid., U.S. State Department, INCSR, March 2005, and ONDCP, March 25, 2005.

[5]   *Coca, Drugs and Social Protest in Bolivia and Peru*, Latin America Report No. 12, International Crisis Group, March 3, 2005.

[6]   Contreras, Joseph, "Failed 'Plan,'"*Newsweek International*, August 29, 2005.

[7]   U.S. Government Accountability Office, *Drug Control. Specific Performance Measures and Long-Term Costs for U.S. Programs in Colombia Have Not Been Developed*, GAO-03-783, June 16, 2003; and Contreras, Joseph, "Failed 'Plan,'"*Newsweek International*, August 29, 2005.

[8]   "Drugs in Latin America: What Kind of Turning Point?," *Latin American Special Reports*, [http://www.latinnews.com], November 2003.

[9]   U.S. Government Accountability Office, *Drug Control: U.S.-Supported Efforts in Colombia and Bolivia*, GAO/NSIAD-89-24, November 1988.

[10] Isaías Rojas, "Peru: Drug Control Policy, Human Rights, and Democracy," in *Drugs and Democracy in Latin America: The Impact of U.S. Policy*; Coletta A. Youngers and Eileen Rosin (Eds.), 2005; and *Coca, Drugs and Social Protest in Bolivia and Peru*, Latin America Report No. 12, International Crisis Group, March 3, 2005.

[11] For more information on Bolivia, see CRS Report RL32580, *Bolivia: Political Developments and Implications for U.S. Policy*, by Connie Veillette.

[12] According to UNODC World Drug Report 2005, there were 124,291 acres in 1990 and 68,446 acres in 2004.

[13] Betsy Marsh, *Going to Extremes: The U.S.-Funded Aerial Eradication Program in Colombia*, Latin America Working Group, March 2004.

[14] Information on USAID programs in Colombia, Peru and Bolivia is drawn from USAID's Congressional Budget Justification for FY2006.

[15] This section prepared by Linda-Jo Schierow, Specialist in Environmental Policy, Research, Science and Industry Division, CRS.

[16] The term "unreasonable" is used in several environmental statutes, including the statute that authorizes EPA to regulate sale and use of pesticides, the Federal Insecticide, Fungicide, and Rodenticide Act (FIFRA). It generally is interpreted to require regulators to balance costs and benefits in making decisions.

[17] The Roundup formulation was determined based on the registration date (1994, according to U.S. EPA, Office of Pesticide Programs, "Details of the 2003 Consultation for the Department of State: Use of Pesticide for Coca and Poppy Eradication Program in Colombia." June 2003. p. 12. (Hereafter cited as U.S. EPA.)) and the concentration of glyphosate (41%, according to the Department of State, Bureau for International Narcotics and Law Enforcement Affairs, "Updated Report on Chemicals Used in the Colombian Aerial Eradication Program," December 2003). Roundup Ultra Herbicide® is the only glyphosate product that fits that description, according to EPA's database, the National Pesticide Information Retrieval System at [http://ppis.ceris.purdue.edu/htbin/rnamset.com], visited Oct. 20, 2005.

[18] Manufacturers improve the performance of their pesticide products by adding substances that increase stickiness, tendency to spread so as to improve coverage, and other properties. "Adjuvant" is the term usually applied to such additives. The identity of these so-called "inert" ingredients often is kept secret to protect business interests, but is known to the federal agency that registers the product, which is EPA in the case of pesticide products.

[19] U.S. EPA, p. 13.

[20] The product name varies depending on concentration of the ingredients, but is most commonly known as Roundup®. Vision® is another name for the glyphosate plus POEA surfactant formulation.

[21] EPA's statements regarding the safety of the herbicide product support the State Department's position, but stipulate that they are based on information provided by the State Department about the pesticide formulation, application rates, and application methods in Colombia. In its 2002 report to the State Department, EPA requested field investigations of health complaints by Colombians, while the 2003 EPA report requested that such investigations be standardized and better documented.

[22] These certifications are available at [http://www.state.gov/p/inl/rls/rpt/aeicc/].

[23] U.S. EPA, Executive Summary.

[24] Charles W. Schmidt, "Battle Scars: Global Conflicts and Environmental Health," *Environmental Health Perspectives*, vol. 112, no. 17, Dec. 2004.

[25] OAS, CICAD, "Environmental and Human Health Assessment of the Aerial Spray Program for Coca and Poppy Control in Colombia," p. 121, at [http://www.cicad.oas.org/en/ glifosateFinalReport.pdf], visited October 20, 2005.

[26] A number of organizations have been active in pressing for further studies of the glyphosate mixture used in Colombia, among them The World Wildlife Fund and Friends of the Earth.

[27] One additive in the blend sprayed in Colombia after 2002 is different from, and less toxic than, the adjuvant used prior to 2002, when EPA recommended a switch to a less toxic mixture.

[28] U.S. EPA, p. 14.

[29] Charles W. Schmidt, "Battle Scars: Global Conflicts and Environmental Health," *Environmental Health Perspectives*, vol. 112, no. 17, December 2004.

[30] Ibid.

[31] U.S. EPA, Executive summary.

[32] Adolfo Maldonado, *Daños Genéticos en la Frontera de Ecuador por las Fumigaciones del Plan Colombia*, November 2003.

[33] For example, see "Are Pesticide 'Inerts' an Unrecognized Environmental Danger?," by Rebecca Renner in *Environmental Science & Technology Online News*, September 7, 2005. Also, the CICAD study cited above concluded that the toxicity of the Roundup plus Cosmo-Flux is greater than the toxicity of Roundup alone. Older studies that found adverse environmental effects due to Roundup or other glyphosate formulations are not cited here because they may have involved additives or contaminants that are no longer constituents of herbicide mixtures being sprayed in Colombia.

[34] Sophie Richard, Safa Moslemi, Herbert Sipahutar, Nora Benachour, and Tilles-Eric Seralini, "Differential Effects of Glyphosate and Roundup® on Human Placental Cells and Aromatase," *Environmental Health Perspectives*, vol. 113, no. 6, June 2005.

[35] M.T. Tsui and L.M. Chu, "Aquatic Toxicity of Glyphosate-Based Formulations: Comparison Between Different Organisms and the Effects of Environmental Factors," *Chemosphere*, vol. 52, no. 7, pp. 1189-1197.

[36] Rick A. Relyea, "The Impact of Insecticides and Herbicides on the Biodiversity and Productivity of Aquatic Communities," *Ecological Applications*, vol. 15, no. 2, 2005, pp. 618-627, and Rick A. Relyea, "The Lethal Impact of Roundup® on Aquatic and

Terrestrial Amphibians," *Ecological Applications*, vol. 15, no. 4, August 2005, pp. 1118-1124.

[37] Rick A. Relyea, Nancy M. Schoeppner, and Jason T. Hoverman, "Pesticides and Amphibians: The Importance of Community Context," *Ecological Applications*, vol. 15, no. 4, August 2005, pp. 1125-1124. For criticism of the earliest of these amphibian studies, see the paper "Response to `The impact of insecticides and herbicides on the biodiversity and productivity of aquatic communities,'" posted on the Monsanto website   at [http://www.monsanto.com/monsanto/content/products/productivity/roundup/ bkg_amphib_05a.pdf]. The biologist's response also is posted on the Internet at [http://www.pitt.edu/~relyea/Roundup.html], visited Oct. 18, 2005. In part, the researcher and pesticide company disagree on the likelihood that concentrations of glyphosate product might approach toxic levels in bodies of water where amphibians lay their eggs and larvae develop.

[38] Kim Housego, "Colombian Cocaine Blight Spreads into Nature Parks, Threatening Their Survival," *Associated Press*, September 27, 2005.

[39] "Alternative Coca Reduction Strategies in the Andean Region," Chapter 6, OTA-F-556, July 1993, at [http://www.wws.princeton.edu/ota/], visited October 27, 2005.

[40] For example, see the press release from the U.S. Embassy in Bogota. "Colombia y ONU tratan cooperación micoherbicida contra coca," at [http://bogota.usembassy.gov/ wwwsfu00.shtml], visited October 27, 2005; and J.A. Gracia-Garza, D. R. Fravel, B. A. Bailey, and P. K. Hebbar, "Dispersal of Formulations of Fusarium oxysporum f. sp. erythroxyli and F. oxysporum f. sp. melonis by Ants," *American Phytopathological Society*, vol. 88, no. 3, pp. 185-189, 1998, [http://www.apsnet.org/phyto/abstract/1998/ pma98ab.htm], visited October 27, 2005.

[41] C.E. Swift, E.R. Wickliffe, and H.F. Schwartz, "Vegetative compatibility groups of fusarium oxysporum f. sp. cepae from onion in Colorado," *Plant Disease*, vol. 86, no. 6, pp. 606-610, 2002; David C. Sands and Alice L. Pilgeram, "Enhancing the Efficacy of Biocontrol Agents Against Weeds," in M. Vurro et al. (eds.) *Enhancing Biocontrol Agents and Handling Risks*, pp. 3-5, 2001; and Eric Fichtl, "Washington's New Weapon in the War on Drugs." *Colombian Journal Online*, 2000, [http://www.colombiajournal.org/colombia21.htm], visited October 29, 2005.

[42] Government Accountability Office, *Drug Control: Coca Cultivation and Eradication Estimates in Colombia*, GAO-03-319R, January 8, 2003.

[43] "Drugs in Latin America: What Kind of Turning Point?,"*Latin American Special Reports*, [http://www.latinnews.com], November 2003, and Pablo Bachelet and Steve Dudley, "Coca Crop Figures Raise Questions Over Drug War," *New York Times*, April 6, 2005.

[44] U.S. Office of National Drug Control Policy, "2004 Coca and Opium Poppy Estimates for Colombia and the Andes," March 25, 2005.

[45] "'Balloon Effect' is Boosting Coca Production in Peru, Bolivia, and Even Colombia," *Weekly Report*, at [http://www.latinnews.com], January 11, 2005, and U.S. Environmental Protection Agency, Office of Pesticide Programs Details of the Consultation for Department of State Use of Pesticide for Coca Eradication Program in Colombia, August 2002.

[46] "More Eradication to Counter 'Balloon Effect,'" *Daily Security and Strategic Review*, Latinnews.com, May 2005.

[47] "Drugs in Latin America: What Kind of Turning Point," *Special Report*, at [http://www.latinnews.com], November 2003.

[48] Ibid., *Weekly Report*, Latinnews.com, January 11, 2005, and *Security and Strategic Review*, at [http://www.latinnews.com], May 2005.

[49] Pablo Bachelet, "Plan Colombia Hampers Drug Trade; The Bush Administration Claimed that Higher Cocaine Prices Showed the Drug War is Being Won," *The Miami Herald*, November 18, 2005.

[50] Boyum, David and Peter Reuter, "An Analytic Assessment of U.S. Drug Policy," American Enterprise Institute for Public Policy Research, 2005.

[51] James Painter, *Bolivia and Coca: A Study in Dependency*, Boulder: Lynne Rienner Publishers, 1994. See also Kathryn Ledebur, "Bolivia: Clear Consequences," in *Drugs and Democracy in Latin America*, edited by Coletta A. Youngers and Eileen Rosin, Lynne Rienner Publishers, 2005.

[52] U.S. Government Accountability Office, *Specific Performance Measures and Long-Term Costs for U.S. Programs in Colombia Have Not Been Developed*, GAO-03-783, June 2003.

[53] It is estimated that up to 40% of the country is controlled to some degree by illegally armed groups. For more information, see CRS Report RL32774, *Plan Colombia: A Progress Report*; and CRS Report RL32250, *Colombia: Issues for Congress*, both by Connie Veillette.

[54] Organization of American States, CICAD — Inter-American Commission on Drugs, *Environmental and Human Health Assessment of the Aerial Spray Program for Coca and Poppy Control in Colombia*, March 31, 2005.

[55] U.S. Department of State, *Chemicals Used for the Aerial Eradication of Illicit Coca in Colombia and Conditions of Application*, September 2002.

[56] "Ecuador: Fumigation Compensation Demanded," *Latinnews Daily*, July 19, 2005, "Ecuador: Talks with Colombia Over Fumigations Achieve Little," *Latinnews Daily*, September 1, 2005, and "Ecuador Concerned by Colombia's Herbicide Use," *Reuters*, September 19, 2005.

[57] These are currently set forth in P.L. 109-102, the FY2006 Foreign Operations Appropriations Act.

[58] Betsy Marsh, *Going to Extremes: The U.S.-Funded Aerial Eradication Program in Colombia*, Latin America Working Group, March 2004.

[59] Contraloria General de la Republica, "Plan Colombia: Quinto Informe de Evaluación," December 2004, and U.S. Department of State, *Memorandum of Justification Concerning the Secretary of State's 2005 Certification of Conditions Related to the Aerial Eradication of Illicit Coca and Opium Poppy in Colombia*, April 22, 2005.

[60] Kathryn Ledebur, "Bolivia: Clear Consequences," in *Drugs and Democracy in Latin America: The Impact of U.S. Policy*, Coletta A. Youngers and Eileen Rosin (Eds.) 2005.

[61] "Policy Clashes and Vacillation Threaten the 'War on Drugs' in the Andes," *Security and Strategic Review*, [http://www.latinnews.com], July 2005.

[62] Coletta A. Youngers and Eileen Rosin (Eds.), 2005; and *Coca, Drugs and Social Protest in Bolivia and Peru*, Latin America Report No. 12, International Crisis Group, March 3, 2005.

[63] Ibid.

[64] James C. Jones, "An Overview of Alternative Development in the South American Andes," U.N. Office on Drugs and Crime, September 2004, and "The Role of Alternative Development in Drug Control and Development Cooperation," U.N. Development Program, International Conference, January 2002.

[65] U.S. Government Accountability Office, *U.S. Nonmilitary Assistance to Colombia Is Beginning to Show Intended Results, But Programs Are Not Readily Sustainable,* GAO-04-726, July 2004.

[66] U.S. Government Accountability Office, *Drug Control: Efforts to Develop Alternatives to Cultivating Illicit Crops in Colombia Have Made Little Progress and Face Serious Obstacles*, GAO-02-29, February 2002.

[67] Testimony of Eduardo Cifuentes, Defensor del Pueblo, before the Colombian Congress, July 2001.

[68] U.S. Government Accountability Office, *U.S. Nonmilitary Assistance to Colombia Is Beginning to Show Intended Results, But Programs Are Not Readily Sustainable,* GAO-04-726, July 2004.

[69] Linda Farthing, "Rethinking Alternative Development in Bolivia," Andean Information Network and Washington Office on Latin America, February 2004.

[70] U.S. Government Accountability Office, *U.S. Nonmilitary Assistance to Colombia Is Beginning to Show Intended Results, But Programs Are Not Readily Sustainable,* GAO-04-726, July 2004.

[71] "Peru: Coca Replacement a Failure," *Latinnews Daily*, May 18, 2004.

In: Illegal Drugs and Governmental Policies
Editor: Lee V. Barton, pp. 59-96

ISBN 978-1-60021-351-9
© 2007 Nova Science Publishers, Inc.

Chapter 4

MEDICAL MARIJUANA: REVIEW AND ANALYSIS OF FEDERAL AND STATE POLICIES[*]

Mark Eddy

SUMMARY

The issue before Congress is whether to continue to support the executive branch's prosecution of medical marijuana patients and their providers, in accordance with marijuana's status as a Schedule I drug under the Controlled Substances Act, or whether to relax federal marijuana prohibition enough to permit the medical use of botanical cannabis products by seriously ill persons, especially in states that have created medical marijuana programs under state law.

Bills have been introduced in recent Congresses to allow patients who appear to benefit from medical cannabis to use it in accordance with the various regulatory schemes that have been approved, since 1996, by the voters and legislatures of 11 states. In the current Congress, the States' Rights to Medical Marijuana Act (H.R. 2087, Frank) would move marijuana from Schedule I to Schedule II of the Controlled Substances Act and make it available under federal law for medical use in states with medical marijuana programs. The Steve McWilliams Truth in Trials Act (H.R. 4272, Farr) would make it possible for defendants in federal court to reveal to juries that their marijuana activity was medically related and legal under state law.

In June 2005, the House defeated, for the third time, the Hinchey-Rohrabacher amendment to prevent federal enforcement of the Controlled Substances Act against medical marijuana patients in states that have approved such use. The amendment is expected to be offered again in the 2nd session of the 109th Congress.

Eleven states, mostly in the West, have enacted laws allowing the use of marijuana for medical purposes, and many thousands of patients, having registered in their state programs, are seeking relief from a variety of serious illnesses by smoking marijuana or using other herbal cannabis preparations. Meanwhile, the federal Drug Enforcement Administration (DEA) continues to investigate and arrest medical marijuana providers in those states as elsewhere.

Claims and counterclaims about medical marijuana — much debated by journalists and academics, policymakers at all levels of government, and interested citizens — include the following: Marijuana is harmful and has no medical value; marijuana effectively treats the symptoms of certain diseases; smoking is an improper route of drug administration; marijuana

---

[*] Excerpted from CRS Report RL33211, Updated December 29, 2005

should be rescheduled to permit medical use; state medical marijuana laws send the wrong message and lead to increased illicit drug use; the medical marijuana movement undermines the war on drugs; patients should not be arrested for using medical marijuana; the federal government should allow the states to experiment and should not interfere with state medical marijuana programs; medical marijuana laws harm the drug approval process; the medical cannabis movement is a cynical ploy to legalize marijuana and other drugs. With strong opinions being expressed on all sides of these complex issues, the debate over medical marijuana does not appear to be approaching resolution.

INTRODUCTION: THE ISSUE BEFORE CONGRESS

The issue before Congress is whether to continue to support the executive branch's prosecution of medical marijuana[1] patients and their providers, in accordance with marijuana's status as a Schedule I drug under the Controlled Substances Act, or whether to relax federal marijuana prohibition enough to permit the medical use of botanical cannabis products by seriously ill persons, especially in those states that have created medical marijuana programs under state law.

Bills have been introduced in recent Congresses to allow patients who appear to benefit from medical cannabis to use it in accordance with the various regulatory schemes that have been approved, since 1996, by the voters and legislatures of 11 states. In the current Congress, the States' Rights to Medical Marijuana Act (H.R. 2087, Frank) would move marijuana from Schedule I to Schedule II of the Controlled Substances Act and make it available under federal law for medical use in states with medical marijuana programs. The bill has not advanced beyond the committee referral stage.

In June 2005, the House of Representatives expressed its opposition to medical marijuana by rejecting an amendment that would have prevented the Department of Justice from arresting and prosecuting patients in states with medical marijuana laws. This and other congressional actions relating to the issue of medical marijuana are discussed below in greater detail.[2]

BACKGROUND: MEDICAL MARIJUANA PRIOR TO 1937

The Cannabis sativa plant has been used for healing purposes throughout history. According to written records from China and India, the use of marijuana to treat a wide range of ailments goes back more than 2,000 years. Ancient texts from Africa, the Middle East, classical Greece, and the Roman Empire also describe the use of cannabis to treat disease.

For most of American history, growing and using marijuana was legal under federal law and the laws of the individual states. By the 1840s, some U.S. physicians began to recognize marijuana's therapeutic potential. From 1850 to the early 1940s, cannabis was included in the *United States Pharmacopoeia* as a recognized medicinal.[3] By the end of 1936, however, all 48 states had enacted laws to regulate marijuana.[4] Its decline in medicine was hastened by the development of aspirin, morphine, and then other opium-derived drugs, all of which helped to replace marijuana in the treatment of pain and other medical conditions in Western medicine.[5]

FEDERAL MEDICAL MARIJUANA POLICY

All three branches of the federal government play an important role in formulating federal policy on medical marijuana. Significant actions of each branch are highlighted here, beginning with the legislative branch.

Congressional Actions

The Marihuana Tax Act of 1937. Spurred by spectacular accounts of marijuana's harmful effects on its users, the drug's alleged connection to violent crime, and a perception that state and local efforts to bring use of the drug under control were not working, Congress enacted the Marihuana Tax Act of 1937.[6] Promoted by Harry Anslinger, Commissioner of the recently established Federal Bureau of Narcotics, the act imposed registration and reporting requirements and a tax on the growers, sellers, and buyers of marijuana. Although the act did not prohibit marijuana outright, its effect was the same. Because marijuana was not included in the Harrison Narcotics Act in 1914,[7] the Marihuana Tax Act of 1937 was the federal government's first attempt to regulate marijuana.

Dr. William C. Woodward, legislative counsel of the American Medical Association (AMA), opposed the measure. In oral testimony before the House Ways and Means Committee, he stated that "there are evidently potentialities in the drug that should not be shut off by adverse legislation. The medical profession and pharmacologists should be left to develop the use of this drug as they see fit."[8] Two months later, in a letter to the Senate Finance Committee, he again argued against the act:

> There is no evidence, however, that the medicinal use of these drugs ["cannabis and its preparations and derivatives"] has caused or is causing cannabis addiction. As remedial agents they are used to an inconsiderable extent, and the obvious purpose and effect of this bill is to impose so many restrictions on their medicinal use as to prevent such use altogether. Since the medicinal use of cannabis has not caused and is not causing addiction, the prevention of the use of the drug for medicinal purposes can accomplish no good end whatsoever. How far it may serve to deprive the public of the benefits of a drug that on further research may prove to be of substantial value, it is impossible to foresee.[9]

Despite the AMA's opposition, the Marihuana Tax Act was approved, causing all medicinal products containing marijuana to be withdrawn from the market and leading to marijuana's removal, in 1941, from *The National Formulary* and the *United States Pharmacopoeia*, in which it had been listed for almost a century.

Controlled Substances Act (1970). In response to the increased use of marijuana and other street drugs during the 1960s, notably by college and high school students, federal drug-control laws came under scrutiny. In July 1969, President Nixon asked Congress to enact legislation to combat rising levels of drug use.[10] Hearings were held, different proposals were considered, and House and Senate conferees filed a conference report in October 1970.[11] The report was quickly adopted by voice vote in both chambers and was signed into law as the Comprehensive Drug Abuse Prevention and Control Act of 1970 (P.L. 91-513).

Included in the new law was the Controlled Substances Act (CSA),[12] which placed marijuana and its derivatives in Schedule I, the most restrictive of five categories. Schedule I substances have a high potential for abuse, no currently accepted medical use in treatment in the United States, and a lack of accepted safety standards for use of the drug under medical supervision.[13] Other recreational drugs also became Schedule I substances at that time, including heroin, amphetamine, methamphetamine, LSD, mescaline, peyote, and psilocybin. Drugs with recognized medical uses were assigned to Schedules II through V, depending on their potential for abuse.[14] Despite its placement in Schedule I, marijuana use increased, as did the number of health-care professionals and their patients who believed in the plant's therapeutic value.

The CSA does not distinguish between the medical and recreational use of marijuana. Under federal statute, simple possession of marijuana for personal use, a misdemeanor, can bring up to one year in federal prison and up to a $100,000 fine for a first offense.[15] Growing marijuana is considered *manufacturing* a controlled substance, a felony.[16] A single plant can bring an individual up to five years in federal prison and up to a $250,000 fine for a first offense.[17]

Under the U.S. system of government, the CSA is not preempted by state medical marijuana laws, nor are state medical marijuana laws preempted by the CSA. States can statutorily create a medical use exception for botanical cannabis and its derivatives under their own, state-level controlled substance laws. At the same time, federal agents can investigate, arrest, and prosecute medical marijuana patients, caregivers, and providers in accordance with the federal Controlled Substances Act, even in those states where medical marijuana programs operate in accordance with state law.

Medical Marijuana Legislation in the 105th Congress (1998). In September 1998, the House debated and passed a resolution (H.J.Res. 117) declaring that Congress supports the existing federal drug approval process for determining whether any drug, including marijuana, is safe and effective and opposes efforts to circumvent this process by legalizing marijuana, or any other Schedule I drug, for medicinal use without valid scientific evidence and without approval of the Food and Drug Administration (FDA). With the Senate not acting on the resolution and adjournment approaching, this language was incorporated into the FY1999 omnibus appropriations act.[18] In a separate amendment to the same act, Congress prevented the District of Columbia government from spending any appropriated funds on a medical marijuana ballot initiative.[19]

The Hinchey-Rohrabacher Amendment (2003-2005). In the 1st session of the 108th Congress, in response to federal Drug Enforcement Administration (DEA) raids on medical cannabis users and providers in California and other states that had approved the medical use of marijuana under a doctor's supervision, Representatives Hinchey and Rohrabacher introduced a bipartisan amendment to the Commerce, Justice, State appropriations bill for FY2004 (H.R. 2799). The amendment would have prevented the Justice Department from using appropriated funds to interfere with the implementation of medical cannabis laws in the nine states that had approved such use. The amendment was debated on the floor of the House on July 22, 2003. When brought to a vote on the following day, it was defeated 152 to 273 (66 votes short of passage).[20]

The amendment was offered again in the 2nd session of the 108th Congress. It was debated on the House floor on July 7, 2004, during consideration of H.R. 4754, the Commerce, Justice, State appropriations bill for FY2005, and would have applied to 10 states, with the recent addition of Vermont to the list of states that had approved the use of medical cannabis. It was again defeated by a similar margin, 148 to 268.[21]

The amendment was voted on again in the 1st session of the 109th Congress and was again defeated, 161-264, on June 15, 2005. During floor debate, a Member stated in support of the amendment that her now-deceased mother had used marijuana to treat her glaucoma. Opponents of the amendment argued, among other things, that its passage would undermine efforts to convince young people that marijuana is a dangerous drug.[22]

The amendment is expected to be offered again as an ongoing measure of sentiment in the House for marijuana law reform.

Medical Marijuana Bills in the 109th Congress (2005). The States' Rights to Medical Marijuana Act (H.R. 2087, Frank) would transfer marijuana from Schedule I to Schedule II of the Controlled Substances Act. It would also provide that, in states in which marijuana may legally be prescribed or recommended by a physician for medical use, under state law, no provisions of the Controlled Substances Act or the Federal Food, Drug, and Cosmetic Act could prohibit or otherwise restrict (1) a physician from prescribing or recommending marijuana for medical use, (2) an individual from obtaining and using marijuana if prescribed or recommended by a physician for medical use, (3) a pharmacy from obtaining and holding marijuana for such a prescription or recommendation, or (4) an entity established by a state from producing and distributing marijuana for such a prescription or recommendation. (Versions of this bill have been introduced in every Congress since the 105th in 1997 but have not seen action beyond the committee referral process.)

The Steve McWilliams Truth in Trials Act (H.R. 4272, Farr) would amend the Controlled Substances Act to provide an affirmative defense for the medical use of marijuana in accordance with the laws of the various states. At the present time, medical marijuana defendants in federal court are not permitted to introduce evidence that their marijuana-related activity was undertaken for a valid medical purpose under state law. First introduced in the 108th Congress, this version of the bill was named for a California medical marijuana provider who took his own life while awaiting federal sentencing for providing medical marijuana to seriously ill patients in San Diego. He had been unable to present jurors with accurate information about his activities; this bill seeks to change that restriction.

Neither bill has seen action beyond the committee referral process.

Executive Branch Actions and Policies

IND Compassionate Access Program (1978). In 1975, a Washington, DC, resident was arrested for growing marijuana to treat his glaucoma. He won his case by using the medical necessity defense,[23] forcing the government to find a way to provide him with his medicine. In 1978, the Investigational New Drug (IND) Compassionate Access Program[24] was established by the FDA, allowing patients whose serious medical conditions could be relieved only by marijuana to apply for and receive marijuana from the federal government. Over the next 14 years, other patients, less than 100 in total, were admitted to the program for conditions including chemotherapy-induced nausea and vomiting (emesis), glaucoma, spasticity, and weight loss. Then, in 1992, in response to a large number of applications from AIDS patients who sought to use medical cannabis to increase appetite and reverse wasting disease, the George H.W. Bush Administration closed the program to all new applicants.

Previously approved patients, who remain in the program today, continue to be provided with their monthly supply of government-grown medical marijuana.

Approval of Marinol (1985). Marinol is the only cannabis-based drug approved by the FDA for use in the United States. Made by Unimed, Marinol is the trade name for dronabinol, a synthetic form of delta-9-tetrahydrocannabinol (THC), one of the principal psychoactive components of botanical marijuana. Marinol was approved in May 1985 for nausea and vomiting associated with cancer chemotherapy in patients who fail to respond to conventional antiemetic treatments. In December 1992, it was approved by the FDA for the treatment of anorexia associated with weight loss in patients with AIDS. Marketed as a capsule, Marinol was originally placed in Schedule II.[25] In July 1999, in response to a rescheduling petition from Unimed, DEA moved it to Schedule III to make it more widely available to patients.[26] The rescheduling was granted after a DEA and Department of Health and Human Services (HHS) review found little evidence of illicit abuse of the drug. In Schedule III, Marinol is now subject to fewer regulatory controls and lesser criminal sanctions for illicit use.

DEA's Administrative Law Judge Ruling (1988). Congressional passage of the Controlled Substances Act in 1970 and its placement of marijuana in Schedule I provoked controversy at the time because it strengthened the federal policy of marijuana prohibition and forced medical marijuana users to buy marijuana of uncertain quality on the black market at inflated prices, subjecting them to fines, arrest, court costs, property forfeiture, incarceration, probation, and criminal records. The new bureaucratic controls on Schedule I substances were also criticized because they would impede research on marijuana's therapeutic potential, making its evaluation and rescheduling through the normal drug approval process unlikely.

These concerns prompted a citizens' petition to the Bureau of Narcotics and Dangerous Drugs (BNDD) in 1972 to reschedule marijuana and make it available by prescription. The petition was summarily rejected.[27] This rejection led to a long succession of appeals, hearing requests, and various court proceedings. Finally, in 1988, after extensive public hearings on marijuana's medicinal value, the chief administrative law judge of the Drug Enforcement Administration (the BNDD's successor agency) ruled on the petition, stating that "Marijuana, in its natural form, is one of the safest therapeutically active substances known to man."[28] Judge Francis L. Young also wrote:

> The evidence in this record clearly shows that marijuana has been accepted as capable of relieving the distress of great numbers of very ill people, and doing so with safety under medical supervision. It would be unreasonable, arbitrary and capricious for DEA to continue to stand between those sufferers and the benefits of this substance in light of the evidence in this record.

Judge Young found that "the provisions of the [Controlled Substances] Act permit and require the transfer of marijuana from schedule I to schedule II," which would recognize its medicinal value and permit doctors to prescribe it. The Judge's findings and recommendation were soon rejected by the DEA Administrator because "marijuana has not been demonstrated as suitable for use as a medicine."[29] Subsequent rescheduling petitions were also rejected, and marijuana remains a Schedule I substance.

NIH-Sponsored Workshop (1997). NIH convened a scientific panel on medical marijuana composed of eight nonfederal experts in fields such as cancer treatment, infectious diseases, neurology, and ophthalmology. Over a two-day period in February, they analyzed available scientific information on the medical uses of marijuana and concluded that "in order to evaluate various hypotheses concerning the potential utility of marijuana in various therapeutic areas, more and better studies would be needed." Research would be justified, according to the panel, into certain conditions or diseases such as pain, neurological and movement disorders, nausea of patients undergoing chemotherapy for cancer, loss of appetite and weight related to AIDS, and glaucoma.[30]

Institute of Medicine Report (1999). In January 1997, shortly after passage of the California and Arizona medical marijuana initiatives, the Director of the Office of National Drug Control Policy (the federal drug czar) commissioned the National Institute of Medicine (IOM) of the National Academy of Sciences to review the scientific evidence on the potential health benefits and risks of marijuana and its constituent cannabinoids. Begun in August 1997, IOM's 257-page report, *Marijuana and Medicine: Assessing the Science Base,* was released in March 1999.[31] A meta-analysis of all existing studies of the therapeutic value of cannabis, the IOM Report was also based on public hearings and consultations with biomedical and social scientists and concerned citizens from across the country.

For the most part, the IOM Report straddled the issue, providing sound bites for both sides of the medical marijuana debate. For example: "Until a nonsmoked rapid-onset cannabinoid drug delivery system becomes available, we acknowledge that there is no clear alternative for people suffering from *chronic* conditions that might be relieved by smoking marijuana, such as pain or AIDS-wasting" (p. 179) and "Smoked marijuana is unlikely to be a safe medication for any chronic medical condition" (p. 126). The report also stated, "There is no conclusive evidence that marijuana causes cancer in humans, including cancers usually related to tobacco use" (p. 119) and "Numerous studies suggest that marijuana smoke is an important risk factor in the development of respiratory disease" (p. 127).

The IOM Report did find more potential promise in synthetic cannabinoid drugs than in smoked marijuana (p. 177):

> The accumulated data suggest a variety of indications, particularly for pain relief, antiemesis, and appetite stimulation. For patients such as those with AIDS or who are undergoing chemotherapy, and who suffer simultaneously from severe pain, nausea, and appetite loss, cannabinoid drugs might offer broad-spectrum relief not found in any other single medication.

In general, the report emphasized the need for well-formulated, scientific research into the therapeutic effects of marijuana and its cannabinoid components on patients with specific disease conditions. To this end, the report recommended that clinical trials be conducted to develop safe delivery systems.

DEA Enforcement Actions Against Cannabis Buyers' Clubs. Most arrests in the United States for marijuana possession are made by state and local police, not the DEA. This means that patients and their caregivers in states that permit medical marijuana are largely protected from prosecution, because their own state's marijuana laws do not apply to them and because federal law is not usually enforced against them.

Federal agents do, however, move against medical cannabis growers and distributors in states with medical marijuana programs. In recent years, more than 20 large-scale raids of cannabis buyers' clubs have occurred in California and a handful of raids have taken place in other states.

DEA's actions to shut down medical marijuana growing and distribution operations have provoked lawsuits and other responses. In April 2003, for example, the city and county of Santa Cruz, CA, along with seven medical marijuana patients, filed a lawsuit in San Jose federal district court in response to the DEA's earlier raid on the Wo/Men's Alliance for Medical Marijuana (WAMM). The court granted the plaintiffs' motion for a preliminary injunction, thereby allowing WAMM to resume growing and producing marijuana medications for its approximately 250 member-patients with serious illnesses, pending the final outcome of the case.[32] The suit is reportedly the first court challenge brought by a local government against the federal war on drugs.

Medical Cannabis in the Courts: Major Cases

Because Congress and the executive branch have not acted to permit seriously ill Americans to use botanical marijuana medicinally, the issue has been considered by the judicial branch, with mixed results. Three significant cases have been decided so far, and other court challenges are moving through the judicial pipeline.[33]

***U.S.* v. *Oakland Cannabis Buyers' Cooperative* (2001).** The U.S. Department of Justice filed a civil suit in January 1998 to close six medical marijuana distribution centers in northern California. A U.S. district court judge issued a temporary injunction to close the centers, pending the outcome of the case. The Oakland Cannabis Buyers' Cooperative fought the injunction but was eventually forced to cease operations and appealed to the Ninth Circuit Court of Appeals. At issue was whether a medical marijuana distributor can use a medical necessity defense against federal marijuana distribution charges.[34]

The Ninth Circuit's decision found in September 1999 that "medical necessity" is a valid defense against federal marijuana trafficking charges if a trial court finds that the patients to whom the marijuana was distributed are seriously ill, face imminent harm without marijuana, and have no effective legal alternatives.[35] The Justice Department appealed to the Supreme Court.

The Supreme Court held, 8-0, that "a medical necessity exception for marijuana is at odds with the terms of the Controlled Substances Act" because "its provisions leave no doubt that the defense is unavailable."[36] This decision had no effect on state medical marijuana laws, which continued to protect patients and primary caregivers from arrest by state and local law enforcement agents in the states with medical marijuana programs.

***Conant* v. *Walters* (2002).** After the 1996 passage of California's medical marijuana initiative, the Clinton Administration threatened to investigate doctors and revoke their licenses to prescribe controlled substances and to participate in Medicaid and Medicare if they recommended medical marijuana to patients under the new state law. A group of California physicians and patients filed suit in federal court, early in 1997, claiming a constitutional free-speech right, in the context of the doctor-patient relationship, to discuss the potential risks and benefits of the medical use of cannabis. A preliminary injunction, issued in April 1997, prohibited federal officials from threatening or punishing physicians for recommending marijuana to patients suffering from HIV/AIDS, cancer, glaucoma, or seizures or muscle spasms associated with a chronic, debilitating condition.[37] The court subsequently made the injunction permanent in an unpublished opinion.

On appeal, the Ninth Circuit affirmed the district court's order entering a permanent injunction. The federal government, the opinion states, "may not initiate an investigation of a physician solely on the basis of a recommendation of marijuana within a bona fide doctor-patient relationship, unless the government in good faith believes that it has substantial evidence of criminal conduct."[38] The first Bush Administration appealed, but the Supreme Court refused to take the case.

***Gonzalez* v. *Raich* (2005).** In response to DEA agents' destruction of their medical marijuana plants, two patients and two caregivers in California brought suit. They argued that applying the Controlled Substances Act (CSA) to a situation in which medical marijuana was being grown locally for no remuneration in accordance with state law exceeded Congress's authority under the Commerce Clause. In December 2003, the Ninth Circuit Court of Appeals in San Francisco agreed, ruling that states are free to adopt medical marijuana laws so long as the marijuana is not sold, transported across state lines, or used for nonmedical purposes.[39] Federal appeal sent the case to the Supreme Court.

The issue before the Supreme Court was whether the CSA, when applied to the *intra*state cultivation and possession of marijuana for personal use under state law, exceeds Congress's power under the Commerce Clause. The Supreme Court, in June 2005, reversed the Ninth Circuit's decision and held, in a 6-3 decision, that Congress's power to regulate commerce extends to purely local activities that are "part of an economic class of activities that have a substantial effect on interstate commerce."[40]

Raich does not invalidate state medical marijuana laws. The decision does mean, however, that DEA may continue to enforce the CSA against medical marijuana patients and their caregivers, even in states with medical marijuana programs.

Although *Raich* did not address the efficacy of medical marijuana or its listing in Schedule I, the majority opinion stated in a footnote: "We acknowledge that evidence proffered by respondents in this case regarding the effective medical uses for marijuana, if found credible after trial, would cast serious doubt on the accuracy of the findings that require marijuana to be listed in Schedule I."[41] The majority opinion, in closing, notes that in the absence of judicial relief for medical marijuana users there remains "the democratic process, in which the voices of voters allied with these respondents may one day be heard in the halls of Congress."[42]

Thus, the Supreme Court reminds that Congress has the power to reschedule marijuana, thereby making it available to patients. Congress, however, does not appear likely to do so. Neither does the executive branch, which could reschedule marijuana through regulatory procedures authorized by the CSA. In the meantime, actions taken by state and local governments continue to raise the issue.

STATE AND LOCAL REFERENDA AND LEGISLATION

In the face of federal intransigence on the issue, advocates of medical marijuana have turned to state and local governments in a mostly successful effort, as outlined below, to pass laws and establish programs that enable patients to obtain and use botanical marijuana therapeutically in a legal and regulated manner.

States Allowing the Use of Medical Marijuana[43]

Eleven states, covering about 22% of the U.S. population, have enacted laws allowing the use of cannabis for medical purposes.[44] These states have removed state-level criminal penalties for the cultivation, possession, and use of medical marijuana, if such use has been recommended by a medical doctor. All of these states (except Arizona) have in place, or are developing, programs to regulate the use of medical marijuana by approved patients. Patients in state programs may be assisted by caregivers, persons who are authorized to help patients grow, acquire, and use the drug. Physicians in these states are immune from liability and prosecution for discussing or recommending medical cannabis to their patients in accordance with the law.

Nine of the 11 states that have legalized medical marijuana are in the West. Among the 37 nonwestern states, only two — Maine and Vermont — have adopted medical cannabis statutes. Hawaii and Vermont have the only programs initiated by an act of the state legislature. The medical marijuana programs in the other nine states were approved by the voters in statewide referenda or ballot initiatives, beginning in 1996 with California and Arizona. Since then, voters have approved medical marijuana initiatives in every state where they have appeared on the ballot. Bills have been introduced in the legislatures of additional states and have received varying levels of consideration but have so far not been enacted.

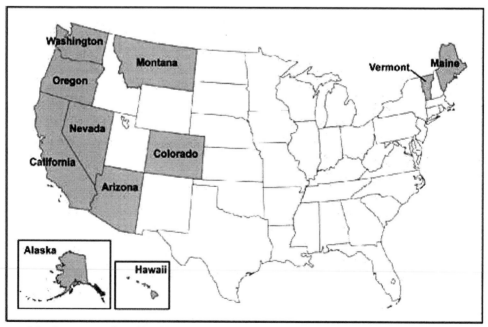

Source: Map Resources, adapted by CRS (K. Yancey 8/05)

Figure 1. States That Have Legalized Medical Marijuana

State medical marijuana laws do not attempt to overturn or otherwise violate federal laws that prohibit doctors from writing prescriptions for marijuana and pharmacies from distributing it. In the 10 states with medical marijuana programs, doctors do not actually prescribe marijuana, and the marijuana products used by patients are not distributed through pharmacies. Rather, doctors *recommend* marijuana to their patients, and the cannabis products are grown by patients or their caregivers, or they are obtained from cooperatives or other alternative dispensaries. The state medical marijuana programs do, however, contravene the federal prohibition of marijuana. Medical marijuana patients, their caregivers, and other marijuana providers can, therefore, be arrested by federal law enforcement agents, and they can be prosecuted under federal law.

Statistics on medical marijuana users. Determining exactly how many patients use medical marijuana with state approval is difficult. According to a 2002 study published in the *Journal of Cannabis Therapeutics*, an estimated 30,000 California patients and another 5,000 patients in eight other states possessed a physician's recommendation to use cannabis medically.[45] Recent estimates are much higher. The *New England Journal of Medicine* reported in August 2005 that an estimated 115,000 people have obtained marijuana recommendations from doctors in the states with programs.[46]

Although 115,000 people may be approved medical marijuana users, the number of patients who have actually registered is much lower. A July 2005 CRS telephone survey of the state programs revealed a total of 14,758 registered medical marijuana users in eight states. (Maine and Washington do not maintain state registries.) This number vastly understates the number of medical marijuana users, however, because California's state registry was in pilot status, with only 70 patients so far registered.

A brief description of the state medical marijuana programs appears below. The programs are discussed in the order in which they were approved by voters or passed by the state legislature.

California (1996). Proposition 215, approved by 56% of the voters in November, removed the state's criminal penalties for medical marijuana use, possession, and cultivation by patients with the "written or oral recommendation or approval of a physician" who has determined that the patient's "health would benefit from medical marijuana." Called the Compassionate Use Act, it legalized cannabis for "the treatment of cancer, anorexia, AIDS, chronic pain, spasticity, glaucoma, arthritis, migraine, or any other illness for which marijuana provides relief." The law permits possession of an amount sufficient for the patient's "personal medical purposes."

Arizona (1996). Arizona's law, approved by 65% of the voters in November, permits marijuana prescriptions, but there is no active program in the state because federal law prohibits doctors from *prescribing* marijuana. Patients cannot, therefore, obtain a valid prescription. (Other states' laws allow doctors to *recommend* rather than *prescribe*.)

Oregon (1998). Voters in November removed the state's criminal penalties for medical marijuana use, possession, and cultivation by patients whose physicians advise that marijuana "may mitigate the symptoms or effects" of a debilitating condition. The law, approved by 55% of Oregon voters, does not provide for distribution of cannabis but allows up to seven plants per patient (changed to 24 plants by act of the state legislature in 2005). The state registry program is supported by patient fees. (In the November 2004 election, Oregon voters rejected a measure that would have expanded the state's existing program.)

Alaska (1998). Voters in November approved a ballot measure to remove state-level criminal penalties for patients diagnosed by a physician as having a debilitating medical condition for which other approved medications were considered. The measure was approved by 58% of the voters. In 1999, the state legislature created a mandatory state registry for medical cannabis users and limited the amount a patient can legally possess to 1 ounce and six plants.

Washington (1998). Approved in November by 59% of the voters, the ballot initiative exempts from prosecution patients who meet all qualifying criteria, possess no more marijuana than is necessary for their own personal medical use (but no more than a 60-day supply), and present valid documentation to investigating law enforcement officers. The state does not issue identification cards to patients.

Maine (1999). Maine's ballot initiative, passed in November by 61% of the voters, puts the burden on the state to prove that a patient's medical use or possession is not authorized by statute. Patients with a qualifying condition, authenticated by a physician, who have been "advised" by the physician that they "might benefit" from medical cannabis, are permitted 1¼ ounces and six plants. There is no state registry of patients.

Hawaii (2000). In June 2000, the Hawaii legislature approved a bill removing state-level criminal penalties for medical cannabis use, possession, and cultivation of up to seven plants. A physician must certify that the patient has a debilitating condition for which "the potential benefits of the medical use of marijuana would likely outweigh the health risks." This was the first state law permitting medical cannabis use that was enacted by a legislature instead of by ballot initiative.

Colorado (2000). A ballot initiative to amend the state constitution was approved by 54% of the voters in November. The amendment provides that lawful medical cannabis users must be diagnosed by a physician as having a debilitating condition and be "advised" by the physician that the patient "might benefit" from using the drug. A patient and the patient's caregiver may possess 2 usable ounces and six plants.

Nevada (2000). To amend the state constitution by ballot initiative, a proposed amendment must be approved by the voters in two separate elections. In November 2000, 65% of Nevada voters passed for the second time an amendment to exempt medical cannabis users from prosecution. The amendment requires the state legislature to develop a program that allows qualified patients to use, possess, and grow marijuana for medicinal purposes.

Vermont (2004). In May, Vermont became the second state to legalize medical cannabis by legislative action instead of ballot initiative. Vermont patients are allowed to grow up to three marijuana plants in a locked room and to possess two ounces of manicured cannabis under the supervision of the Department of Public Safety, which maintains a patient registry. The law went into effect without the signature of the governor, who declined to sign it but also refused to veto it, despite pressure from Washington.

Montana (2004). In November 2004, 62% of state voters made Montana the 11th state in the country to allow medical cannabis and the 10th to establish a program for patients. The public health department has begun accepting applications for the state medical marijuana registry and is issuing ID cards to qualifying patients.

Other State and Local Medical Marijuana Laws

Maryland (2003). Maryland's General Assembly became the second state legislature to protect medical cannabis patients from the threat of jail in March 2003 when it approved a bill, later signed by the governor, providing that patients using marijuana preparations to treat the symptoms of illnesses such as cancer, AIDS, and Cohn's disease would be subject to no more than a $100 fine.[47] Falling short of full legalization, patients in Maryland can still be arrested and forced to prove in court that they use cannabis for legitimate medical needs, but the law does create a medical necessity defense in court for people who use marijuana on their own for medical purposes.

Other state laws. Laws favorable to medical marijuana have been enacted in 36 states since 1978.[48] Except for the state laws mentioned above, however, the laws do not currently protect medical marijuana users from state prosecution. For example, some states have laws that allow patients to acquire and use cannabis through therapeutic research programs, although none of these programs has been operational since 1985, due in large part to federal opposition. Other states have enacted laws that allow doctors to prescribe marijuana or that allow patients to possess marijuana if it has been obtained through a prescription, but the federal Controlled Substances Act prevents these laws from being implemented. Several states have placed marijuana in a controlled drug schedule that recognizes its medical value. State legislatures continue to consider medical marijuana bills, some favorable to its use by patients, others not.

District of Columbia (1998). In the nation's capitol, 69% of voters approved a medical cannabis initiative to allow patients a "sufficient quantity" of marijuana to treat illness and to permit nonprofit marijuana suppliers. Congress, however, has blocked the initiative from taking effect.

Local Measures. Medical cannabis measures have been adopted in several localities throughout the country. San Diego is the country's largest city to do so. One day after the Supreme Court's antimarijuana ruling in *Gonzalez* v. *Raich* was issued, Alameda County in California approved an ordinance to regulate medical marijuana dispensaries, becoming the 17th locality in the state to do so. Localities in nonmedical marijuana states have also acted. In November 2004, for example, voters in Ann Arbor, MI, and Columbia, MO, approved medical cannabis measures. Although largely symbolic, such local laws can influence the priorities of local law enforcement officers and prosecutors.

PUBLIC OPINION ON MEDICAL MARIJUANA

Voters have approved every medical marijuana initiative that has appeared on state ballots. Likewise, American public opinion has consistently favored access to medical marijuana by seriously ill patients. ProCon.org, a nonprofit and nonpartisan public education foundation, has identified 21 national public opinion polls that asked questions about medical marijuana from 1995 to the present. Respondents in every poll were in favor of medical marijuana by substantial margins, ranging from 60% to 80%.[49]

The *Journal of the American Medical Association* analyzed public opinion on the War on Drugs in a 1998 article. The authors' observations concerning public attitudes toward medical marijuana remain true today:

> While opposing the use or legalization of marijuana for recreational purposes, the public apparently does not want to deny very ill patients access to a potentially helpful drug therapy if prescribed by their physicians. The public's support of marijuana for medical purposes is conditioned by their belief that marijuana would be used only in the treatment of serious medical conditions.[50]

ANALYSIS OF ARGUMENTS FOR AND AGAINST MEDICAL MARIJUANA

At least in public opinion polls, the majority of Americans appear to hold that seriously ill or terminal patients should be able to use marijuana if recommended by their doctors. In 9 of the 11 states with medical marijuana laws, a majority has supported that belief in the voting booth. The federal government and most state governments, however, remain strongly opposed to medical marijuana.

In the ongoing debate over cannabis as medicine, certain arguments are frequently made on both sides of the issue. These arguments are briefly stated below and analyzed in turn. Equal weight is not given to both sides of every argument. Instead, the analysis is weighted according to the preponderance of evidence as currently understood. CRS takes no position on the claims or counterclaims in this debate.

What follows, then, is an attempt to analyze objectively the arguments frequently made about the role that herbal cannabis might play in the symptomatic treatment of certain diseases and about the possible societal consequences should its role in the practice of modern medicine be expanded beyond the handful of states where it is now permitted.

Marijuana Is Harmful and Has No Medical Value

> Suitable and superior medicines are currently available for treatment of all symptoms alleged to be treatable by crude marijuana. (Brief of the Drug Free America Foundation et al., 2004[51])

The federal government — along with many state governments and private antidrug organizations — staunchly maintains that botanical marijuana is a dangerous drug without any legitimate medical use. Marijuana intoxication can impair a person's coordination and decision-making skills and alter behavior. Chronic marijuana smoking can adversely affect the lungs, the cardiovascular system, and possibly the immune and reproductive systems.[52]

Of course, the FDA's 1985 approval of Marinol proves that the principal psychoactive ingredient of marijuana — THC — has therapeutic value. But that is not the issue in the medical marijuana debate. Botanical marijuana remains a plant substance, an herb, and its opponents say it cannot substitute for legitimate pharmaceuticals. Just because one molecule found in marijuana has become an approved medicine, they argue, does not make crude marijuana a medicine. The Drug Free America Foundation calls medical marijuana "a step backward to the times of potions and herbal remedies."[53]

The federal government's argument that marijuana has no medical value is straightforward. A drug, in order to meet the standard of the Controlled Substances Act as having a "currently accepted medical use in treatment in the United States," must meet a five-part test:

(1) The drug's chemistry must be known and reproducible,
(2) there must be adequate safety studies,
(3) there must be adequate and well-controlled studies proving efficacy,
(4) the drug must be accepted by qualified experts, and
(5) the scientific evidence must be widely available.[54]

According to the DEA, botanical marijuana meets none of these requirements. First, marijuana's chemistry is neither fully known nor reproducible. Second, adequate safety studies have not been done. Third, there are no adequate, well-controlled scientific studies proving marijuana is effective for any medical condition. Fourth, marijuana is not accepted by even a significant minority of experts qualified to evaluate drugs. Fifth, published scientific evidence concluding that marijuana is safe and effective for use in humans does not exist.[55]

The same DEA Final Order that set forth the five requirements for currently accepted medical use also outlined scientific evidence that would be considered irrelevant by the DEA in establishing currently accepted medical use. These include individual case reports, clinical data collected by practitioners, studies conducted by persons not qualified by scientific training and experience to evaluate the safety and effectiveness of the substance at issue, and studies or reports so lacking in detail as to preclude responsible scientific evaluation. Such information is inadequate for experts to conclude responsibly and fairly that marijuana is safe and effective for use as medicine.[56] The DEA and other federal drug control agencies can thereby disregard medical literature and opinion that claim to show the therapeutic value of marijuana because they do not meet the government's standards of proof.

The official view of medical marijuana is complicated by the wider War on Drugs. It is difficult to disentangle the medical use of locally grown marijuana for personal use from the overall policy of marijuana prohibition, as the Supreme Court made clear in *Raich*. To make an exemption for medical marijuana, the Court decided, "would undermine the orderly enforcement of the entire regulatory scheme ... The notion that California law has surgically excised a discrete activity that is hermetically sealed off from the larger interstate marijuana market is a dubious proposition...."[57]

The federal government maintains the position, then, that the Schedule I substance marijuana is harmful — not beneficial — to human health. Its use for any reason, including medicinal, should continue to be prohibited and punished. Despite possible signs of a more tolerant public attitude toward medical marijuana, its therapeutic benefits, if any, will continue to be officially unacknowledged and largely unrealized in the United States so long as this position prevails at the federal level.

Marijuana Effectively Treats the Symptoms of Some Diseases

[I]t cannot seriously be contested that there exists a small but significant class of individuals who suffer from painful chronic, degenerative, and terminal conditions, for whom marijuana provides uniquely effective relief. (Brief of the Leukemia & Lymphoma Society et al., 2004[58])

Proponents of medical marijuana point to a large body of reports and journal articles from around the world that support the therapeutic value of marijuana in treating a variety of disease-related problems, including

- relieving nausea,
- increasing appetite,
- reducing muscle spasms and spasticity,
- relieving chronic pain,

- reducing intraocular pressure, and
- relieving anxiety.[59]

Given these properties, marijuana has been used successfully to treat the debilitating symptoms of cancer and cancer chemotherapy,[60] AIDS, multiple sclerosis, epilepsy, glaucoma, anxiety, and other serious illnesses.[61] As opponents to medical marijuana assert, existing FDA-approved pharmaceuticals for these conditions are generally more effective than marijuana. Nevertheless, as the IOM Report acknowledged, the approved medicines do not work for everyone.[62] Many medical marijuana users report trying the drug only reluctantly and as a last resort after exhausting all other treatment modalities. A distinct subpopulation of patients now relies on whole cannabis for a degree of relief that FDA-approved synthetic drugs do not provide.

Medical cannabis proponents claim that single-cannabinoid, synthetic pharmaceuticals like Marinol are poor substitutes for the whole marijuana plant, which contains more than 400 known chemical compounds, including about 60 active cannabinoids in addition to THC. They say that scientists are a long way from knowing for sure which ones, singly or in combination, provide which therapeutic effects. Many patients have found that they benefit more from the whole plant than from any synthetically produced chemical derivative.[63] Furthermore, the natural plant is easily grown, whereas Marinol and any other cannabis-based pharmaceuticals that might be developed in the future will likely be expensive — prohibitively so for some patients.[64]

In recognition of the therapeutic benefits of botanical marijuana products, various associations of health professionals have passed resolutions in support of medical cannabis. These include the American Public Health Association, the American Nurses Association, and the California Pharmacists Association. The *New England Journal of Medicine* has editorialized in favor of patient access to marijuana.[65] Other groups, such as the American Medical Association, are more cautious. Their position is that not enough is known about botanical marijuana and that more research is needed.[66]

The recent discovery of cannabinoid receptors in the human brain and immune system provides a biological explanation for the claimed effectiveness of marijuana in relieving multiple disease symptoms. The human body produces its own cannabis-like compounds, called endocannabinoids, that react with the body's cannabinoid receptors. Like the better known opiate receptors, the cannabinoid receptors in the brain stem and spinal cord play a role in pain control. Cannabinoid receptors, which are abundant in various parts of the human brain, also play a role in controlling the vomiting reflex, appetite, emotional responses, motor skills, and memory formation. The presence of endogenous cannabinoids in the human nervous system and immune system, which some scientists believe holds the key to many promising drugs in the future,[67] provides the basis for the therapeutic value of marijuana.

The federal government's own IND Compassionate Access Program, which has provided government-grown medical marijuana to a select group of patients since 1978, would seem to affirm that marijuana has medicinal value and can be used safely. A scientist and organizer of the California medical marijuana initiative, along with two medical-doctor colleagues, has written:

> Nothing reveals the contradictions in federal policy toward marijuana more clearly than the fact that there are still eight patients in the United States who receive a tin of marijuana

'joints' (cigarettes) every month from the federal government. ... These eight people can legally possess and use marijuana, at government expense and with government permission. Yet hundreds of thousands of other patients can be fined and jailed under federal law for doing exactly the same thing.[68]

Smoking is an Improper Route of Drug Administration

Can you think of any other untested, home-made, mind-altering medicine that you self-dose, and that uses a burning carcinogen as a delivery vehicle?"[69] (General Barry McCaffrey, U.S. Drug Czar, 1996-2000)

That medical marijuana is smoked is probably the biggest obstacle preventing its acceptance. Opponents of medical marijuana argue that smoking is a poor way to take a drug, that inhaling smoke is an unprecedented drug delivery system. DEA Administrator Karen Tandy writes:

The scientific and medical communities have determined that smoked marijuana is a health danger, not a cure. There is no medical evidence that smoking marijuana helps patients. In fact, the Food and Drug Administration (FDA) has approved no medications that are smoked, primarily because smoking is a poor way to deliver medicine. Morphine, for example has proven to be a medically valuable drug, but the FDA does not endorse smoking opium or heroin.[70]

Medical marijuana opponents argue that chronic marijuana smoking is harmful to the lungs, the cardiovascular system, and possibly the immune and reproductive systems. These claims may be overstated to preserve marijuana prohibition. For example, neither epidemiological nor aggregate clinical data show higher rates of lung cancer in people who smoke marijuana.[71] The other alleged harms also remain unproven. However, even if smoking marijuana is proven harmful, the immediate benefits of smoked marijuana could outweigh the potential long-term harms for terminally ill patients.[72]

The therapeutic value of *smoked* marijuana is supported by existing research and experience. For example, the following statements appeared in the American Medical Association's (AMA's) "Council on Scientific Affairs Report 10 —Medicinal Marijuana,"[73] adopted by the AMA House of delegates on December 9, 1997:

- "Smoked marijuana was comparable to or more effective than oral THC [Marinol], and considerably more effective than prochlorperazine or other previous antiemetics in reducing nausea and emesis." (p. 10)
- "Anecdotal, survey, and clinical data support the view that smoked marijuana and oral THC provide symptomatic relief in some patients with spasticity associated with multiple sclerosis (MS) or trauma." (p. 13)
- "Smoked marijuana may benefit individual patients suffering from intermittent or chronic pain." (p. 15)

The IOM Report, however, expressed concerns about smoking (p. 126): "Smoked marijuana is unlikely to be a safe medication for any chronic medical condition." Despite this concern, the IOM Report's authors, were willing to recommend smoked marijuana under certain limited circumstances. For example, the report states (p. 154):

> Until the development of rapid-onset antiemetic drug delivery systems, there will likely remain a subpopulation of patients for whom standard antiemetic therapy is ineffective and who suffer from debilitating emesis. It is possible that the harmful effects of smoking marijuana for a limited period of time might be outweighed by the antiemetic benefits of marijuana, at least for patients for whom standard antiemetic therapy is ineffective and who suffer from debilitating emesis. Such patients should be evaluated on a case-by-case basis and treated under close medical supervision.

The IOM Report makes another exception for terminal cancer patients (p. 159):

> Terminal cancer patients pose different issues. For those patients the medical harm associated with smoking is of little consequence. For terminal patients suffering debilitating pain or nausea and for whom all indicated medications have failed to provide relief, the medical benefits of smoked marijuana might outweigh the harm.

Smoking can actually be a preferred drug delivery system for patients whose nausea prevents them from taking anything orally. Such patients *need* to inhale their antiemitic drug. Other patients *prefer* inhaling because the drug is absorbed much more quickly through the lungs, so that the beneficial effects of the drug are felt almost at once. This rapid onset also gives patients more control over dosage. For a certain patient subpopulation, then, the advantages of inhalation may prevail over both edible marijuana preparations and pharmaceutical drugs in pill form, such as Marinol.

Moreover, medical marijuana advocates argue that there are ways to lessen the risks of smoking. Any potential problems associated with smoking, they argue, can be reduced by using higher potency marijuana, which means that less has to be inhaled to achieve the desired therapeutic effect. Furthermore, marijuana does not have to be smoked to be used as medicine. It can be cooked in various ways and eaten.[74] Like Marinol, however, taking marijuana orally can be difficult for patients suffering from nausea. Many patients are turning to vaporizers, which offer the benefits of smoking — rapid action, ease of dose titration — without having to inhale smoke. Vaporizers are devices that take advantage of the fact that cannabinoids vaporize at a lower temperature than that required for marijuana to burn. Vaporizers heat the plant matter enough for the cannabinoids to be released as vapor without having to burn the marijuana preparation. Patients can thereby inhale the beneficial cannabinoids without also having to inhale the potentially harmful by-products of marijuana combustion.[75]

Marijuana Should Be Rescheduled to Permit Medical Use

> [T]he administrative law judge concludes that the provisions of the [Controlled Substances] Act permit and require the transfer of marijuana from Schedule I to Schedule II. The Judge realizes that strong emotions are aroused on both sides of any discussion concerning the use of marijuana. Nonetheless it is essential for this Agency [DEA], and its Administrator, calmly and dispassionately to review the evidence of record, correctly apply the law, and act accordingly. (Francis L. Young, DEA Administrative Law Judge, 1988[76])

Proponents of medical marijuana believe its placement in Schedule I of the CSA was an error from the beginning. Cannabis is one of the safest therapeutically active substances known.[77] No one has ever died of an overdose.[78] Petitions to reschedule marijuana have been received by the federal government, and rejected, ever since the original passage of the Controlled Substances Act in 1970.

Rescheduling can be accomplished administratively or it can be done by an act of Congress. Administratively, the federal Department of Health and Human Services (HHS) could find that marijuana meets sufficient standards of safety and efficacy to warrant rescheduling. Even though THC, the most prevalent cannabinoid in marijuana, was administratively moved to Schedule III in 1999, no signs exist that botanical marijuana will similarly be rescheduled by federal agency ruling anytime soon.

An act of Congress to reschedule marijuana is only slightly less likely, although such legislation has been introduced in recent Congresses, including the 109th.[79] The States' Rights to Medical Marijuana Act (H.R. 2087, Frank), which would move marijuana from Schedule I to Schedule II of the Controlled Substances Act, has seen no action beyond committee referral.[80]

Schedule II substances have a high potential for abuse and may lead to severe psychological or physical dependence but have a currently accepted medical use in treatment in the United States. Cocaine, methamphetamine, morphine, and methadone are classified as Schedule II substances. Many drug policy experts and laypersons alike believe that marijuana should also reside in Schedule II.

Others think marijuana should be properly classified as a Schedule III substance, along with THC and its synthetic version, Marinol. Substances in Schedule III have less potential for abuse than the drugs in Schedules I and II, their abuse may lead to moderate or low physical dependence or high psychological dependence, and they have a currently accepted medical use in treatment in the United States.

Rescheduling seems to be supported by public opinion. A nationwide Gallup Poll conducted in March 1999 found that 73% of American adults favor "making marijuana legally available for doctors to prescribe in order to reduce pain and suffering." An AARP poll of American adults age 45 and older conducted in mid-November 2004 found that 72% agree that adults should be allowed to legally use marijuana for medical purposes if recommended by a physician.[81]

Few Members of Congress, however, publicly support the rescheduling option. The States' Rights to Medical Marijuana Act (H.R. 2087, Frank), which would move marijuana from Schedule I to Schedule II of the Controlled Substances Act, currently has 37 cosponsors.

State Medical Marijuana Laws Increase Illicit Drug Use

> The natural extension of this myth [that marijuana is good medicine] is that, if marijuana is medicine, it must also be safe for recreational use. (Karen P. Tandy, DEA Administrator, 2005[82])

It is the position of the federal government that to permit the use of medical marijuana affords the drug a degree of legitimacy it does not deserve. America's youth are especially vulnerable, it is said, and state medical marijuana programs send the wrong message to our youth, many of whom do not recognize the very real dangers of marijuana.

Studies show that the use of an illicit drug is inversely proportional to the perceived harm of that drug. That is, the more harmful a drug is perceived to be, the fewer the number of people who will try it.[83] Opponents of medical marijuana argue that "surveys show that perception of harm with respect to marijuana has been dropping off annually since the renewal of the drive to legalize marijuana as medicine, which began in the early 1990s when legalization advocates first gained a significant increase in funding and began planning the state ballot initiative drive to legalize crude marijuana as medicine."[84] They point to the 1999 National Household Survey on Drug Abuse (NHSDA), which "reveals that those states which have passed medical marijuana laws have among the highest levels of past-month marijuana use, of past-month other drug use, of drug addiction, and of drug and alcohol addiction."[85]

Indeed, all eleven states that have passed medical marijuana laws ranked above the national average in the percentage of persons 12 or older reporting past-month use of marijuana in 1999, as shown in **Table 3**. It is at least possible, however, that this analysis confuses cause with effect. It is logical to assume that the states with the highest prevalence of marijuana usage would be more likely to approve medical marijuana programs, because the populations of those states would be more knowledgeable of marijuana's effects and more tolerant of its use.

It is also the case that California, the state with the largest and longest-running medical marijuana program, ranked 34th in the percentage of persons age 12-17 reporting marijuana use in the past month during the period 2002-2003, as shown in **Table 2**. In fact, between 1999 and 2002-2003, of the 10 states with active medical marijuana programs, 5 states (AK, HI, ME, MT, VT) rose in the state rankings of past-month marijuana use by 12- to 17-year-olds and 5 states fell (CA, CO, NV, OR, WA).[86] Of the five states that had approved medical marijuana laws before 1999 (AK, AZ, CA, OR, WA), only Alaska's ranking rose between 1999 and 2002-2003, from 7th to 4th, with 11.08% of youth reporting past-month marijuana use in 2002-2003, compared with 10.4% in 1999. No clear patterns are apparent in the state-level data. Clearly, more important factors are at work in determining a state's prevalence of recreational marijuana use than whether the state has a medical marijuana program.

The IOM Report found no evidence for the supposition that state medical marijuana programs lead to increased use of marijuana or other drugs (pp. 6-7):

> Finally, there is a broad social concern that sanctioning the medical use of marijuana might increase its use among the general population. At this point there are no convincing data to support this concern. The existing data are consistent with the idea that this would not be a problem if the medical use of marijuana were as closely regulated as other medications with abuse potential. [T]his question is beyond the issues normally considered for medical uses of drugs and should not be a factor in evaluating the therapeutic potential of marijuana or cannabinoids.

The IOM Report further states (p. 126):

> Even if there were evidence that the medical use of marijuana would decrease the perception that it can be a harmful substance, this is beyond the scope of laws regulating the approval of therapeutic drugs. Those laws concern scientific data related to the safety and efficacy of drugs for individual use; they do not address perceptions or beliefs of the general population.

Tables 1 and 2. States Ranked by Percentage of Youth Age 12-17 Reporting Past-Month Marijuana Use, 1999 and 2002-2003

Table 1. 1999			Table 2. 2002-2003		
Rank	**State**	**%**	**Rank**	**State**	**%**
1	Delaware	13.9	1	**Vermont**	13.32
2	Massachusetts	11.9	2	**Montana**	12.07
3	**Nevada**	11.6	3	New Hampshire	11.79
4	**Montana**	11.4	4	**Alaska**	11.08
5	Rhode Island	10.8	5	Rhode Island	10.86
6	New Hampshire	10.7	6	**Maine**	10.56
7	**Alaska**	10.4	7	Massachusetts	10.53
8	**Colorado**	10.3	8	New Mexico	10.35
9	Minnesota	9.9	9	**Hawaii**	10.23
9	**Washington**	9.9	10	**Colorado**	9.82
11	**Oregon**	9.6	11	**Nevada**	9.58
	District of Columbia	9.6	12	South Dakota	9.57
12	Illinois	9.2	13	Delaware	9.41
12	New Mexico	9.2	14	**Oregon**	9.31
14	Maryland	8.8	15	Michigan	9.23
15	Indiana	8.7	16	Connecticut	9.22
16	Connecticut	8.6	17	Nebraska	9.13
17	**Vermont**	8.4	18	**Washington**	9.11
18	**Hawaii**	8.3	19	Minnesota	8.92
18	Wisconsin	8.3	20	New York	8.76
20	Michigan	7.8	21	Ohio	8.74
20	Wyoming	7.8	22	West Virginia	8.62
22	**California**	7.7	23	Florida	8.52
23	North Dakota	7.6	24	North Carolina	8.44
	National	7.4	25	Virginia	8.43
24	South Carolina	7.4	26	Pennsylvania	8.18
27	**Arizona**	7.3	27	Kentucky	8.16
27	Arkansas	7.3	28	Oklahoma	8.13
27	New Jersey	7.3		*National*	8.03
28	**Maine**	7.2	29	Arkansas	7.97
29	West Virginia	7.1	30	Idaho	7.92
31	Ohio	6.9	31	Maryland	7.87
31	South Dakota	6.9	32	**Arizona**	7.74
33	New York	6.8	33	Wisconsin	7.71
33	North Carolina	6.8	34	**California**	7.66
34	Mississippi	6.7	35	Illinois	7.61
37	Kansas	6.6	36	North Dakota	7.58
37	Louisiana	6.6	37	Missouri	7.43
37	Missouri	6.6		District of Columbia	7.43
38	Georgia	6.4	38	Kansas	7.39
40	Oklahoma	6.3	39	Indiana	7.37
40	Pennsylvania	6.3	40	New Jersey	7.33
41	Florida	6.2	41	South Carolina	7.25
43	Nebraska	6.1	42	Wyoming	7.14
43	Utah	6.1	43	Iowa	7.10
45	Idaho	5.9	44	Louisiana	6.92
45	Virginia	5.9	45	Georgia	6.87
46	Texas	5.7	46	Texas	6.38
47	Alabama	5.6	47	Alabama	6.37
48	Kentucky	5.3	47	Tennessee	6.37
50	Iowa	5.2	49	Mississippi	6.04
50	Tennessee	5.2	50	Utah	5.30

Source: SAMHSA, Office of Applied Studies, National Household Survey on Drug Abuse, 1999, Table 3B, at [http://www.oas. samhsa.gov/NHSDA/99StateTabs/tables2.htm]. Rankings calculated by CRS.

Source: SAMHSA, Office of Applied Studies, National Survey on Drug Use and Health, 2002 and 2003, Table B.3, at [http://www.oas.samhsa.gov/2k3State/ appB.htm#tabB.3]. Rankings calculated by CRS.

Tables 3 and 4. States Ranked by Percentage of Persons 12 or Older Reporting Past-Month Marijuana Use, 1999 and 2003-2004

Table 3. 1999				Table 4. 2003-2004		
Rank	**State**	**%**		**Rank**	**State**	**%**
1	Maryland	7.9		1	New Hampshire	10.23
2	**Colorado**	7.7		2	**Alaska**	9.78
3	Massachusetts	7.5		3	**Vermont**	9.77
4	Rhode Island	7.4			District of Columbia	9.60
5	**Alaska**	7.1		4	Rhode Island	9.56
	District of Columbia	7.1		5	**Montana**	9.17
6	**Washington**	6.8		6	**Oregon**	8.88
7	**Oregon**	6.6		7	**Colorado**	8.49
8	Delaware	6.5		8	**Maine**	7.95
8	New Mexico	6.5		9	Massachusetts	7.80
10	**California**	6.0		10	**Nevada**	7.62
11	**Montana**	5.9		11	**Washington**	7.41
11	New Hampshire	5.9		12	New Mexico	7.37
13	**Hawaii**	5.8		13	New York	7.34
13	**Maine**	5.8		14	Michigan	7.20
15	**Nevada**	5.6		15	**Hawaii**	6.95
15	Wyoming	5.6		16	Connecticut	9.94
17	**Vermont**	5.4		17	Delaware	6.89
18	Michigan	5.3		18	Missouri	6.76
18	Minnesota	5.3		19	Florida	6.58
20	**Arizona**	5.2		20	**California**	6.50
21	Wisconsin	5.1		21	Ohio	6.49
22	Connecticut	5.0		22	Minnesota	6.37
22	Florida	5.0			*National*	6.18
22	New Jersey	5.0		23	Indiana	6.12
25	New York	4.9		24	Nebraska	5.97
25	Utah	4.9		25	Virginia	5.96
	National	4.9		26	North Carolina	5.89
27	Illinois	4.8		27	Louisiana	5.77
29	Missouri	4.7		28	Maryland	5.73
29	North Carolina	4.7		29	**Arizona**	5.68
30	Indiana	4.6		30	South Carolina	5.65
31	Pennsylvania	4.5		31	Pennsylvania	5.64
32	Ohio	4.3		32	Arkansas	5.63
34	Georgia	4.2		33	Kentucky	5.62
34	Idaho	4.2		34	Illinois	5.60
35	South Dakota	4.1		35	Oklahoma	5.58
36	Virginia	4.0		36	Wyoming	5.45
38	Nebraska	3.9		37	Wisconsin	5.40
38	North Dakota	3.9		38	North Dakota	5.35
39	South Carolina	3.8		39	South Dakota	5.24
40	Kansas	3.7		40	West Virginia	5.12
43	Kentucky	3.6		41	Idaho	5.09
43	Tennessee	3.6		42	New Jersey	5.05
43	West Virginia	3.6		43	Georgia	4.93
47	Arkansas	3.5		44	Kansas	4.91
47	Louisiana	3.5		45	Iowa	4.90
47	Oklahoma	3.5		46	Texas	4.79
47	Texas	3.5		47	Mississippi	4.64
50	Alabama	3.3		48	Tennessee	4.59
50	Iowa	3.3		49	Alabama	4.32
50	Mississippi	3.3		50	Utah	4.00

Source: SAMHSA, Office of Applied Studies, National Household Survey on Drug Abuse, 1999, Table 3B, at [http://www.oas.samhsa.gov/NHSDA/99StateTabs/tables2.htm]. Rankings calculated by CRS.

Source: SAMHSA, Office of Applied Studies, National Survey on Drug Use and Health, 2002 and 2003, Table B.3, at [http://www.oas.samhsa.gov/2k3State/appB.htm#tabB.3]. Rankings calculated by CRS.

The IOM Report also found that "No evidence suggests that the use of opiates or cocaine for medical purposes has increased the perception that their illicit use is safe or acceptable"(p. 102). Doctors can prescribe cocaine, morphine, amphetamine, and methamphetamine, but this is not seen as weakening the war on drugs. Why is doctors' recommending medical marijuana to their patients any different?

A June 2005 editorial in the *Washington Examiner* had a slightly different take on this issue:

> Studies show higher increases in overall marijuana use in states that have passed medical marijuana initiatives. The solution is to go after the estimated 15 million people who smoke marijuana for recreation, not the sick people these laws were intended to help.[87]

The so-called "Gateway Theory" of marijuana use is also cited to explain how medical marijuana will increase illicit drug use. With respect to the rationale behind the argument that marijuana serves as a "gateway" drug, the IOM Report offered the following (p. 6):

> In the sense that marijuana use typically precedes rather than follows initiation of other illicit drug use, it is indeed a "gateway" drug. But because underage smoking and alcohol use typically precede marijuana use, marijuana is not the most common, and is rarely the first, "gateway" to illicit drug use. There is no conclusive evidence that the drug effects of marijuana are causally linked to the subsequent abuse of other illicit drugs.

Medical Marijuana Undermines the War on Drugs

> The DEA and its local and state counterparts routinely report that large-scale drug traffickers hide behind and invoke Proposition 215, even when there is no evidence of any medical claim. In fact, many large-scale marijuana cultivators and traffickers escape state prosecution because of bogus medical marijuana claims. Prosecutors are reluctant to charge these individuals because of the state of confusion that exists in California. Therefore, high-level traffickers posing as 'care-givers' are able to sell illegal drugs with impunity. (California Medical Marijuana Information, DEA Web page[88])

Many opponents to medical marijuana argue that state laws related to this issue weaken the fight against drug abuse by making the work of police officers more difficult. This undermining of law enforcement can occur in at least three ways: by diverting medical marijuana into the recreational drug market, by causing state and local law enforcement priorities to diverge from federal priorities, and by complicating the job of law enforcement by forcing officers to distinguish medical users from recreational users.

Diversion. Marijuana grown for medical purposes, according to DEA and other federal drug control agencies, can be diverted into the larger, illegal marijuana market, thereby undermining law enforcement efforts to eliminate the marijuana market altogether. This point was emphasized by the Department of Justice (DOJ) in its prepublication review of a report by the Government Accountability Office (GAO) on medical marijuana. DOJ criticized the GAO draft report on the grounds that the "report did not mention that state medical marijuana laws are routinely abused to facilitate traditional illegal trafficking."[89]

GAO responded that in their interviews with federal officials regarding the impact of state medical marijuana laws on their law enforcement efforts, "none of the federal officials we spoke with provided information that abuse of medical marijuana laws was routinely occurring in any of the states, including California."[90] The government also failed to establish this in the *Raich* case. (It is of course possible that significant diversion is taking place yet remains undetected.)

Just as with many pharmaceuticals, some diversion is inevitable. Some would view this as an acceptable cost of implementing a medical marijuana program. Every public policy has its costs and benefits. Depriving seriously ill patients of their medical marijuana is seen by some as a small price to pay if doing so will help to protect America's youth from marijuana. Others balance the harms and benefits of medical marijuana in the opposite direction. Legal analyst Stuart Taylor Jr. recently wrote, "As a matter of policy, Congress as well as the states should legalize medical marijuana, with strict regulatory controls. The proven benefits to some suffering patients outweigh the potential costs of marijuana being diverted to illicit uses."[91]

Changed state and local law enforcement priorities. Following the passage of California's and Arizona's medical marijuana initiatives, federal officials expressed concern that the measures would seriously affect the federal government's drug enforcement effort because federal drug policies rely heavily on the state's enforcement of their own drug laws to achieve federal objectives. For instance, in hearings before the Senate Judiciary Committee, the head of the Drug Enforcement Administration stated

> I have always felt ... that the federalization of crime is very difficult to carry out; that crime, just in essence, is for the most part a local problem and addressed very well locally, in my experience. We now have a situation where local law enforcement is unsure.... The numbers of investigations that you would talk about that might be presently being conducted by the [Arizona state police] at the gram level would be beyond our capacity to conduct those types of individual investigations without abandoning the major organized crime investigations.[92]

State medical marijuana laws arguably feed into the deprioritization movement, by which drug reform advocates seek to influence state and local law enforcement to give a low priority to the enforcement of marijuana laws. This movement to make simple marijuana possession the lowest law enforcement priority has made inroads in such cities as San Francisco, Seattle, and Oakland, but it extends beyond the medical marijuana states to college towns such as Ann Arbor, MI, Madison, WI, Columbia, MO, and Lawrence, KS.[93] Federal officials fear that jurisdictions that "opt out" of marijuana enforcement "will quickly become a haven for drug traffickers."[94]

Distinguishing between legal and illegal providers and users.

Police officers in medical marijuana states have complained about the difficulty of distinguishing between legitimate patients and recreational marijuana smokers. According to the DEA

> Local and state law enforcement counterparts cannot distinguish between illegal marijuana grows and grows that qualify as medical exemptions.
> Many self-designated medical marijuana growers are, in fact, growing marijuana for illegal, "recreational" use.[95]

This reasoning is echoed in the *Raich* amicus brief of Community Rights Counsel (p. 12):

> Creating an exception for medical use [of marijuana] could undermine enforcement efforts by imposing an often difficult burden on prosecutors of establishing the violator's subjective

motivation and intent beyond a reasonable doubt. Given that marijuana used in response to medical ailments is not readily distinguishable from marijuana used for other reasons, Congress rationally concluded that the control of all use is necessary to address the national market for controlled substances.

Patients and caregivers, on the other hand, have complained that their marijuana, which is lawful under state statute, has been seized by police and not returned. In some cases, patients and caregivers have been unexpectedly arrested by state or local police officers. A November 2002 GAO report on medical marijuana stated that "Several law enforcement officials in California and Oregon cited the inconsistency between federal and state law as a significant problem, particularly regarding how seized marijuana is handled."[96]

This inconsistency has especially been a problem in California where the California Highway Patrol (CHP) has, on numerous occasions, arrested patients or confiscated their medical marijuana during routine traffic stops. "Although voters legalized medical marijuana in California nearly nine years ago," reports the *Los Angeles Times*, "police statewide have wrangled with activists over how to enforce the law."[97]

As a result of a lawsuit brought against the CHP by a patient advocacy group, CHP officers will no longer seize patients' marijuana as long as they possess no more than 8 ounces and can show a certified user identification card or their physician's written recommendation. The CHP's new policy, announced in August 2005, will likely also influence the behavior of other California law enforcement agencies.

The Committee on Drugs and the Law of the Bar of the City of New York concluded its 1997 report "Marijuana Should be Medically Available" with this statement: "The government can effectively differentiate medical marijuana and recreational marijuana, as it has done with cocaine. The image of the Federal authorities suppressing a valuable medicine to maintain the rationale of the war on drugs only serves to discredit the government's effort."[98]

Patients Should Not Be Arrested for Using Medical Marijuana

Centuries of Anglo-American law stand against the imposition of criminal liability on individuals for pursuing their own lifesaving pain relief and treatment ... Because the experience of pain can be so subversive of dignity — and even of the will to live — ethics and legal tradition recognize that individuals pursuing pain relief have special claims to non-interference. (Brief of the Leukemia & Lymphoma Society et al., 2004[99])

Medical marijuana advocates believe that seriously ill people should not be punished for acting in accordance with the opinion of their physicians in a bona fide attempt to relieve their suffering, especially when acting in accordance with state law. Even if marijuana were proven to be more harmful than now appears, prison for severely ill patients is believed to be a worse alternative. Patients have enough problems without having to fear the emotional and financial cost of arrest, legal fees, prosecution, and a possible prison sentence.

The American public appears to agree. The Institute of Medicine found that "public support for patient access to marijuana for medical use appears substantial; public opinion polls taken during 1997 and 1998 generally reported 60-70 percent of respondents in favor of allowing medical uses of marijuana."[100]

The federal penalty for possessing one marijuana cigarette — even for medical use — is up to one year in prison and up to a $100,000 fine,[101] and the penalty for growing a cannabis plant is up to five years and up to a $250,000 fine.[102] That patients are willing to risk these severe penalties to obtain the relief that marijuana provides appears to present strong evidence for both the substance's therapeutic effectiveness and their urgent need for relief.

Although the Supreme Court ruled differently in *Raich*, the argument persists that medical marijuana providers and patients are engaging in a class of activity totally different from those persons trafficking in marijuana for recreational use and that patients should not be arrested for using medical marijuana in accordance with the laws of the states in which they reside.

With its position affirmed by *Raich*, however, the DEA continues to investigate — and sometimes raid and shut down — medical marijuana distribution operations in California and other medical marijuana states. DEA's position is that

> [F]ederal law does not distinguish between crimes involving marijuana for claimed "medical" purposes and crimes involving marijuana for any other purpose. DEA likewise does not so distinguish in carrying out its duty to enforce the CSA and investigate possible violations of the Act. Rather, consistent with the agency's mandate, DEA focuses on large-scale trafficking organizations and other criminal enterprises that warrant federal scrutiny. If investigating CSA violations in this manner leads the agency to encounter persons engaged in criminal activities involving marijuana, DEA does not alter its approach if such persons claim at some point their crimes are "medically" justified. To do so would be to give legal effect to an excuse considered by the text of federal law and the United States Supreme Court to be of no moment.[103]

Because nearly all arrests and prosecutions for marijuana possession are handled by state and local law enforcement officers, patients and caregivers in the medical marijuana states can, as a practical matter, possess medical marijuana without fear of arrest and imprisonment. DEA enforcement actions against medical marijuana dispensaries — as occurred in San Francisco shortly after the *Raich* decision was announced[104] — can, however, make it more difficult for patients to obtain the drug. The situation that Grinspoon and Bakalar described in 1995 in the

Journal of the American Medical Association persists a decade later: "At present, the greatest danger in medical use of marihuana is its illegality, which imposes much anxiety and expense on suffering people, forces them to bargain with illicit drug dealers, and exposes them to the threat of criminal prosecution."[105]

The States Should Be Allowed To Experiment

> Doctors, not the federal government, know what's best for their patients. If a state decides to allow doctors to recommend proven treatments for their patients, then the federal government has no rightful place in the doctor's office. (Attorney Randy Barnett, 2004[106])

Three States — California, Maryland, and Washington — filed an amicus curiae brief supporting the right of states to institute medical marijuana programs.

Their brief argued, "In our federal system States often serve as democracy's laboratories, trying out new, or innovative solutions to society's ills."[107]

The *Raich* case shows that the federal government has zero tolerance for state medical marijuana programs. The Bush Administration appealed the decision of the Ninth Circuit Court of Appeals to the Supreme Court, which reversed the Ninth Circuit and upheld the federal position against the states. Framed as a Commerce Clause issue, the case became a battle for states' rights against the federal government.

The *Raich* case created unusual political alliances. Three southern states that are strongly opposed to any marijuana use, medical or otherwise — Alabama, Louisiana, and Mississippi — filed an amici curiae brief supporting California's medical marijuana users on the grounds of states' rights. Their brief argued

> As Justice Brandeis famously remarked, "[i]t is one of the happy incidents of the federal system that a single courageous State may, if its citizens choose, serve as a laboratory; and try novel social and economic experiments without risk to the rest of the country."[108] Whether California and the other compassionate-use States are "courageous — or instead profoundly misguided — is not the point. The point is that, as a sovereign member of the federal union, California is entitled to make for itself the tough policy choices that affect its citizens.[109]

States' rights advocates argue that authority to define criminal law and the power to make and enforce laws protecting the health, safety, welfare, and morals reside at the state level and that a state has the right to set these policies free of congressional interference.

For Justice O'Connor, the *Raich* case exemplified "the role of States as laboratories."[110] She wrote in her dissenting opinion that

> If I were a California citizen, I would not have voted for the medical marijuana ballot initiative; if I were a California legislator I would not have supported the Compassionate Use Act. But whatever the wisdom of California's experiment with medical marijuana, the federalism principles that have driven our Commerce Clause cases require that room for experiment be protected in this case.[111]

Medical Marijuana Laws Harm the Drug Approval Process

> The current efforts to gain legal status of marijuana through ballot initiatives seriously threaten the Food and Drug Administration statutorily authorized process of proving safety and efficacy. (Brief of the Drug Free America Foundation et al., 2004[112])

Although the individual states regulate the practice of medicine, the federal government has taken primary responsibility for the regulation of medical products, especially those containing controlled substances. Pharmaceutical drugs must be approved for use in the United States by the Food and Drug Administration (FDA), an agency of the Department of Health and Human Services (HHS). The Federal Food, Drug, and Cosmetics Act gives HHS and FDA the responsibility for determining that drugs are safe and effective, a requirement that all medicines must meet before they can enter interstate commerce and be made available for general medical use.[113] Clinical evaluation is required regardless of whether the drug is synthetically produced or originates from a natural botanical or animal source.

Opponents of medical marijuana say that the FDA's drug approval process should not be circumvented. To permit states to decide which medical products can be made available for therapeutic use, they say, would undercut this regulatory system. State medical marijuana initiatives are seen as inconsistent with the federal government's responsibility to protect the public from unsafe, ineffective drugs.

The Bush Administration argued in its brief in the *Raich* case that "excepting drug activity for personal use or free distribution from the sweep of [federal drug laws] would discourage the consumption of lawful controlled substances and would undermine Congress's intent to regulate the drug market comprehensively to protect public health and safety."[114]

Three prominent drug abuse experts argued the following in their Amici brief:

> This action by the state of California did not create a "novel social and economic experiment," but rather chaos in the scientific and medical communities. Furthermore, under Court of Appeals ruling, such informal State systems could be replicated, and even expanded, in a manner that puts at risk the critical protections so carefully crafted under the national food and drug legislation of the 20th century.[115]

The FDA itself has stated that

> FDA is the sole Federal agency that approves drug products as safe and effective for particular indications, and efforts that seek to bypass the FDA drug approval process would not serve the interests of public health. FDA has not approved marijuana for any indication. Only the disciplined, systematic, scientific conduct of clinical trials can establish whether there is any medicinal value to marijuana, smoked or otherwise.[116]

The Drug Free America *Raich* brief elaborates further (pp. 12-13):

> The ballot initiative-led laws create an atmosphere of medicine by popular vote, rather than the rigorous scientific and medical process that all medicines must undergo. Before the development of modern pharmaceutical science, the field of medicine was fraught with potions and herbal remedies. Many of those were absolutely useless, or conversely were harmful to unsuspecting subjects. Thus evolved our current Food and Drug Administration and drug scheduling processes, which Congress has authorized in order to create a uniform and reliable system of drug approval and regulation. This system is being intentionally undermined by the legalization proponents through use of medical marijuana initiatives.

The organizers of the medical marijuana state initiatives deny that it was their intent to undermine the federal drug approval process. Rather, in their view, it became necessary for them to *bypass* the FDA and go to the states because of the federal government's resistance to marijuana research requests and rescheduling petitions.

As for the charge that politics should not play a role in the drug approval and controlled substance scheduling processes, medical marijuana supporters point out that marijuana's original listing as a Schedule I substance in 1970 was itself a political act on the part of Congress.

Scientists on both sides of the issue say more research needs to be done, yet some researchers charge that the federal government has all but shut down marijuana clinical trials for reasons based on politics and ideology rather than science.[117]

In any case, as the IOM Report pointed out, "although a drug is normally approved for medical use only on proof of its 'safety and efficacy,' patients with life-threatening conditions are sometimes (under protocols for 'compassionate use') allowed access to unapproved drugs whose benefits and risks are uncertain."[118] This was the case with the IND Compassionate

Access Program established by the FDA in 1978, under which a limited number of patients are provided government-grown medical marijuana to treat their serious medical conditions.

Some observers believe the pharmaceutical industry and many politicians oppose medical marijuana to protect pharmaceutical industry profits. Because the whole marijuana plant cannot be patented, research efforts must be focused on the development of *synthetic* cannabinoids such as Marinol. But even if additional cannabinoid drugs are developed and marketed, some believe that doctors and patients should still not be criminalized for recommending and using the natural substance.

The New England Journal of Medicine has editorialized that

[A] federal policy that prohibits physicians from alleviating suffering by prescribing marijuana for seriously ill patients is misguided, heavy-handed, and inhumane. Marijuana may have long-term adverse effects and its use may presage serious addictions, but neither long-term side effects nor addiction is a relevant issue in such patients. It is also hypocritical to forbid physicians to prescribe marijuana while permitting them to use morphine and meperidine to relieve extreme dyspnea and pain. With both of these drugs the difference between the dose that relieves symptoms and the dose that hastens death is very narrow; by contrast, there is no risk of death from smoking marijuana. To demand evidence of therapeutic efficacy is equally hypocritical. The noxious sensations that patients experience are extremely difficult to quantify in controlled experiments. What really counts for a therapy with this kind of safety margin is whether a seriously ill patient feels relief as a result of the intervention, not whether a controlled trial "proves" its efficacy.[119]

Some observers suggest that until the federal government relents and becomes more hospitable to marijuana research proposals and more willing to consider moving marijuana to a less restrictive schedule, the medical marijuana issue will continue to be fought at state and local levels of governance. As one patient advocate has stated, "As the months tick away, it will become more and more obvious that we need to continue changing state laws until the federal government has no choice but to change its inhumane medicinal marijuana laws."[120]

The Medical Marijuana Movement Is Politically Inspired

Advocates have tried to legalize marijuana in one form or another for three decades, and the "medical marijuana" concept is a Trojan Horse tactic towards the goal of legalization. (Brief of the Drug Free America Foundation et al., 2004[121])

Medical marijuana opponents see the movement to promote the use of medical marijuana as a cynical attempt to subvert the Controlled Substances Act and legalize the recreational use of marijuana for all. They see it as a devious tactic in the more than 30-year effort by marijuana proponents to bring an end to marijuana prohibition in the United States and elsewhere.

They point out that between 1972 and 1978, the National Organization for the Reform of Marijuana Laws (NORML) successfully lobbied 11 state legislatures to decriminalize the drug, reducing penalties for possession in most cases to that of a traffic ticket. Also, in 1972, NORML began the first of several unsuccessful attempts to petition the DEA to reschedule marijuana from Schedule I to Schedule II on the grounds that crude marijuana had use in medicine.[122]

Later, beginning with California in 1996, "drug legalizers" pushed successfully for passage of medical marijuana voter initiatives in several states, prompting then-Drug Czar Barry McCaffrey, writing in *Newsweek*, to warn that "We're on a Perilous Path." "I think it's clear," he wrote, "that a lot of the people arguing for the California proposition and others like it are pushing the legalization of drugs, plain and simple."[123]

Is it cynical or smart for NORML and other drug reform organizations to simultaneously pursue the separate goals of marijuana decriminalization for all, on the one hand, and marijuana rescheduling for the seriously ill, on the other? It is not unusual for political activists tactically to press for — and accept — half-measures in pursuit of a larger strategic goal. Pro-life activists work to prohibit partial-birth abortions and to pass parental notification laws. Gay rights activists seek limited domestic partner benefits as a stepping stone to full marriage equality. The tactic is used on both sides of the cultural divide in America, to the alarm of those opposed.

It is certainly true that the medical cannabis movement is an offshoot of the marijuana legalization movement. Many individuals and organizations that support medical marijuana also support a broader program of drug law reform. It is also true, however, that many health professionals and other individuals who advocate medical access to marijuana do not support any other changes in U.S. drug control policy. In the same way, not everyone in favor of parental notification laws supports banning abortions for everyone. And not every supporter of domestic partner benefits believes in same-sex marriage.

In these hot-button issues, ideology and emotion often rule. Marijuana users in general, and medical marijuana users in particular, are demonized by some elements of American society. The ideology of the "Drug Warriors" intrudes on the science of medical marijuana, as pointed out by Grinspoon and Bakalar in the *Journal of the American Medical Association*:

> Advocates of medical use of marihuana are sometimes charged with using medicine as a wedge to open a way for "recreational" use. The accusation is false as applied to its target, but expresses in a distorted form a truth about some opponents of medical marihuana: they will not admit that it can be a safe and effective medicine largely because they are stubbornly committed to exaggerating its dangers when used for nonmedical purposes.[124]

The authors of the IOM Report were aware of the possibility that larger ideological positions could influence one's stand on the specific issue of patient access to medical marijuana when they wrote that

> [I]t is not relevant to scientific validity whether an argument is put forth by someone who believes that all marijuana use should be legal or by someone who believes that any marijuana use is highly damaging to individual users and to society as a whole. (p. 14)

In other words, it is widely believed that science should rule when it comes to medical issues. Both sides in the medical marijuana debate claim adherence to this principle. The House Government Reform Committee's April 2004 hearing on medical marijuana was titled "Marijuana and Medicine: The Need for a Science-Based Approach." And medical marijuana advocates plead with the federal government to permit scientific research on medical marijuana to proceed.

Rescheduling marijuana and making it available for medical use and research is not necessarily a step toward legalizing its recreational use. Such a move would put it on a par with cocaine, methamphetamine, morphine, and methadone, all of which are Schedule II substances that are not close to becoming legal for recreational use. Proponents of medical marijuana ask why marijuana should be considered differently than these other scheduled substances.

It is also arguable that marijuana should indeed be considered differently than cocaine, methamphetamine, morphine, and methadone. Scientists note that marijuana is less harmful and less addictive than these other Schedule II substances. Acceptance of medical marijuana could in fact pave the way for its more generalized use. Ethan Nadelmann, head of the Drug Policy Alliance, has observed, "As medical marijuana becomes more regulated and institutionalized in the West, that may provide a model for how we ultimately make marijuana legal for all adults."[125] Medical marijuana opponents have trumpeted his candor as proof of the hypocrisy of those on the other side of the issue. Others note, however, that his comment may be less hypocritical than astute.

REFERENCES

[1]   The term *medical marijuana*, as used in this report, refers to marijuana (Cannabis sativa) and to marijuana use that qualifies for a medical use exception under the laws of certain states and under the federal Investigational New Drug Compassionate Access Program.

[2]   The author would like to acknowledge the assistance of summer intern Broocks Andrew Meade in preparing this report.

[3]   Gregg A. Bliz, "The Medical Use of Marijuana: The Politics of Medicine," *Hamline Journal of Public Law and Policy*, vol. 13, spring 1992, p. 118.

[4]   Oakley Ray and Charles Ksir, *Drugs, Society, and Human Behavior*, 10th ed. (New York: McGraw-Hill, 2004), p. 456.

[5]   Bill Zimmerman, *Is Marijuana the Right Medicine for You? A Factual Guide to Medical Uses of Marijuana* (New Canaan, CT: Keats Publishing, 1998), p. 19.

[6]   [P.L. 75-]238, 50 Stat. 551, Aug. 2, 1937. In *Leary* v. *United States* (395 U.S. 6 [1968]), the Supreme Court ruled the Marihuana Tax Act unconstitutional because it compelled self-incrimination, in violation of the Fifth Amendment.

[7]   [P.L. 63-]223, December 17, 1914, 38 Stat. 785. This law was passed to implement the Hague Convention of 1912 and created a federal tax on opium and coca leaves and their derivatives.

[8]   U.S. Congress, House Committee on Ways and Means, *Taxation of Marihuana*, hearings on H.R. 6385, 75th Cong., 1st sess., May 4, 1937 (Washington: GPO, 1937), p. 114.

[9]   U.S. Congress, Senate Committee on Finance, Taxation of Marihuana, hearing on H.R. 6906, 75th Cong., 1st sess., July 12, 1937 (Washington: GPO, 1937), p. 33.

[10]   U.S. President, 1969-1974 (Nixon), "Special Message to the Congress on Control of Narcotics and Dangerous Drugs," July 14, 1969, *Public Papers of the Presidents of the United States 1969* (Washington: GPO, 1971), pp. 513-518.

[11]   U.S. Congress, Conference Committees, *Comprehensive Drug Abuse Prevention and Control Act of 1970*, conference report to accompany H.R. 18583, 91st Cong., 2d sess., H.Rept. 91-1603 (Washington: GPO, 1970).

[12] Title II of the Comprehensive Drug Abuse Prevention and Control Act of 1970, P.L. 91-513, October 27, 1970, 84 Stat. 1242, 21 U.S.C. §801, et seq.

[13] Ibid., Sec. 202, 84 Stat. 1247, 21 U.S.C. §812.

[14] Amphetamine and methamphetamine have since been moved to Schedule II, in recognition of their accepted medical use in treatment. Cocaine was put in Schedule II in 1970 and remains there today.

[15] Sec. 404 of the CSA (21 U.S.C. §844) and 18 U.S.C. §3571. Sec. 404 also calls for a minimum fine of $1,000, and Sec. 405 (21 U.S.C. §844a) permits a civil penalty of up to $10,000.

[16] Sec. 102(15), (22) of the CSA (21 U.S.C. §802[15], [22]).

[17] Sec. 401(b)(1)(D) of the CSA (21 U.S.C. §841[b][1][D]).

[18] Omnibus Consolidated and Emergency Supplemental Appropriations Act, 1999, P.L. 105-277, Oct. 21, 1998, 112 Stat. 2681-760.

[19] Ibid., District of Columbia Appropriations Act, 1999, Sec. 171, 112 Stat. 2681-150. This recurring provision of D.C. appropriations acts is known as the Barr Amendment.

[20] "Amendment No. 1 offered by Mr. Hinchey," *Congressional Record*, daily edition, vol. 149 (July 22, 2003), pp. H7302-H7311. Ibid., vol. 149, (July 23, 2003), pp. H7354-H7355.

[21] "Amendment No. 6 Offered by Mr. Farr," *Congressional Record*, daily edition, vol. 150 (July 7, 2004), pp. H5300-H5306, H5320.

[22] "Amendment Offered by Mr. Hinchey," *Congressional Record*, daily edition, vol. 151 (July 15, 2005), pp. H4519-H4524, H4529.

[23] The necessity defense argues that the illegal act committed (in this case, growing marijuana) was necessary to avert a greater harm (blindness).

[24] Despite the program's name, it was not a clinical trial to test the drug for eventual approval, but a means for the government to provide medical marijuana to patients demonstrating necessity. Some have criticized the government for its failure to study the safety and efficacy of the medical-grade marijuana it grew and distributed to this patient population.

[25] U.S. Dept. of Justice, Drug Enforcement Administration, "Schedules of Controlled Substances: Rescheduling of Synthetic Dronobinol in Sesame Oil and Encapsulation in Soft Gelatin Capsules From Schedule I to Schedule II; Statement of Policy," 51 *Federal Register* 17476, May 13, 1986.

[26] Ibid., "Schedules of Controlled Substances: Rescheduling of the Food and Drug Administration Approved Product Containing Synthetic Dronabinol [(-)-delta nine-(trans)-Tetrahydrocannabinol] in Sesame Oil and Encapsulated in Soft Gelatin Capsules From Schedule II to Schedule III," 64 *Federal Register* 35928, July 2, 1999.

[27] Ibid., Bureau of Narcotics and Dangerous Drugs, "Schedule of Controlled Substances: Petition to Remove Marijuana or in the Alternative to Control Marijuana in Schedule V of the Controlled Substances Act," 37 *Federal Register* 18097, Sept. 7, 1972.

[28] Ibid., Drug Enforcement Administration, "In the Matter of Marijuana Rescheduling Petition, Docket No. 86-22, Opinion and Recommended Ruling, Findings of Fact, Conclusions of Law and Decision of Administrative Law Judge," Francis L. Young, Administrative Law Judge, Sept. 6, 1988. Hereinafter cited as "the Young Opinion." This quote and the following two quotes are at pp. 58-59, p. 68, and p. 67, respectively.

This opinion is online at [http://www.druglibrary.org/olsen/MEDICAL/YOUNG/young.html].

[29] Ibid., "Marijuana Scheduling Petition; Denial of Petition," 54 *Federal Register* 53767 at 53768, Dec. 29, 1989. The petition denial was appealed, eventually resulting in yet another DEA denial to reschedule. See Ibid., "Marijuana Scheduling Petition; Denial of Petition; Remand," 57 *Federal Register* 10499, Mar. 26, 1992.

[30] National Institutes of Health. The Ad Hoc Group of Experts. *Workshop on the Medical Utility of Marijuana: Report to the Director*, August 1997. Hereinafter cited as NIH Workshop. [http://www.nih.gov/news/medmarijuana/MedicalMarijuana.htm]

[31] Janet E. Joy, Stanley J. Watson, Jr., and John A. Benson, Jr., eds., *Marijuana and Medicine: Assessing the Science Base* (Washington: National Academy Press, 1999). [http://www.nap.edu/books/0309071550/html/] Hereinafter cited as "the IOM Report."

[32] *County of Santa Cruz* v. *Ashcroft*, 314 F.Supp.2d 1000 (N.D.Cal. 2004); the decision, however, rests on the 9th Circuit's ruling in *Raich*, subsequently overthrown by the Supreme Court.

[33] For a legal analysis of all three cases mentioned here, see CRS Report RL31100, *Marijuana for Medical Purposes: The Supreme Court's Decision in United States v. Oakland Cannabis Buyers' Cooperative and Related Legal Issues*, by Charles Doyle.

[34] The necessity defense argues that the illegal act committed (distribution of marijuana in this instance) was necessary to avert a greater harm (withholding a helpful drug from seriously ill patients).

[35] 523 U.S. 483 (2001).

[36] Ibid. at 494 n. 7.

[37] *Conant* v. *McCaffrey*, 172 F.R.D. 681 (N.D. Cal. 1997).

[38] *Conant* v. *Walters*, 309 F.3d 629, 636 (9th Cir. 2002); the parties agreed that "a doctor who actually prescribes or dispenses marijuana violates federal law," ibid. at 634.

[39] *Raich* v. *Ashcroft*, 352 F.3d 1222 (9th Cir. 2003).

[40] *Gonzalez* v. *Raich*, 125 S.Ct. 2195, 2205 (2005).

[41] Ibid. at 2211 n. 37. For a legal analysis of this case, see Gonzales *v.* Raich: *Congress's Power Under the Commerce Clause to Regulate Medical Marijuana*, by Todd B. Tatelman.

[42] Ibid. at 2215.

[43] The information in this and the following section is drawn largely from: *State-by-State Medical Marijuana Laws: How to Remove the Threat of Arrest*, Marijuana Policy Project, July 2004, available at [http://www.mpp.org/statelaw/index.html]. More recent information is from press reports.

[44] Alaska (Stat. §11.71.090); Arizona (Ariz.Rev.Stat.Ann. §13-3412.01[A]); California (Cal.Health & Safety Code Ann. §11362.5); Colorado (Colo.Const. Art. XVIII §4); Hawaii (Rev.Stat. §§329-121 to 329-128); Maine (Me.Rev.Stat.Ann. tit.22 §1102 or 2382-B[5]); Montana (Mont.Code Ann. §§50-46-101 to 50-46-210); Nevada (Nev.Rev.Stat.Ann. §§453A.010 to 453A.400); Oregon (Ore.Rev.Stat. §§475.300 to 475.346); Vermont (Vt.Stat.Ann. tit. 18, §§4472-4474d); Washington (Wash.Rev.Code Ann. §§69.51A.005 to 69.51A.902).

[45] Dale Gieringer, "The Acceptance of Medical Marijuana in the U.S.," *Journal of Cannabis Therapeutics*, vol. 3, no. 1 (2003), pp. 53-67. The author later estimated that

there were more than 100,000 medical marijuana patients in California alone (personal communication dated April 30, 2004).

[46] Susan Okie, "Medical Marijuana and the Supreme Court," *New England Journal of Medicine*, vol. 353, no. 7 (Aug. 18, 2005), p. 649.

[47] Md. Crim. Code Ann. §5-601.

[48] *State-by-State Medical Marijuana Laws: How to Remove the Threat of Arrest*, Marijuana Policy Project, July 2004, p. 3. The laws in some of these states have expired or been repealed.

[49] The questions asked and the results obtained can be viewed at [http://www.medicalmarijuanaprocon.org/pop/votesNat.htm].

[50] Robert J. Blend on and John T. Young, "The Public and the War on Illicit Drugs," *Journal of the American Medical Association*, vol. 279, no. 11 (Mar. 18, 1998), p. 831.

[51] Brief for the Drug Free America Foundation, Inc., et al. as Amici Curiae Supporting Petitioners at 13, *Gonzalez v. Raich*, 125 S.Ct. 2195 (2005) (No. 03-1454). The *amicus curiae* briefs filed in *Raich* contain a wealth of information and arguments on both sides of the medical marijuana debate. They are available online at [http://www.angeljustice.org].

[52] See, for example, "Exposing the Myth of Medical Marijuana," on the DEA Web site at [http://www.usdoj.gov/dea/ongoing/marijuanap.html].

[53] Ibid at 25.

[54] This test was first formulated by the DEA in 1992 in response to a marijuana rescheduling petition. See U.S. Department of Justice, Drug Enforcement Administration, "Marijuana Scheduling Petition; Denial of Petition; Remand," 57 *Federal Register* 10499, March 26, 1992, at 10506.

[55] Ibid., p. 10507.

[56] Ibid., pp. 10506-10507.

[57] *Gonzalez v. Raich*, 125 S.Ct. 2195, at 2212 and 2213 (2005).

[58] Brief for the Leukemia & Lymphoma Society, et al. as Amici Curiae Supporting Respondents at 4, Gonzalez v. Raich, 125 S.Ct. 2195 (2005) (No. 03-1454).

[59] Ibid., at 1-2.

[60] A 1990 survey of oncologists found that 54% of those with an opinion on medical marijuana favored the controlled medical availability of marijuana and 44% had already broken the law by suggesting at least once that a patient obtain marijuana illegally. R. Doblin and M. Kleiman, "Marijuana as Antiemetic Medicine," *Journal of Clinical Oncology*, vol. 9 (1991), pp. 1314-1319.

[61] There is evidence that marijuana might also be useful in treating arthritis, migraine, menstrual cramps, alcohol and opiate addiction, and depression and other mood disorders.

[62] IOM Report, pp. 3-4: "The effects of cannabinoids on the symptoms studied are generally modest, and in most cases there are more effective medications. However, people vary in their responses to medications, and there will likely always be a subpopulation of patients who do not respond well to other medications."

[63] Brief for the Leukemia & Lymphoma Society et al. as Amici Curiae Supporting Respondents at 18, *Gonzalez v. Raich*, 125 S.Ct. 2195 (2005) (No. 03-1454).

[64] Marinol currently sells at retail for about $17 per pill.

[65] "Federal Foolishness and Marijuana," *New England Journal of Medicine*, vol. 336, no. 5 (Jan. 30, 1997), pp. 366-367.

[66] The Web site "Medical Marijuana ProCon" [http://www.medicalmarijuanaprocon.org] contains information on organizations that both support and oppose medical marijuana.

[67] For a summary of the growing body of research on endocannabinoids, see Roger A. Nicoll and Bradley N. Alger, "The Brain's Own Marijuana," *Scientific American*, Dec. 2004, pp. 68-75.

[68] Bill Zimmerman, *Is Marijuana the Right Medicine For You? A Factual guide to Medical Uses of Marijuana* (Keats Publishing, New Canaan, CT: 1998), p. 25.

[69] Barry R. McCaffrey, "We're on a Perilous Path," *Newsweek*, Feb. 3, 1997, p. 27.

[70] Karen Tandy, "Marijuana: The Myths Are Killing Us," *Police Chief Magazine*, Mar. 2005, available at [http://www.usdoj.gov/dea/pubs/pressrel/pr042605p.html].

[71] Lynn Zimmer and John P. Morgan, *Marijuana Myths Marijuana Facts* (New York: Lindesmith Center, 1997), p. 115.

[72] Medicines do not have to be completely safe to be approved. In fact, no medicine is completely safe; every drug has toxicity concerns. All pharmaceuticals have potentially harmful side effects, and it would be startling, indeed, if botanical marijuana were found to be an exception. The IOM Report states that "[E]xcept for the harms associated with smoking, the adverse effects of marijuana use are within the range of effects tolerated for other medications." (p. 5)

[73] American Medical Association, Council on Scientific Affairs Report: *Medical Marijuana (A-01)*, June 2001. An unpaginated version of this document can be found on   the   Web   at [http://www.mfiles.org/Marijuana/medicinal_use/b2_ama_csa_report.html].

[74] Cannabis preparations are also used topically as oils and balms to soothe muscles, tendons, and joints.

[75] Several companies offer vaporizers for sale in the United States, but their marketing is complicated by marijuana prohibition and by laws prohibiting drug paraphernalia. The advantages of the vaporizer were brought to the attention of the IOM panel. The IOM Report, however, devoted only a single sentence to such devices, despite its recommendation for research into safe delivery systems. The IOM Report said, "Vaporization devices that permit inhalation of plant cannabinoids without the carcinogenic combustion products found in smoke are under development by several groups; such devices would also require regulatory review by the FDA." (p. 216)

[76] The Young Opinion, p. 67.

[77] Ibid., pp. 58-59.

[78] Ibid., p. 56.

[79] When Congress directly schedules a drug, as it did marijuana in 1970, it is not bound by the criteria in section 202(b) of the CSA (21 U.S.C. 812[b]).

[80] Congress could also follow the lead of some states that have a dual scheduling scheme for botanical marijuana, whereby its recreational use is prohibited (Schedule I) but permitted when used for medicinal purposes (Schedules II or III). Congress could achieve the same effect by leaving marijuana in Schedule I but removing criminal penalties for the medical use of marijuana, commonly called *decriminalization*. Congress could also opt for *legalization* by removing marijuana from the CSA entirely and subjecting it to federal and state controls based on the tobacco or alcohol regulatory

models or by devising a regulatory scheme unique to marijuana. None of these options seem likely given the current political climate in which both political parties support marijuana prohibition.

[81] These   and   other   poll   results   can   be   consulted   at [http://www.medicalmarijuanaprocon.org/ pop/votes.htm]. This Web site states: "Because 100% of the voter initiatives and polls we located were favorable (50.01% or more pro) towards the medical use of marijuana, we contacted several organizations decidedly "con" to medical marijuana — two of which were federal government agencies — and none knew of any voter initiatives or polls that were 'con' (50.01% or more con) to medical marijuana."

[82] Karen Tandy, "Marijuana: The Myths Are Killing Us," *Police Chief Magazine*, March 2005, available at [http://www.usdoj.gov/dea/pubs/pressrel/pr042605p.html].

[83] See, for example, J.G. Bachman et al. "Explaining Recent Increases in Students' Marijuana Use: Impacts of Perceived Risks and Disapproval, 1976 through 1996," *American Journal of Public Health*, vol. 88 (1998), pp. 887-892.

[84] Brief for the Drug Free America Foundation, Inc., et al. as Amici Curiae Supporting Petitioners at 26, Gonzalez v. Raich, 125 S.Ct. 2195 (2005) (No. 03-1454).

[85] Ibid. at 27. The 1999 NHSDA was the first to include state-level estimates for various measures of drug use. Unfortunately, comprehensive state-level data prior to 1999 are not available from other sources.

[86] Care should be taken in comparing NHSDA data for 1999 with NSDUH data for 2002 and after, due to changes in survey methodology made in 2002. The trend observations drawn here from these data should therefore be considered suggestive rather than definitive.

[87] "Congress Should Amend Drug Laws," *Washington Examiner* editorial, June 16, 2005.

[88] Available at [http://www.usdoj.gov/dea/ongoing/calimarijuanap.html].

[89] U.S. General Accounting Office, *Marijuana: Early Experiences with Four States' Laws That Allow Use for Medical Purposes*, GAO-03-189, Nov. 2002, p. 36.

[90] Ibid., p. 37.

[91] Stuart Taylor, Jr., "Liberal Drug Warriors! Conservative Pot-Coddlers!," *National Journal*, June 11, 2005, p. 1738.

[92] Testimony of Thomas A. Constantine in U.S. Congress, Senate Committee on the Judiciary, *Prescription for Addiction? The Arizona and California Medical Drug Use Initiatives*, hearing, 104th Cong., 2nd sess., Dec. 2, 1996 (Washington: GPO, 1997), pp. 42-43, 45.

[93] "Marijuana: Lawrence, Kansas, Ponders City Marijuana Ordinance — Impact of HEA Cited," available at [http://stopthedrugwar.org/chronicle/401/lawrence.shtml].

[94] Brief for U.S. Representative Mark E. Souder et al., as Amici Curiae Supporting Petitioners at 20, *Gonzalez v. Raich*, 125 S.Ct. 2195 (2005) (No. 03-1454).

[95] "California Medical Marijuana Information," available on DEA's Web site at [http://www.usdoj.gov/dea/ongoing/calimarijuanap.html].

[96] U.S. General Accounting Office, *Marijuana: Early Experiences with Four States' Laws That Allow Use for Medical Purposes*, GAO-03-189, Nov. 2002, p. 64. GAO interviewed 37 law enforcement agencies and found that the majority indicated that "medical-marijuana laws had not greatly affected their law enforcement activities" (p. 4).

[97] Eric Bailey, "CHP Revises Policy on Pot Seizures," *Los Angeles Times* (national edition), August 28, 2005, p. A12.

[98] Committee on Drugs and the Law, "Marijuana Should be Medically Available," *Record of the Association of the Bar of the City of New York*, vol. 52, no. 2 (March 1997), p. 238.

[99] Brief for the Leukemia & Lymphoma Society et al., as Amici Curiae Supporting Respondents at 1,2, *Gonzalez v. Raich*, 125 S.Ct. 2195 (2005) (No. 03-1454).

[100] IOM report, p. 18.

[101] U.S.C. §844 and 18 U.S.C. §3571. 21 U.S.C. §844 also calls for a minimum fine of $1,000, and 21 U.S.C. §844a permits a civil penalty of up to $10,000.

[102] U.S.C. §841(b)(1)(D)

[103] Communication from DEA Congressional Affairs to author dated September 27, 2005.

[104] Stacy Finz, "19 Named in Medicinal Pot Indictment, More than 9,300 Plants Were Seized in Raids," *San Francisco Chronicle*, June 24, 2005, p. B4.

[105] Lester Grinspoon and James B. Bakalar, "Marihuana as Medicine: A Plea for Reconsideration," *Journal of the American Medical Association*, vol. 273, no. 23 (June 21, 1995), p. 1876.

[106] Angel Wings Patient OutReach press release, Nov. 29, 2004. Barnett represented Raich et al., in Supreme Court oral argument on this date.

[107] Brief for the States of California, Maryland, and Washington et al., as Amici Curiae Supporting Respondents at 3, *Gonzalez v. Raich*, 125 S.Ct. 2195 (2005) (No. 03-1454).

[108] *New State Ice Co.* v. *Liebmann*, 285 U.S. 262, 311 (1932) (Brandeis, J., dissenting)

[109] Brief for the States of Alabama, Louisiana, and Mississippi et al., as Amici Curiae Supporting Respondents at 3, *Gonzalez v. Raich*, 125 S.Ct. 2195 (2005) (No. 03-1454).

[110] *Gonzales* v. *Raich*, 125 S.Ct. 2195, 2220 (2005) (O'Connor, J., dissenting)

[111] Ibid. at 2229

[112] Brief for the Drug Free America Foundation, Inc., et al. as Amici Curiae Supporting Petitioners at 12, *Gonzalez v. Raich*, 125 S.Ct. 2195 (2005) (No. 03-1454).

[113] U.S.C. §351-360

[114] Brief for Petitioners at 11, *Gonzales v. Raich*, 125 S.Ct. 2195 (2002) (No. 03-1454).

[115] Brief for Robert L. DuPont, M.D., et al. as Amici Curiae Supporting Petitioners at 19, *Gonzalez v. Raich*, 125 S.Ct. 2195 (2005) (No. 03-1454).

[116] FDA, "FDA Statement Re: Marijuana Legislation," provided to Rep. Mark E. Souder on July 7, 2004, available at[http://reform.house.gov/UploadedFiles/Medical%20 Marijuana% 20Statement.pdf].

[117] See, for example, Lila Guterman, "The Dope on Medical Marijuana," *Chronicle of Higher Education*, June 2, 2000, p. A21.

[118] IOM Report, p. 14.

[119] "Federal Foolishness and Marijuana," *New England Journal of Medicine*, vol. 336, no. 5 (Jan. 30, 1997), p. 366.

[120] Chuck Thomas, Marijuana Policy Project press release dated Apr. 20, 1999. Available at [http://www.mpp.org/releases/nr042099.html].

[121] Brief for the Drug Free America Foundation, Inc., et al. as Amici Curiae Supporting Petitioners at 9, *Gonzalez v. Raich*, 125 S.Ct. 2195 (2005) (No. 03-1454).

[122] For example, the Amici Curiae Brief of the Drug Free America Foundation et al., reveals this history to discredit the medical marijuana movement (pp. 9-11). Actually,

NORML and some other drug reform organizations are open in acknowledging that they support patient access to marijuana as a first step toward decriminalizing or legalizing marijuana for use by adults in general. See, for example, Joab Jackson, "Medical Marijuana: From the Fringe to the Forefront," *Baltimore City Paper*, March 28, 2002[http://www.alternet.org/print.html? StoryID=12714].

[123] Barry R. McCaffrey, "We're on a Perilous Path," *Newsweek*, Feb. 3, 1997, p. 27.

[124] Lester Grinspoon and James B. Bakalar, "Marihuana as Medicine: A Plea for Reconsideration," *Journal of the American Medical Association*, vol. 273, no. 23 (June 21, 1995), p. 1876.

[125] Quoted in MSNBC.com story, "Western States Back Medical Marijuana," Nov. 4, 2004, available at [http://msnbc.msn.com/id/6406453].

In: Illegal Drugs and Governmental Policies
Editor: Lee V. Barton, pp. 97-135

ISBN 978-1-60021-351-9
© 2007 Nova Science Publishers, Inc.

Chapter 5

AFGHANISTAN: NARCOTICS AND U.S. POLICY[*]

Christopher M. Blanchard

SUMMARY

Opium poppy cultivation and drug trafficking have become significant factors in Afghanistan's fragile political and economic order over the last 25 years. In 2005, Afghanistan remained the source of 87% of the world's illicit opium, in spite of ongoing efforts by the Afghan government, the United States, and their international partners to combat poppy cultivation and drug trafficking. U.N. officials estimate that in-country illicit profits from the 2005 opium poppy crop were equivalent in value to 50% of the country's legitimate GDP, sustaining fears that Afghanistan's economic recovery continues to be underwritten by drug profits.

Across Afghanistan, regional militia commanders, criminal organizations, and corrupt government officials have exploited opium production and drug trafficking as reliable sources of revenue and patronage, which has perpetuated the threat these groups pose to the country's fragile internal security and the legitimacy of its embryonic democratic government. The trafficking of Afghan drugs also appears to provide financial and logistical support to a range of extremist groups that continue to operate in and around Afghanistan, including remnants of the Taliban regime and some Al Qaeda operatives. Although coalition forces may be less frequently relying on figures involved with narcotics for intelligence and security support, many observers have warned that drug related corruption among appointed and newly elected Afghan officials may create new political obstacles to further progress.

The initial failure of U.S. and international counternarcotics efforts to disrupt the Afghan opium trade or sever its links to warlordism and corruption after the fall of the Taliban led some observers to warn that without redoubled multilateral action, Afghanistan would succumb to a state of lawlessness and reemerge as a sanctuary for terrorists. Following his election in late 2004, Afghan president Hamid Karzai identified counternarcotics as the top priority for his administration and since has stated his belief that "the fight against drugs is the fight for Afghanistan." In 2005, U.S. and Afghan officials implemented a new strategy to provide viable economic alternatives to poppy cultivation and to disrupt corruption and narco-terrorist linkages. According to a U.N. survey, these new initiatives contributed to a 21% decrease in the amount of opium poppy cultivation across Afghanistan in the 2004-2005 growing season. However, better weather and higher crop yields ensured that overall opium

---

[*] Excerpted from CRS Report RL32686, Updated January 25, 2006

output remained nearly static at 4,100 metric tons. Survey results and official opinions suggest output may rise again in 2006.

In addition to describing the structure and development of the Afghan narcotics trade, this report provides current statistical information, profiles the trade's various participants, explores alleged narco-terrorist linkages, and reviews U.S. and international policy responses since late 2001. The report also considers current policy debates regarding the role of the U.S. military in counternarcotics operations,

INTRODUCTION

In spite of ongoing international efforts to combat Afghanistan's narcotics trade, U.N. officials estimate that Afghanistan produced a massive opium poppy crop in 2005 that supplied 87% of the world's illicit opium for the second year in a row.[1] Afghan, U.S., and international officials have stated that opium poppy cultivation and drug trafficking constitute serious strategic threats to the security and stability of Afghanistan and jeopardize the success of post-9/11 counterterrorism and reconstruction efforts there. In light of the 9/11 Commission's recommendation that the United States make a long-term commitment to the security and stability of Afghanistan, counternarcotics policy has emerged as a focal point of recurring debate in the Bush Administration and in Congress concerning the United States' strategic objectives in Afghanistan and the global war against terrorism.

Concerns include the role of U.S. military personnel in counternarcotics activities and strategies for continuing the simultaneous pursuit of counterterrorism and counternarcotics goals, which may be complicated by practical necessities and emerging political realities. Coalition forces pursuing regional security and counterterrorism objectives may rely on the cooperation of commanders, tribal leaders, and local officials who may be involved in the narcotics trade. Similarly, U.S. officials and many observers believe that the introduction of a democratic system of government to Afghanistan has likely been accompanied by the election and appointment of narcotics-associated individuals to positions of public office.

Efforts to combat the opium trade in Afghanistan face the challenge of ending a highly-profitable enterprise that has become deeply interwoven with the economic, political, and social fabric of a war-torn country. Afghan, U.S., and international authorities are engaged in a campaign to reverse an unprecedented upsurge of opium poppy cultivation and heroin production: they have begun implementing a multifaceted counternarcotics initiative that includes public awareness campaigns, judicial reform measures, economic and agricultural development assistance, drug interdiction operations, and more robust poppy eradication. The Bush Administration and Congress continue to consider options for upgrading U.S. support for counternarcotics efforts in Afghanistan in order to meet the challenges posed by the Afghan opium economy to the security of Afghanistan and the international community. Questions regarding the likely effectiveness, resource requirements, and implications of new counternarcotics strategies in Afghanistan are likely to arise as such options continue to be debated.

AFGHANISTAN'S OPIUM ECONOMY

Opium production has become an entrenched element of Afghanistan's fragile political and economic order over the last 25 years in spite of ongoing local, regional, and international efforts to reverse its growth. At the time of Afghanistan's proCommunist coup in 1978, narcotics experts estimated that Afghan farmers produced 300 metric tons (MT) of opium annually, enough to satisfy most local and regional demand and to supply a handful of heroin production facilities whose products were bound for Western Europe.[2] Since the early 1980s, a trend of increasing opium poppy cultivation and opium production has unfolded during successive periods of insurgency, civil war, fundamentalist government, and recently, international engagement (Figures 1 and 2). In 2004, Afghanistan produced a world record opium poppy crop that yielded 4200 MT of illicit opium — an estimated 87% of the world's supply. A slightly smaller crop in 2005 produced a similar volume of opium, and estimated 4,100 MT, due to improved weather and environmental conditions.

Narcotics experts describe Afghanistan's opium economy as the backbone of a multibillion dollar drug trade that stretches throughout Central and Southwest Asia and supplies heroin to consumption markets in Europe, Russia, the Middle East, and the United States. Millions of Afghans remain involved with various aspects of the opium trade, including farmers, laborers, traffickers, warlords, and government officials. Some experts have warned that the consolidation of existing relationships between these groups supports negative trends such as warlordism and corruption and threatens to transform Afghanistan into a failed narco-state.

Current Production Statistics

According to the 2005 Afghanistan Opium Survey conducted by the United Nations Office on Drugs and Crime (UNODC) and the Afghan Ministry of Counternarcotics (MCN):

- Opium poppy cultivation took place in fewer Afghan provinces in 2005 than in 2004, with significant decreases occurring in some provinces and significant increases occurring in others (see **Figure 3**). Afghan farmers cultivated opium poppy on 104,000 hectares of land during the 2004-2005 growing season, a 21% decrease from the 131,000 hectares cultivated in 2004. The area under cultivation was equal to 2.3% of Afghanistan's arable land. U.S. government estimates placed the area under cultivation at a similar level of 107,400 hectares.

- The 2005 opium poppy crop produced 4,100 MT of illicit opium, a small decrease from the 4,200 MT produced in 2004. Although the area of land dedicated to opium poppy cultivation decreased by 21%, crop yields improved due to better weather and other environmental factors. A range of accepted opium to heroin conversion rates indicate that the 2005 opium yield of 4,100 MT could have produced 400 to 650 MT of refined heroin.[3] U.S. government estimates placed overall opium output lower at 3,375 MT.

- Approximately 309,000 Afghan families cultivated opium poppy in 2005, a number equal to roughly 2.0 million people or 8.7% of the Afghan population. An estimated

500,000 laborers and an unknown number of traffickers, warlords, and officials also participate.

- The estimated $2.7 billion value of Afghanistan's 2005 illicit opium harvest is equivalent to approximately 50% of the country's licit GDP. Many licit and emerging industries are financed or supported by profits from narcotics trafficking.[4]

The 2005 UNODC report credits the public outreach efforts of President Karzai, who has characterized opium as shameful and demanded that regional and local officials take direct action to curb poppy cultivation and opium trafficking. The report also indicates that farmers fear crop eradication and notes that the largest declines in opium poppy cultivation occurred in provinces that received the largest investments of alternative livelihood assistance. Other observers have pointed to the steady increase in opium production volume that has occurred since late 2001 and argued that excess opium supply had reduced raw opium price levels **(Table 1)** and price incentives for farmers to cultivate poppy. Price levels have shown signs of increase since late 2005 which may reinvigorate price incentives in some areas.

Experts have identified two factors that may affect Afghanistan's future opium output regardless of reported declines in cultivation. Intensified interdiction and eradication efforts by Afghan authorities may fuel a renewed increase in opium prices that could enrich traffickers who control large existing stocks of opium and encourage farmers to resume cultivation in the future. In addition, drought and crop disease problems that limited the output of the 2004 poppy crop may not affect the output of future poppy crops. Smaller nationwide poppy crops may yield higher opium outputs if weather and irrigation improve productivity in cultivated areas.

Table 1. Recent Opium Prices in Afghanistan
(regionally weighted fresh opium farmgate[a] price US$/kilogram)

	1999	2000	2001[b]	2002	2003	2004	2005
Opium Price	$40	$28	$301	$350	$283	$92	$102

Source: United Nations Office on Drugs and Crime, Afghanistan Opium Survey 2004-5.

a. Farmgate price for fresh opium is the price paid to farmers for non-dried opium. b. Dry opium prices skyrocketed to nearly $700/kg immediately following the September 11, 2001 terrorist attacks and fell to $93/kg after U.S. airstrikes began.

Note: The following figures display trends in poppy cultivation and opium production in Afghanistan over the last 25 years. The sharp decline in cultivation and production in the 2000-2001 growing season is related to the Taliban regime's decision to ban opium poppy cultivation. According to U.S. officials, opium trafficking continued unabated during this period, and Taliban authorities and their allies collected higher profits from the sale of opium and heroin stockpiles.[5]

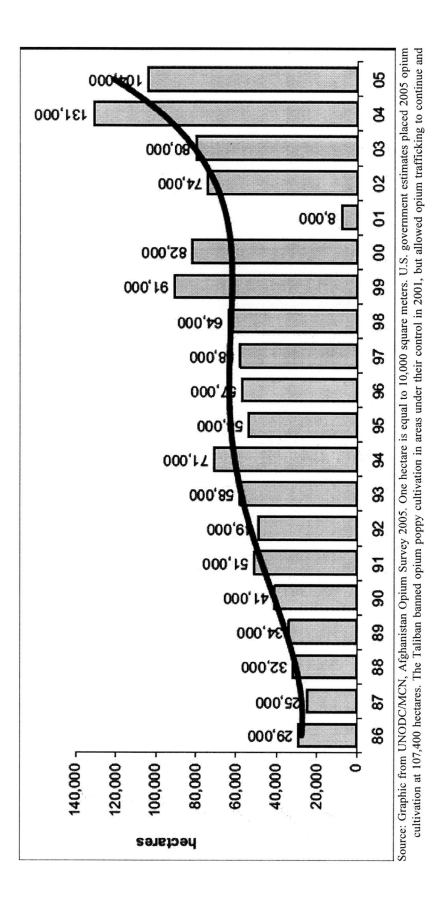

Source: Graphic from UNODC/MCN, Afghanistan Opium Survey 2005. One hectare is equal to 10,000 square meters. U.S. government estimates placed 2005 opium cultivation at 107,400 hectares. The Taliban banned opium poppy cultivation in areas under their control in 2001, but allowed opium trafficking to continue and profited from the sale of regime-controlled opium stocks. Limited cultivation continued in areas under Northern Alliance control.

Figure 1. Opium Poppy Cultivation, 1986-2005 (hectares)

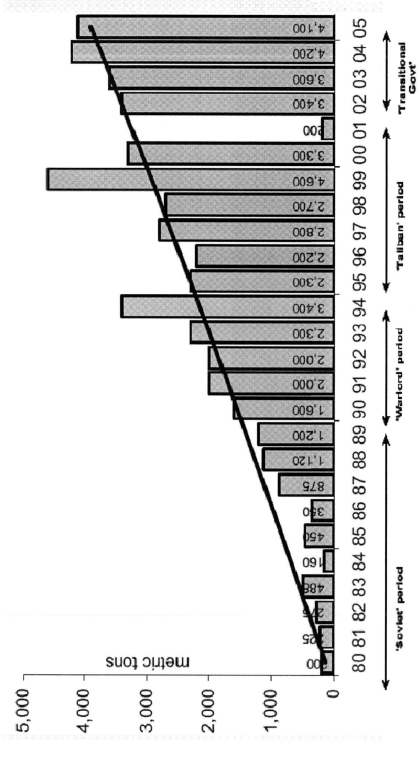

Source: Graphic adapted from UNODC/MCN, Afghanistan Opium Surveys 2004 and 2005. One metric ton is equal to 2,200 pounds. U.S. government estimates placed 2005 opium production at .3375 metric tons. The Taliban banned opium poppy cultivation in areas under their control in 2001 but allowed opium trafficking to continue and profited from the sale of regime-controlled opium stocks. Limited cultivation continued in areas under Northern Alliance control.

Figure 2. Opium Production, 1980-2005 (metric tons)

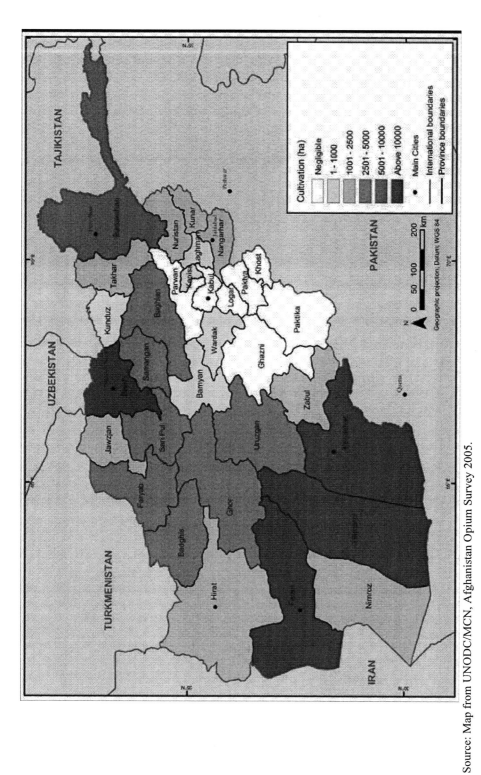

Source: Map from UNODC/MCN, Afghanistan Opium Survey 2005.

Figure 3. Opium Poppy Cultivation by Province, 2005

Historical Development

During the more than two decades of occupation, foreign interference, and civil war that followed the 1979 Soviet invasion, opium poppy cultivation and drug trafficking served as central parts of Afghanistan's war economy, providing revenue to individuals and groups competing for power and an economic survival mechanism to a growing segment of the impoverished population. In December 2001, Afghan leaders participating in the Bonn conference that formed Afghanistan's interim post-Taliban government echoed pleas issued by their pro-Communist predecessors decades earlier:[6] They strongly urged that "the United Nations, the international community, and regional organizations cooperate with the Interim Authority to combat international terrorism, cultivation, and trafficking of illicit drugs and provide Afghan farmers with financial, material and technical resources for alternative crop production."[7] In spite of renewed efforts on the part of Afghan and international authorities to combat opium poppy cultivation since the fall of the Taliban, Afghanistan remains the world's leading producer of opium.

Opium and Afghanistan's War Economy. Following the Soviet invasion of 1979 and during the civil war that ensued in the aftermath of the Soviet withdrawal, opium poppy cultivation expanded in parallel with the gradual collapse of state authority across Afghanistan. As the country's formal economy succumbed to violence and disorder, opium became one of the few available commodities capable of both storing economic value and generating revenue for local administration and military supplies. Some anti-Soviet mujahideen commanders encouraged and taxed opium poppy cultivation and drug shipments, and, in some instances, participated in the narcotics trade directly as a means of both economic survival and military financing.[8] Elements of Pakistan's Inter-Services Intelligence (ISI) agency and Afghan rebel commanders to which the ISI channeled U.S. funding and weaponry are also alleged to have participated in the Afghan narcotics trade during the Soviet occupation and its aftermath, including in the production and trafficking of refined heroin to U.S. and European markets.[9] After the withdrawal of Soviet troops and a drop in U.S. and Soviet funding, opium poppy cultivation, drug trafficking, and other criminal activities increasingly provided local leaders and military commanders with a means of supporting their operations and establishing political influence in the areas they controlled.

Taliban Era. The centralization of authority under the Taliban movement during the mid-to-late 1990s further fueled Afghan opium poppy cultivation and narcotic production, as Taliban officials coopted their military opponents with promises of permissive cultivation policies and mirrored the practices of their warlord predecessors by collecting tax revenue and profits on the growing output.[10] In 1999, Afghanistan produced a peak of over 4500 MT of raw opium, which led to growing international pressure from states whose populations were consuming the end products of a seemingly endless supply of Afghan drugs. In response, the Taliban announced a ban on opium poppy cultivation in late 2000, but allowed the opiate trade to continue, fueling speculation that the decision was designed to contribute to their marginalized government's campaign for international legitimacy. Under the ban, opium poppy cultivation was reduced dramatically and overall opium output fell to 185 MT, mainly because of continued cultivation and production in areas under the control of Northern Alliance forces. Individual Northern Alliance commanders also taxed opium production and transportation within their zones of control and continued producing opium and trafficking heroin following the Taliban prohibition.[11] Although U.S. and international officials initially applauded the Taliban policy shift, many experts now believe that the ban was designed to increase the market price for and potential revenue from stocks of Afghan opium maintained by the Taliban and its powerful trafficking allies within the country.[12]

Post-Taliban Resurgence. Following 9/11, Afghan farmers anticipated the fall of the Taliban government and resumed cultivating opium poppy as U.S.-led military operations began in October 2001. International efforts to rebuild Afghanistan's devastated society began with the organization of an interim administration at the Bonn Conference in December 2001, and Afghan leaders committed their new government to combat the resurgence of opium poppy cultivation and requested international counternarcotics assistance from the United States, the United Kingdom and others.[13] The United Kingdom was designated the lead nation for international counternarcotics assistance and policy in Afghanistan. On January 17, 2002, the Afghan Interim Administration issued a ban on opium poppy cultivation that was enforced with a limited eradication campaign in April 2002. In spite of these efforts, the 2001-2002 opium poppy crop produced over 3400 MT of opium, reestablishing Afghanistan as the world's leading producer of illicit opium. Since 2002, further government bans and stronger interdiction and eradication efforts failed to reverse an overall trend of increasing opium poppy cultivation and opium output, although year-on-year reductions occurred in 2005.

Actors in Afghanistan's Opium Economy

Farmers, laborers, landowners, and traffickers each play roles in Afghanistan's opium economy. Ongoing field research indicates that the motives and methods of each group vary considerably based on their geographic location, their respective economic circumstances, their relationships with ethnic groups and external parties, and prevailing political conditions.[14] Studies suggest that profit is not the universal motivating factor fueling opium poppy cultivation in Afghanistan: opium trade field researcher David Mansfield argues that the "great diversity in the socio-economic groups involved in opium poppy in Afghanistan and the assets at their disposal" ensures that "there is great disparity in the revenues that they can accrue from its cultivation."[15] Household debt and land access needs also motivate opium poppy cultivation.

Farmers. Field studies have identified several structural barriers that limit the profitability of opium poppy cultivation for the average Afghan farmer. Many Afghan farming households cultivate opium poppy in order to improve their access to land, water, agricultural supplies, and credit — inputs that remain in short supply in many of the rural areas where opium poppy is grown. Experts have identified high levels of household debt as a powerful structural determinant of the continuation of opium poppy cultivation among some Afghan farmers. An opium-for-credit system, known as *salaam*, allows farmers to secure loans to buy necessary supplies and provisions if they agree in advance to sell future opium harvests at rates as low as half their expected market value. Crop failures that occurred as a result of a severe four-year nationwide drought (1998-2001) reportedly caused many farming households to accumulate large amounts of debt in the form of *salaam* loans based on future cultivation of opium poppy. In some cases, the introduction of strict poppy cultivation bans and crop eradication policies by the Taliban in 2001 and the Afghan Interim Authority in

2002 and 2003 increased the debt levels of many Afghan farmers by destroying opium crops that served as collateral for *salaam* arrangements.

Although the Afghan government issued a decree banning opium-based loans and credit in April 2002, the 2005 UNODC/MCN opium survey reports that *salaam* lending has continued. Increased debt has led some farmers to mortgage land and to agree to cultivate opium poppy in the future through sharecropping arrangements. Other landless farmers have reportedly been forced to accept the crop selection choices of landowners who control their access to land and water and who favor opium poppy over other traditional crops. According to experts, this combination of drought-induced debt, predatory traditional lending systems, and the unintended side-effects from government cultivation bans and eradication programs has fueled opium poppy cultivation in Afghanistan. The 2005 UNODC/MCN opium survey warns that in areas where farmers carry high salaam and other loan debt, significant decreases in opium poppy cultivation and associated revenue may be "potentially problematic" and could create "severe financial pressure on to farmers to resume opium production [in 2006] in order not to default."

Land Owners. Afghan land owners are better positioned to profit from opium poppy cultivation because of the labor intensive nature of the opium production process. Land owners who control vital opium cultivation inputs like land, water, and fertilizers enjoy an economic advantage in the opium production cycle, which places heavy demands on Afghanistan's rural agricultural labor market during annual opium poppy planting, maintenance, and harvesting seasons. Wealthy land owners secure the services of skilled itinerant laborers to assist in the complex opium harvesting process, which improves their crop yields and profits. Itinerant laborers, in turn, contribute to the spread of opium cultivation expertise around Afghanistan.[16] Although opium prices have fallen since reaching a peak of $350/kg in 2002, farmers have experienced greater profit loss than land owners.[17] Land owners also have benefitted from consolidation of property related to rising debt levels among Afghan farmers. Land valuation based on potential opium yields also benefits land owners.

Traffickers. International market prices for heroin and intermediate opiates such as morphine ensure that individuals and groups engaged in the shipment and distribution of refined opium products earn substantially higher profits than those involved with cultivating and producing raw opium gum.[18] Although opium refining facilities that produce morphine base and heroin traditionally have been located in tribal areas along the Afghan border with Pakistan, the growth and spread of opium cultivation in recent years has led to a corresponding proliferation of opiate processing facilities, particularly into northeastern Badakhshan province.[19] The large proportion of heroin in the composition of drugs seized in countries neighboring Afghanistan reflects this proliferation and suggests that the profitability of opiate trafficking for Afghan groups has increased significantly in recent years.

Although Afghan individuals and groups play a significant role in trafficking opiates within Afghanistan and into surrounding countries, relatively few Afghans have been identified as participants in the international narcotics trafficking operations that bring finished opiate products such as heroin to Middle Eastern, European, or North American consumer markets.[20] Ethnic and tribal relationships facilitate the opium trade within Afghanistan, while relationships between ethnic Tajik, Uzbek, Pashtun, and Baluchi Afghans and their counterparts in Central Asia, Pakistan, and Iran provide a basis for the organization and networking needed to deliver Aghan opiates to regional markets and into the hands of international trafficking organizations.[21] Some observers argue that trafficking profits are a source of economic and political instability and that interdiction and prosecution should precede eradication efforts so that increased post-eradication opium prices do not enrich trafficking groups further. Multilateral intelligence gathering and interdiction operations have been initiated since 2001 and are described in further detail below.

NARCOTICS AND SECURITY

Experts and officials have identified three areas of concern about the potential impact of the Afghan narcotics trade on the security of Afghanistan, the United States, and the international community. Each is first summarized, and then more fully developed below.

- **Prospects for State Failure:** Afghan, U.S., and international officials have identified several correlations between the narcotics trade and negative political and economic trends that undermine efforts to stabilize Afghanistan, establish the rule of law, and restore a functioning and licit economy. These trends include corruption and the existence of independent armed groups opposed to the Afghan government's reform and counternarcotics agendas. Similar drug-related trends threaten countries neighboring Afghanistan. Political observers have warned that figures involved with the drug trade have been elected or appointed to public office and may oppose or undermine current and future counternarcotics initiatives.
- **"Narco-Terrorism":** Afghan and U.S. officials believe that Taliban insurgents and regional groups associated with Al Qaeda continue to profit from Afghanistan's burgeoning narcotics trade. Officials also suspect that drug profits provide some Al Qaeda operatives with financial and logistical support. U.S. officials believe that financial and logistical relationships between narcotics traffickers, terrorists, and criminal groups pose threats to the security of Afghanistan and the wider international community.
- **Consumption and Public Health:** World health officials believe that Afghan narcotics pose social and public health risks for populations in Afghanistan, its neighbors, Russia, Western Europe, and, to a limited extent, the United States. Increased use of Afghan opiates has been closely associated with increased addiction and HIV infection levels in heroin consumption markets.

Narcotics and Prospects for State Failure in Afghanistan

Afghan authorities and international observers have identified negative trends associated with the narcotics trade as barriers to the reestablishment of security, the rule of law, and a legitimate economy throughout Afghanistan — goals which U.S. and Afghan authorities have characterized as essential for the country's long term stability. In a September 2004 report on Afghanistan's economic development, the World Bank described these related trends as "a vicious circle" (**Figure 5**) that constitute "a grave danger" to the "entire state-building and reconstruction agenda."[22]

Anti-Government Elements and Popular Violence. Authorities fear that heavily armed trafficking groups and regional militia may join Afghan farmers in violently resisting expanded drug interdiction and crop eradication efforts. Opium production remains a source of revenue and patronage for some armed groups and militia leaders seeking to maintain their power and influence over areas of the country at the expense of the extension of national government authority.[23] According to U.N. and Afghan officials, some armed groups impose informal taxes and checkpoint fees of 10% to 40% on farmers, traffickers, and opiate processing laboratories within their areas of control, receiving cash or payment in opium.[24] Although much of the outright conflict between regional and factional militias that motivated opium cultivation in the past has ended, long-established political and commercial networks linking armed groups, landowning elites, transportation guilds, and drug syndicates continue to constitute the foundation of the opium economy.

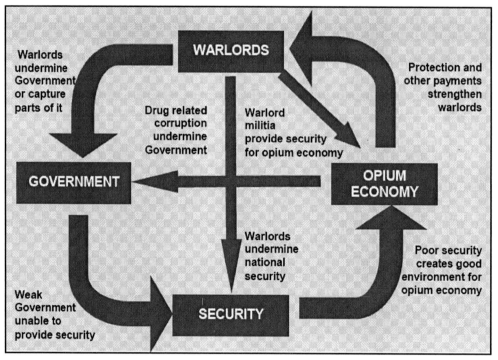

Source: World Bank, Afghanistan: State Building, Sustaining Growth, and Reducing Poverty, Country Economic Report No. 29551-AF September 9, 2004, p. 87.

Figure 4. Narcotics and Security in Afghanistan

Fears of widespread violence are based in large part on patterns of clashes between Afghan farmers and counternarcotics authorities seeking to eradicate crops. In April 2005, a large government eradication force clashed with approximately 2,000 villagers demonstrating against the destruction of opium crops in the southern district of Maiwand, leading to the death of one security officer and the wounding of several civilians. Afghan soldiers and police also were killed during 2005 by attackers firing on government eradication forces in Uruzgan and Kandahar. These clashes and attacks follow a pattern evident in previous years, in which eradication teams employed by provincial authorities faced demonstrations, small arms fire, and mined poppy fields.[25] At the outset of the Afghan government's first eradication campaign in April 2002, for example, Pashtun farmers barricaded the major highway linking Pakistan and Afghanistan, and clashes between opium farmers and Afghan eradication teams killed 16 people.[26]

Corruption and Challenges to Afghan Democracy. According to the State Department, national government officials are generally "believed to be free of direct criminal connection to the drug trade," although among provincial and district level officials, "drug-related corruption is pervasive."[27] In December 2004, Afghan counternarcotics official Mirwais Yasini indicated that "high government officials, police commanders, governors are involved" in the drug trade.[28] Government authorities and security forces in Afghanistan have accused each other of involvement in opium production and trafficking, and militia commanders have clashed over opium production and profits in various regions of the country, threatening the country's stability and the lives of civilians.[29] Although most of Afghanistan's prominent political figures have publicly condemned the country's opium economy, some political figures and their powerful supporters are alleged to have links with the trade or hold responsibility for areas of Afghanistan where opium poppy cultivation and drug trafficking take place. Commanders under the control of former cabinet members and former presidential candidates are alleged to participate in the opium trade.[30]

Some observers fear that as the Afghan government develops stronger counternarcotics policies and capabilities, groups that are involved with the opium trade will join others in seeking to corrupt or subvert Afghanistan's democratic process. Although no major attempts were made to disrupt the Afghan national presidential or parliamentary elections, armed factions and local militia leaders continue to exert political influence across Afghanistan.[31] With regard to recent parliamentary elections, some experts have argued that drug money may have financed the campaigns of candidates, and at least one expert warned that "drug lords" were candidates.[32]

Opium Profits and Afghanistan's Economic Recovery. Reports continue to indicate that profits from Afghanistan's opium trade may be overwhelming efforts to reestablish a functioning, licit economy. According to the UNODC/MCN 2005 opium survey, the value of the 2005 opium harvest, an estimated $2.7 billion, was equal to 50% of the country's licit GDP from 2004. The World Bank reports that the opium economy has produced significant increases in rural wages and income and remains a significant source of credit for low income rural households. Opium profits fuel consumption of domestic products and support imports of high value goods such as automobiles and appliances from abroad. Funds from the drug trade are also a major source of investment for infrastructure development projects, including major projects in "building construction, trade, and transport."[33] Analysts argue that efforts to combat narcotics must address Afghanistan's economic dependence on opium and replace drug profits with licit capital and investment. In February 2005, the IMF warned that new counternarcotics efforts, if successful, "could adversely affect GDP growth, the balance of payments, and government revenue" by lowering drug income and weakening its support for domestic consumption and taxed imports.[34]

Table 2. Afghan Extremists' Links to the Drug Trade

Afghan Extremists	Are they receiving money from the trade?	Do traffickers provide them with logistical support?	Are they telling farmers to grow opium poppy?
Hizb-i Islami/ Gulbuddin (HIG)[a]	**Almost Definitely:** HIG commanders involved in trafficking have led attacks on Coalition forces, and U.S. troops have raided labs linked to the HIG.	**Most Likely:** HIG commanders involved in the drug trade may use those ties to facilitate weapons smuggling and money laundering.	**Probably:** Afghan government officials say the Taliban encourage and in some instances force poppy cultivation. Existing State Department estimates suggest other groups interested in weakening the government in Kabul — like the HIG — may have followed suit.
Taliban	**Almost Definitely:** U.N. and Afghan Transitional Authority officials report the group earns money from trafficking and gets donations form drug lords.	**Most Likely:** Major drug barons who supported the Taliban when it was in power remain at large, and may be moving people, equipment, and money on the group's behalf.	
Islamic Movement of Uzbekistan (IMU)	**Probably:** Uzbek officials have accused the group of involvement in the drug trade, and its remnants in Afghanistan may turn to trafficking to raise funds.	**Probably:** Members with drug ties may turn to traffickers for help crossing borders.	**Possibly:** No reports, and these groups — as foreigners in Afghanistan — may lack the moral and political authority needed to influence farmers' planting decisions.
Al Qaeda	**Possibly:** Only scattered reports, but fighters in Afghanistan may be engaged in low-level — but still lucrative — drug deals.	**Probably:** Traffickers stopped during December 2003 in the Arabian Sea were linked to Al Qaeda. Al Qaeda may hire criminals in South Asia to transfer weapons, explosives, money, and people through the region.	

Source: Robert Charles, Assistant Secretary of State for International Narcotics and Law Enforcement Affairs, Testimony Before the House Committee on Government Reform Subcommittee on Criminal Justice, Drug Policy and Human Resources, April 1, 2004.

[a]. Hizb-i Islami's leader — former anti-Soviet mujahideen commander Gulbuddin Hekmatyar — is alleged to have been involved in the Afghan narcotics trade since the 1980s.

Narcotics, Insurgency, and Terrorism

Afghan and U.S. officials believe that linkages between insurgents, terrorists, and narcotics traffickers threaten the security of Afghanistan and the international community. In addition to moving deadly opiates, sophisticated drug transportation and money laundering networks may also facilitate the movement of wanted individuals and terrorist funds and support illicit trafficking in persons and weapons. Although some U.S. officials have made unequivocal statements about the existence of narco-terrorist linkages, most officials address the issue in general terms and indicate that intelligence agencies are continually developing more complete pictures of these relationships. In late 2005 and early 2006, Afghan president Hamid Karzai made several statements indicating that drug profits were providing financial support to the ongoing Taliban insurgency, including funding suicide bombing operations that killed Afghan civilians. According to U.S. officials, senior Al Qaeda leaders considered and subsequently rejected the idea of becoming directly involved in managing and profiting from aspects of Afghanistan's narcotics trade. Ideological considerations and fear of increased visibility and vulnerability to foreign intelligence and law enforcement services reportedly were the predominant factors in their decision.[35] Al Qaeda operatives and the local tribal and criminal networks in the Afghanistan-Pakistan border region that are suspected of supporting and sheltering them are thought to have some involvement with the regional narcotics trade. **Table 2** describes known linkages between groups involved in terrorism and the drug trade as presented by State Department officials to Members of Congress in April 2004 and February 2005.

Taliban and Al Qaeda Financiers. Afghan individuals serve as middlemen between the groups described in **Table 2** and narcotics producers and traffickers. Press reports and U.S. officials have identified two prominent figures involved in Afghanistan's drug trade that reportedly have financed Taliban insurgents and some low-level Al Qaeda operatives:

- **Haji Bashir Noorzai** is a former confidant of ousted Taliban leader Mullah Omar who served as a military commander during the Taliban era and was reportedly a "major financial supporter of the Taliban."[36] In June 2004, the Bush Administration added Haji Bashir Noorzai to the U.S. government's drug kingpin list. In April 2005, Noorzai was arrested by DEA officials and charged with conspiracy to import heroin into the United States over a 15-year period. The indictment charges that Noorzai and his organization "provided demolitions, weaponry, and manpower to the Taliban" in return for "protection for its opium crops, heroin laboratories, drug-transportation routes, and members and associates."[37]
- **Haji Baz Mohammed** is an alleged drug organization leader from the eastern province of Nangarhar who was extradited to the United States in October 2005 to face charges of importing Afghan heroin into the United States. According to his indictment, Mohammed's organization was "closely aligned with the Taliban" and "provided financial support to the Taliban and other associated Islamic-extremist organizations in Afghanistan" in return for protection.[38]
- **Haji Juma Khan** has been identified as an alleged drug lord and Al Qaeda financier. In August 2004, then-U.S. Assistant Secretary of State for International Narcotics

and Law Enforcement (INL) Robert Charles told *Time Magazine* that Haji Juma Khan is "obviously very tightly tied to the Taliban." Afghan Counter Narcotics Directorate chief Mirwais Yasini added that "there are central linkages among Khan, Mullah Omar and [Osama] Bin Laden."[39]

U.S. forces reportedly detained and released both Haji Juma Khan and Haji Bashir Noorzai in late 2001 and early 2002. Press accounts state that Noorzai voluntarily provided intelligence about his Taliban and Al Qaeda colleagues during questioning at Kandahar's airport prior to his release.[40] DEA officials reportedly were unable to question him at the time.[41] Noorzai's forces later surrendered a large number of weapons to coalition and Afghan authorities and provided security for Qandahar province governor Gul Agha Sherzai.[42] Juma Khan remains at large, and Department of Defense officials indicate that U.S. military forces are not directly pursuing major figures in the Afghan opium trade, although U.S., Afghan, and coalition authorities continue to monitor and collect intelligence on their activities and support Afghan authorities and their operations.[43]

Consumption Markets

Afghan opium presents significant public health and internal security challenges to downstream markets where refined heroin and other opiates are consumed, including the United States. Russia and Europe have been the main consumption markets for Afghan opiates since the early 1990s, and estimates place Afghan opium as the source of over 90% of the heroin that enters the United Kingdom and Western Europe annually. Russian and European leaders have expressed concern over the growth of Afghanistan's opium trade as both a national security threat as well as a threat to public health and safety.

Trafficking to the United States. Heroin originating in southwest Asia (Afghanistan, Pakistan, Iran, and Turkey) "was the predominant form of heroin available in the United States" from 1980 to 1987,[44] and the DEA's Heroin Signature Program has indicated that southwest Asia-derived heroin currently constitutes up to 10% of the heroin available in the United States.[45] Since the 1980s, several figures involved in the Afghan drug trade have been convicted of trafficking illegal drugs, including heroin, into the United States.[46] Afghan and Pakistani nationals have been indicted and convicted on heroin trafficking and money laundering charges in U.S. courts as recently as April 2005. In addition to the cases of Haji Bashir Noorzai and Haji Baz Mohammed noted above, the following other recent cases involve links to the Taliban and Al Qaeda:

- In the mid-1990s, several Pakistani nationals were extradited to the United States and convicted of heroin and hashish trafficking, including Haji Ayub Afridi, a former member of Pakistan's Parliament and alleged drug baron.[47]
- Since 2001, DEA and FBI investigators have prosecuted several Afghan and Pakistani nationals in connection with heroin trafficking and money laundering charges, including members of Pakistan's Afridi clan.[48] Officials have indicated that some of the individuals involved in these recent cases may have relationships with Taliban insurgents and members of Al Qaeda.[49]

- Al Qaeda operatives and sympathizers have been captured trafficking large quantities of heroin and hashish and attempting to trade drugs for Stinger missiles.[50]

Russia. Afghan opiates have been a concern for Russian leaders since the 1980s, when Afghan drug dealers targeted Soviet troops and many Russian soldiers returned from service in Afghanistan addicted to heroin.[51] More recently, the Russian government has expressed deep concern about "narco-terrorist" linkages that are alleged to exist between Chechen rebel groups, their Islamist extremist allies, and Caucasian criminal groups that traffic and distribute heroin in Russia. Since 1993, HIV infection and heroin addiction rates have skyrocketed in Russia, and these trends have been linked to the influx and growing use of Afghan opiates. These concerns make the Afghan narcotics trade an issue of priority interest to Russian decision makers, and motivate attention and initiative on the part of Russian security services in the region. The head of Russia's counternarcotics service has announced plans to open a counternarcotics field office in Kabul.[52]

Western Europe. In Europe, press outlets and public officials in several countries have devoted significant attention to Afghanistan's opium trade since the 1990s. In the United Kingdom, where British officials estimate that 90-95% of the heroin that enters the country annually is derived from Afghan opium, the public places a high priority on combating the Afghan opiate trade. In October 2001, British Prime Minister Tony Blair cited the Taliban regime's tolerance for opium cultivation and heroin production as one justification for the United Kingdom's involvement in the U.S.-led military campaign in Afghanistan. Some British citizens and officials have criticized the Blair Administration's counternarcotics efforts in Afghanistan and argued that more should be done to stem the flow of Afghan opiates in the future.[53] The United Kingdom currently serves as the lead nation for international counternarcotics efforts in Afghanistan, and British government officials assist Afghan counternarcotics authorities in intelligence gathering and targeting operations for interdiction and eradication. British defense officials have announced plans to send up to 4,000 British troops to the key opium-producing province of Helmand province in southern Afghanistan, where their mission reportedly will include efforts to support security operations and target narcotic traffickers.

Regional Security Implications

Afghanistan's opiate trade presents a range of policy challenges for Afghanistan's neighbors, particularly for the Central Asian republics of the former Soviet Union. As a security issue, regional governments face the challenge of securing their borders and populations against the inflow of Afghan narcotics and infiltration by armed trafficking and terrorist groups. Regional terrorist organizations and international criminal syndicates that move Afghan opiates throughout the region have been linked to insecurity, corruption, and violence in several countries.[54] As a public health issue, Afghan narcotics have contributed to a dramatic upsurge in opiate use and addiction rates in countries neighboring Afghanistan, a factor that also has been linked to dramatic increases in HIV infection rates in many of Afghanistan's neighbors. According to the UNODC, by 2001, "Afghan opiates represented: almost 100% of the illicit opiates consumed in... Iran, Pakistan, Turkey, Kazakhstan, Turkmenistan, Kyrgyzstan, Tajikistan, Uzbekistan, Azerbaijan, and the Russian Federation."

[55] With the exception of Turkey, intravenous use of Afghan opiates is the dominant driver of growing HIV infection rates in each of these countries.[56] These destabilizing factors could provide a powerful pretext for increased attention to and possible intervention in Afghan affairs on the part of regional powers such as Iran and Pakistan.

Central Asia.[57] The emergence of the so-called "Northern Route" of opiate trafficking through Central Asia and the Caucasus in the mid-1990s transformed the region's previously small and relatively self-contained opiate market into the center of global opium and heroin trafficking. Ineffective border control, civil war, and corruption facilitated this trend, and opiate trafficking and use in Kazakhstan, Uzbekistan, Turkmenistan, and Kyrgyzstan now pose significant security and public health threats to those countries. U.S. officials have implicated the Islamic Movement of Uzbekistan in the regional drug trade, as well as well-organized and heavily armed criminal syndicates that threaten U.S. interests.

Tajikistan has emerged as the primary transit point for Afghan opiates entering Central Asia and being trafficked beyond. From 1998 to 2003, Tajikistan's Drug Control Agency seized 30 MT of drugs and narcotics, including 16 MT of heroin. U.N. authorities estimate that the European street value of the 5,600 kg of heroin seized by Tajik authorities in 2003 was over $3 billion.[58] The 201st Russian Army Division stationed troops along the Afghan-Tajik border to disrupt the activities of criminals, narcotics traffickers, and terrorist groups from 1993 through late 2004. Tajik and Russian authorities have begun replacing these Russian military forces with Tajik border security guards and are scheduled to complete the process by the end of 2006.[59] Some observers have expressed concern that the relatively poor training and inexperience of the Tajik forces may result in an increase in the flow of opium and heroin into Central Asia and onward to Russia and Europe. Others fear that Tajik security forces may prove more vulnerable to corruption than their Russian counterparts.[60] In January 2005, Russian press sources reported that Russian border guards seized 2.5 MT of heroin on the Tajik-Afghan border in 2004. A Russian-led Collective Security Treaty Organization interdiction effort known as Channel-2005 seized close to 9 MT of drugs in 2005, including over 200 kg of heroin.[61]

Pakistan. According to the 2005 State Department International Narcotics Control Strategy Report (INCSR), "Pakistan remains a substantial trafficking country for heroin, morphine, and hashish from Afghanistan," and Pakistani narcotics traffickers "play a very prominent role in all aspects of the drug trade" in regions of Afghanistan that border Pakistan. Trafficking groups routinely use western areas of Afghanistan and Pakistan as staging areas for the movement of opiates into and through Iran. Efforts to control the narcotics trade in Pakistan have historically been complicated by the government's limited ability to assert authority over autonomous tribal zones, although recent cooperative border security efforts with the United States have increased the presence of government authorities in these regions. The Pakistani government's efforts to reduce opium poppy cultivation and heroin production since 2001 have been moderately successful; however, drug usage remains relatively high among some elements of Pakistani society. In March 2003, former U.S. Ambassador to Pakistan Wendy Chamberlain told a House International Relations Committee panel that the role of Pakistan's Inter-Services Intelligence (ISI) agency in the heroin trade from 1997-2003 had been "substantial."[62] The 2003 State Department INCSR stated that U.S. officials have "no evidence" that any senior government officials were involved with the narcotics trade or drug money laundering, although the report also stated that narcotics remained a source of "persistent corruption" among lower level officials.

Iran. Narcotics trafficking and use continue to present serious security and public health risks to Iran, which the State Department has called "a major transit route for opiates smuggled from Afghanistan." According to the 2003 State Department INCSR, over 3200 Iranian security personnel have been killed in clashes with heavily-armed narcotics trafficking groups over the last twenty years, and 67% of HIV infections in Iran are related to intravenous drug use by the country's more than 1 million estimated addicts. Iran's interdiction efforts along its eastern borders with Afghanistan and Pakistan are widely credited with forcing opiate traffickers to establish and maintain the "Northern Route" through Central Asia. According to the State Department, Iranian officials seized 181 MT of opiates in the first six months of 2004.

The 2005 INCSR states that the Iranian government "has demonstrated sustained national political will and taken strong measures against illicit narcotics, including cooperation with the international community." Although the absence of bilateral diplomatic relations prevents the United States from directly supporting counternarcotics initiatives in Iran, the INSCR indicates that United States and Iran "have worked together productively" in the UN's multilateral "Six Plus Two" group. Shared interest in interdiction has led the United Kingdom to support the Iranian government's counternarcotics efforts since 1999 by providing millions of dollars in grants for security equipment purchases, including bullet-proof vests for Iran's border patrol guards.[63]

THE INTERNATIONAL POLICY RESPONSE

The Bonn Agreement that established the Afghan Interim Authority committed Afghanistan's new government to cooperation with the international community "in the fight against terrorism, drugs and organized crime."[64] After taking office in early 2002, Hamid Karzai's transitional administration took a series of steps to combat the growth of the Afghan narcotics trade, including issuing a formal ban on opium cultivation, outlining a national counternarcotics strategy, and establishing institutions and forces tasked with eradicating poppy crops and interdicting drug traffic. Karzai's government places a high priority on creating alternative livelihoods and sources of income for opium growing farmers. Many countries have contributed funding, equipment, forces, and training to various counternarcotics programs in Afghanistan, including crop eradication and judicial reform. The United States and others work closely with Afghanistan's neighbors in an effort to contain the flow of narcotics and strengthen interdiction efforts.

The United Kingdom serves as the lead coalition nation for international counternarcotics policy and assistance in Afghanistan. Under British leadership, basic eradication, interdiction, and alternative livelihood development measures began in the spring of 2002. The State Department's International Narcotics and Law Enforcement (INL) Bureau administers U.S. counternarcotics and law enforcement assistance programs in Afghanistan and coordinates with the U.S. Agency for International Development (USAID), the Drug Enforcement Administration (DEA), the Government of Afghanistan, the United Kingdom, Italy, Germany, and the United Nations Office on Drugs and Crime (UNODC). To date, U.S. forces in Afghanistan have engaged in some counternarcotics activities based on limited rules of engagement, although military officials indicate that the role of the U.S. military in counternarcotics has expanded in 2005 to include police training and interdiction mission support. British military units carry out interdiction missions in cooperation with Afghan authorities that target drug production laboratories and trafficking infrastructure. The United States also provides counternarcotics assistance to other countries in the region.

The Bush Administration has begun a "five pillar" inter-agency initiative to reinvigorate U.S. support for the implementation of Afghanistan's national counternarcotics strategy. The initiative has been accompanied by a substantial increase in spending on counternarcotics programs, with particular emphasis on alternative livelihood development and greater U.S. support for crop eradication efforts. Training of and equipment for Afghan counternarcotics forces and prosecution teams also have figured prominently in the new strategy. Most observers and officials expect that a long-term, sustained international effort will be necessary to reduce the threat posed by the opium trade to the security and stability of Afghanistan and the international community.

Afghan Counternarcotics Policies, Programs, and Forces

Bans, Prohibitions, and Policy Statements. Among the first acts of the newly established Afghan Interim Authority created by the Bonn Agreement was the issuance of a decree that banned the opium poppy cultivation, heroin production, opiate trafficking, and drug use on January 17, 2002. On April 3, 2002, Afghan authorities released a second decree that described the scope and goals of an eradication program designed to destroy a portion of the opium poppy crop that had been planted during late 2001. In order to prevent further cultivation during the autumn 2002 planting season, the government issued a third, more specific decree in September 2002 that spelled out plans for the enforcement of bans on opium cultivation, production, trafficking, and abuse.

Religious and political leaders have also spoken out adamantly against involvement in the drug trade. Islamic leaders from Afghanistan's General Council of Ulema issued a *fatwa* or religious ruling in August 2004 that declared poppy cultivation to be contrary to Islamic *sharia* law.[65] Following his election in October 2004, President Hamid Karzai has made a number of public statements characterizing involvement in opium cultivation and trafficking as shameful and stating that provincial and district leaders would be held accountable by the central government for failure to combat drug activity in areas under their control.

Afghan authorities developed a national counternarcotics strategy in 2003 in consultation with experts and officials from the United States, the United Kingdom, and the UNODC.[66] The strategy declares the Afghan government's commitment to reducing opium poppy cultivation by 70% by 2008 and to completely eliminating poppy cultivation and drug trafficking by 2013. The strategy identifies five key tactical goals to support its broader commitments: "the provision of alternative livelihoods for Afghan poppy farmers, the extension of drug law enforcement throughout Afghanistan, the implementation of drug control legislation, the establishment of effective institutions, and the introduction of prevention and treatment programs for addicts." In 2005, the Afghan government released an implementation plan for the strategy that outlines specific initiatives planned in each of the five policy areas, as well as for regional cooperation, eradication, and public information campaigns.[67] Afghanistan's new counternarcotics law clarifies administrative authorities for counternarcotics policy and establishes clear procedures for investigating and prosecuting major drug offenses.

Institutions and Forces. In October 2002, then-Interim President Hamid Karzai announced that the Afghan National Security Council would take responsibility for counternarcotics policy and would oversee the creation and activities of a new Counternarcotics Directorate (CND). The CND subsequently established functional units to analyze data and coordinate action in five areas: judicial reform, law enforcement, alternative livelihood development, demand reduction, and public awareness. Following its establishment in late 2002, the CND worked with other Afghan ministries, local leaders, and international authorities to develop counternarcotics policies and coordinate the creation of counternarcotics institutions and the training of effective personnel. The CND was transformed into a new Ministry of Counternarcotics (MCN) in December 2004. Habibullah Qaderi currently serves as Afghanistan's Minister for Counternarcotics.

Counternarcotics enforcement activities have been directed from within the Ministry of Interior since 2002. General Mohammed Daud was named Deputy Ministry of Interior for Counternarcotics in December 2004. General Daud and his staff work closely with U.S. and British officials in implementing the Afghan government's expanded counternarcotics enforcement plan. The Ministry of Interior directs the activities of the following Afghan counternarcotics and law enforcement entities.

- **Counternarcotics Police-Afghanistan (CNP-A).** The CNP-A consists of investigative and enforcement divisions whose officers work closely with U.S. and British counternarcotics authorities. CNP-A officers continue to receive U.S. training to support their ability to plan and execute counternarcotics activities independently.

- **National Interdiction Unit (NIU).** The NIU was established as an element of CNP-A in October 2004 and continues to conduct significant raids across Afghanistan. Approximately 200 NIU officers have received U.S. training and now operate in cooperation with DEA Foreign Advisory Support Teams (FAST teams, for more see below).[68]

- **Central Eradication Planning Cell (CPEC).** The CPEC is a U.K.-supported targeting and intelligence center that uses sophisticated technology and surveying to target poppy crops and monitor the success of eradication operations. The CPEC provides target data for the Central Poppy Eradication Force (CPEF).

- **Central Poppy Eradication Force (CPEF).** The U.S.-supported CPEF conducts ground-based eradication of poppy crops throughout Afghanistan based on targeting data provided by the Central Eradication Planning Cell (CPEC). The force is made up of approximately 1,000 trained eradicators and is supported by security personnel. Plans called for 3,000 CPEF officers to be trained by the end of 2005; however, Afghan and U.S. officials have expressed a preference for locally led and administered eradication efforts for 2006, after the CPEF failed to meet its targets for 2005.[69]

- **Afghan Special Narcotics Force (ASNF).** The elite ASNF, or "Force 333," has received special training from the British military and carries out interdiction missions against high value targets and in remote areas. The U.S. military provides some intelligence and airlift support for the ASNF. According to the Ministry of Counternarcotics, the ASNF has destroyed over 150 MT of opium, 45 MT of precursor chemicals, and 191 drug laboratories.

- **Border Police, National Police, and Highway Police.** Approximately 27,000 Afghan police have graduated from U.S.-sponsored training facilities, and elements of all three forces have received training, equipment, and communications support from British, German, and U.S. authorities to improve their counternarcotics enforcement capabilities. U.S. and German authorities planned to train 50,000 border and national police by December 2005.

U.S. Policy Initiatives: The "Five-Pillar" Plan

In spite of limited efforts on the part of Afghan, U.S., and international authorities, the land area used for opium poppy cultivation in Afghanistan and Afghanistan's corresponding opiate output increased annually from late 2001 through 2004. Although public awareness of government opium poppy cultivation bans and laws outlawing participation in the narcotics trade is widespread, until recently, counternarcotics enforcement activities have been hindered by the Afghan government's tactical inability to carry out nationwide, effective eradication and interdiction campaigns as well as a lack of adequate legal infrastructure to support drug-related prosecutions. International development agencies have made positive, but limited, efforts to address structural economic issues associated with rural livelihoods and drug production, such as household debt and the destruction of local agricultural market infrastructure. These efforts were not centrally coordinated or linked directly to counternarcotics goals and initiatives until late 2004.

Substantial growth in opium poppy cultivation and narcotics trafficking led U.S. officials, in consultation with their Afghan and coalition partners, to develop a more comprehensive, complementary plan to support the implementation of the Afghan national counternarcotics strategy. The evolving policy initiative developed by U.S. agencies consists of five key elements, or pillars, that mirror Afghan initiatives and call for increased interagency and international cooperation.[70] The five pillars of the U.S. initiative are public information, judicial reform, alternative livelihood development, interdiction, and eradication. New initiatives in these areas are building upon a range of preexisting policy initiatives being implemented by U.S., Afghan, and coalition authorities.

Public Information. Afghan and U.S. authorities have initiated public information campaigns to reach out to ordinary Afghans and raise public awareness about the threat of narcotics and the danger of participation in the illegal drug trade.[71] The efforts build on the Afghan government's public awareness strategy, which enlists local community and religious leaders to support the government's counternarcotics policies and encourages them to speak out in their communities against drug use and involvement the opium trade. As noted above, Islamic leaders from Afghanistan's General Council of Ulema have supported this effort by publicly condemning poppy cultivation and involvement in the drug trade.[72]

The U.S. campaigns supplement existing public information efforts designed to reduce demand for illegal drugs within Afghan society and spread awareness of the Afghan government's opium poppy cultivation bans and drug laws. The UNODC/MCN 2005 Opium Survey found that farmers across Afghanistan were well aware of the government's ban on opium poppy cultivation and that many farmers who declined to cultivate opium poppy did so because they feared eradication or incarceration. An earlier survey also reported that farmers in provinces where opium poppy cultivation was found to have increased believed that the government could not or would not enforce the ban.

Judicial Reform. Department of State (INL office) and Department of Justice personnel are undertaking judicial reform efforts to further enable Afghan authorities to enforce counternarcotics laws and prosecute prominent individuals involved in narcotics trafficking. A Counternarcotics Vertical Prosecution Task Force (CNVPTF) is under development and will feature integrated teams of Afghan judges, prosecutors, and enforcement officials that are being specially trained to handle complex, high-profile cases. Some U.S. federal prosecutors are participating in CNVPTF training activities in Afghanistan. In 2005, an Afghan team of ten investigators, seven prosecutors, and three judges began serving under the jurisdiction of the Kabul criminal court and are currently processing cases against narcotics suspects and detainees. The U.S. Department of Defense is supporting construction activities for a maximum-security wing at the Pol-i-Charki prison near Kabul to hold narcotics offenders prosecuted by the Task Force. Afghan and coalition officials are currently working to identify targets for prosecution, although, according to U.S. officials, political concerns and security considerations will play a role in the targeting of individuals.

The April 2005 arrest of Haji Bashir Noorzai by U.S. officials and the extradition of Haji Baz Mohammed raised concern about the readiness and ability of Afghan authorities to investigate, prosecute, and incarcerate drug suspects independently. According to an Afghan Interior Ministry official, "Afghan police had no role in [Noorzai's] arrest," and Afghan authorities were constrained because of "a lack of concrete evidence against him."[73] Discussion of a limited amnesty program for prominent narcotics traffickers surfaced in January 2005 but is reportedly no longer under consideration.[74] With U.S. and coalition support, the government of Afghanistan drafted and issued a new counternarcotics law in December 2005 that clarifies administrative authorities for counternarcotics policy and establishes clear procedures for investigating and prosecuting major drug offenses.

Alternative Livelihood Development.[75] In order to provide viable economic alternatives to opium poppy cultivation and drug production, U.S. officials have developed a three-phased plan that directly links development initiatives to overall counternarcotics efforts through a comprehensive program targeted to opium producing areas. The first phase of the alternative livelihoods plan accelerated existing agricultural development initiatives, including improvements to agricultural market infrastructure, farmer education programs, and micro-credit lending systems to support rural families. The new efforts build on existing USAID programs to develop integrated systems of crop processing facilities, storage areas, roads, and markets, and to restore wheat and other cereal crop production levels. Work began on phase one projects in early 2005 and will continue through 2006.

The second phase of the plan consists of a one-year "immediate needs"/ "cash-for-work" program that is sponsoring labor intensive work projects to provide non-opium incomes to rural laborers and to rehabilitate agricultural infrastructure. The program began in December 2004 and has been renewed for 2006. USAID personnel design "immediate needs" projects in consultation with local councils and tribal leaders in districts where crop eradication has been planned or where farmers have agreed to cease poppy cultivation.[76] According to USAID, in main opium producing provinces, USAID-sponsored alternative livelihood cash-for-work programs generated 4.5 million work days in 2005 and paid $15.7 million in salaries to 194,000 people who otherwise may have engaged in or supported opium poppy cultivation. Over 6,00 km of irrigation canals, drainage ditches, nd traditional water transportation systems were repaired and cleaned in a number of provinces, improving irrigation and supporting high value agriculture on an estimated 290,000 hectares of land.[77]

The third, "comprehensive development" phase of the plan began in six key poppy-producing provinces during 2005 and is scheduled to be implemented through 2009. Current and planned projects include long-term infrastructure development for urban and rural areas, credit and financial services expansion, agricultural diversification, and private investment support. The Afghan government requested that USAID expand alternative livelihood programs into the provinces of Ghor, Dai Kundi, Konar, Farah, and Uruzgan, and USAID personnel have consulted with contractors and security officials and initiated preliminary projects in some of those provinces.

Table 3. Alternative Livelihood Proposed Spending
Targets by Province, FY2005-2007 ($ millions)

Province	Immediate Needs	Comprehensive Development	2004 Province Share of Nationwide Poppy Cultivated Area
Nangarhar and Laghman	$18	$110	21.1%
Helmand and Kandahar	$19	$120	34.2%
Badakhshan and Takhar	$1.5	$60	8.6%

Source: USAID, Alternative Livelihoods Update: Issue 2, March 16 — 31, 2005.

Accountability standards have been built into the USAID alternative livelihood programs, including seed and fertilizer distributions and cash-for-work programs. Seed and fertilizer recipients, including government officials, are required to agree in writing not to grow poppy in exchange for program support. Cash-for-work program participants must make similar commitments, and program staff monitor participant activities outside of the program to ensure compliance. According to USAID, all alternative livelihood program assistance is 100% conditional on the reduction of poppy cultivation within one year of the receipt of assistance.[78] For example, alternative livelihood assistance was denied to the border district of Achin in eastern Nangarhar province during 2005 because its inhabitants refused to halt poppy cultivation. Some villages in Achin that subsequently agreed to abandon poppy farming during the current season are scheduled to receive alternative livelihood assistance on a conditional basis in 2006.

Interdiction. Reflecting on the absence of effective counternarcotics institutions and authorities in post-Taliban Afghanistan, international authorities led by the United States Drug Enforcement Administration (DEA) established a series of cooperative interdiction initiatives in countries neighboring Afghanistan beginning in early 2002. The primary U.S.-led effort, known as "Operation Containment," is designed to "implement a joint strategy to deprive drug trafficking organizations of their market access and international terrorist groups of financial support from drugs, precursor chemicals, weapons, ammunition and currency."[79] Operation Containment has continued since early 2002 and currently involves "nineteen countries from Central Asia, the Caucasus, Europe and Russia."[80] According to the DEA, Operation Containment activities were responsible for the seizure of "2.4 metric tons of heroin, 985 kilograms of morphine base, three metric tons of opium gum, 152.9 metric tons of cannabis, and 195 arrests" in the first quarter of 2005.[81] A similar multinational DEA-led effort named Operation Topaz has focused on interdicting acetic anhydride — a primary heroin production precursor chemical — to Afghanistan.

In addition to ongoing international narcotics and precursor interdiction initiatives under Operation Containment and Operation Topaz, U.S. officials are providing increased support to Afghan government interdiction efforts through intelligence cooperation, training programs, equipment transfers, and joint operations. The DEA has expanded its presence in Afghanistan since January 2003, although in the past DEA officials have cited restrictions on the capabilities and freedom of movement of their staff in Afghanistan due to a general lack of security outside of Kabul. DEA Foreign Advisory and Support Teams (FAST) have been deployed to Afghanistan "to provide guidance and conduct bilateral investigations that will identify, target, and disrupt illicit drug trafficking organizations." The FAST teams receive Defense Department support and are currently conducting operations and providing mentoring to newly-trained Afghan recruits. DEA received new FY2006 funding to expand its operational presence in Afghanistan and Central Asia, including support for FAST teams, Operation Containment activities, and new field officers.

Current U.S. Department of Defense directives state that U.S. military forces in Afghanistan do not and will not directly target drug production facilities or pursue drug traffickers as a distinct component of ongoing U.S. counternarcotics initiatives.[82] Current rules of engagement allow U.S. forces to seize and destroy drugs and drug infrastructure discovered during the course of routine military operations carried out in pursuit of conventional counterterrorism and stability missions.[83] U.S. forces continue to provide limited intelligence and air support to Afghan and British forces during interdiction missions, including the destruction of heroin laboratories and opiate storage warehouses. U.S. initiatives that supply Afghan police with tents, boots, communication equipment, mobility support, infrastructure improvements, and training are expected to continue. Defense Department and military personnel plan to focus future efforts on further improving Afghanistan's border security and providing greater intelligence support to Afghan law enforcement officials through joint military/DEA/Afghan "intelligence fusion centers" located at U.S. facilities in Kabul and the Afghan Ministry of Interior.[84]

British forces currently contribute to a central targeting operation that identifies opiate warehouses and processing facilities for destruction. British Customs and Excise authorities also work with Afghan officials through mobile heroin detection units in Kabul. British military forces reportedly will operate under more permissive rules of engagement that will allow them to carry out "opportunistic strikes" against narcotics infrastructure and to support Afghan eradication teams with a "rapid-reaction force." British defense officials have announced plans to send up to 4,000 British troops to the key opium-producing province of Helmand province in southern Afghanistan, where their mission reportedly will include efforts to support security operations and target narcotic traffickers. [85]

Eradication. Critics have cited growth in opium poppy cultivation figures as evidence that manual eradication campaigns have failed to serve as a credible deterrent for Afghan farmers. Plans developed by the Department of State, in consultation with Afghan authorities, called for early and more robust opium poppy eradication measures for the 2004-2005 growing season to provide a strong deterrent to future cultivation. The Afghan Central Poppy Eradication Force (CPEF) carried out limited operations with support from U.K. intelligence officers, U.S. advisors, and international contractors in early 2005. Field reports indicated that

CPEF personnel met violent resistance from farmers in some instances and largely failed to meet their eradication targets for the 2004-2005 season[86]

The centrally organized and executed eradication plan marked a departure from previous eradication campaign strategies, which largely relied upon governors and local authorities to target and destroy crops. Most governors pledged to support President Karzai's eradication initiatives in 2005, and U.S. officials report that areas where governors and local leaders embraced and enforced the central government's eradication demands saw significant reductions in poppy cultivation. During the current season, "poppy elimination programs" (PEPs) are being established in select Afghan provinces. The PEPs are led by small U.S. interagency and international teams that will direct and monitor locally led and administered counternarcotics activities, including eradication. U.S. officials have stressed the importance of early season, locally executed eradication in order to minimize violent farmer resistance and give Afghan farmers time to plant licit replacement cash crops.

ISSUES FOR CONGRESS

Experts and government officials have warned that narcotics trafficking may jeopardize the success of international efforts to secure and stabilize Afghanistan. U.S. officials believe that efforts to reverse the related trends of opium cultivation, drug trafficking, corruption, and insecurity must expand if broader strategic objectives are to be achieved. A broad interagency initiative to assist Afghan authorities in combating the narcotics trade has been developed, but the effectiveness of new U.S. efforts will not be apparent until later this year. Primary issues of interest to the Congress include program funding, the role of the U.S. military, and the scope and nature of eradication and development assistance initiatives. The 108th Congress addressed the issue of counternarcotics in Afghanistan in intelligence reform proposals, and the first session of the 109th Congress considered new counternarcotics policy proposals in relation to FY2006 appropriation and authorization requests.

Breaking the Narcotics-Insecurity Cycle

As noted above, narcotics trafficking and political instability remain intimately linked across Afghanistan. U.S. officials have identified narcotics trafficking as a primary barrier to the establishment of security and consider insecurity to be a primary barrier to successful counternarcotics operations. Critics of existing counternarcotics efforts have argued that Afghan authorities and their international partners remain reluctant to directly confront prominent individuals and groups involved in the opium trade because of their fear that confrontation will lead to internal security disruptions or armed conflict with drug-related groups. Afghan authorities have expressed their belief that "the beneficiaries of the drugs trade will resist attempts to destroy it," and have argued that "the political risk of internal instability caused by counternarcotics measures" must be balanced "with the requirement to project central authority nationally" for counternarcotics purposes.[87] Conflict and regional security disruptions have accompanied recent efforts to expand crop eradication programs and previous efforts to implement central government counternarcotics policies.

U.S. officials have identified rural security and national rule of law as prerequisites for effective counternarcotics policy implementation, while simultaneously identifying narcotics as a primary threat to security and stability.[88] Although an increasing number of Afghan police, security forces, and counternarcotics authorities are being trained by U.S. and coalition officials, the size and capability of Afghan forces may limit their power to effectively challenge entrenched drug trafficking groups and regional militia in the short term. Specifically, questions remain as to whether Afghan security and counternarcotics forces alone will be able to establish the security conditions necessary for the more robust eradication, interdiction, and alternative livelihood programs planned by U.S. and Afghan officials. From a political perspective, U.S. officials expect that parliamentary and provincial elections will contribute to the political legitimacy of government counternarcotics initiatives; however, the creation of sufficient political and military stability for effective counternarcotics operations is likely to remain a significant challenge. The death of several local contractor employees working on USAID alternative livelihood projects in May 2005 brought renewed urgency to these concerns.

Balancing Counterterrorism and Counternarcotics

In pursuing counterterrorism objectives, Afghan and coalition authorities also must consider difficult political choices when confronting corrupt officials, militia leaders, and narcotics traffickers. Regional and local militia commanders with alleged links to the opium trade played significant roles in coalition efforts to undermine the Taliban regime and capture Al Qaeda operatives, particularly in southeastern Afghanistan. Since late 2001, some of these figures have been incorporated into government and security structures, including positions of responsibility for enforcing counternarcotics policies.[89] According to Afghanistan scholar Barnett Rubin, "the empowerment and enrichment of the warlords who allied with the United States in the anti-Taliban efforts, and whose weapons and authority now enabled them to tax and protect opium traffickers," have provided the opium trade "with powerful new protectors."[90]

Pragmatic decisions taken since 2001 to prioritize counterterrorism operations and current plans to enforce counternarcotics policies more strictly may conflict with each other, forcing Afghan and coalition authorities to address seemingly difficult contradictions. "Tactical" coalition allies in militia and other irregular forces with ties to the drug trade may inhibit the ability of the central government to extend its authority and enforce its counternarcotics policies. These issues may weigh strongly in decision concerning the feasibility and prospects for success of continuing counterterrorism and counternarcotics operations. One senior Defense Department official has argued that U.S. counternarcotics strategy in Afghanistan must recognize "the impact the drug trade has on our other policy objectives, while complementing (and not competing with) our other efforts in furtherance of those objectives."[91]

Defining the Role of the U.S. Military

Some observers have argued that U.S. and coalition military forces should play an active, direct role in targeting the leaders and infrastructure of the opiate trade. Although U.S. Central Command (CENTCOM) officials have indicated that "the DoD counter-narcotics program in Afghanistan is a key element of our campaign against terrorism,"[92] military officials reportedly have resisted the establishment of a direct counternarcotics enforcement role for U.S. forces in Afghanistan. Critics claim that a direct enforcement role for U.S. or coalition forces may alienate them from the Afghan population, jeopardize ongoing counterterrorism missions that require Afghan intelligence support, and divert already stretched military resources from direct counter-insurgent and counterterrorism operations. According to the Defense Department, U.S. military forces are authorized to seize narcotics and related supplies encountered during the course of normal stability and counterterrorism operations.

Current U.S. policy calls for an expanded role for U.S. military forces in training, equipping, and providing intelligence and airlift support for Afghan counternarcotics teams but stops short of elevating narcotics targets to a direct priority for U.S. combat teams. Defense Department officials agreed in March 2005 to provide limited airlift assistance (four operations per month) to U.S. and Afghan interdiction teams using U.S. Blackhawk and Soviet-era Mi-8 helicopters. Successful interdiction operations in remote areas have been carried out on this basis since mid-March 2005, and further helicopter leasing and pilot training arrangements have been made.

The conference report (H.Rept. 109-360) on the National Defense Authorization Act for Fiscal Year 2006 (P.L. 109-163) did not include a provision included in the Senate version of the bill (S. 1042, Section 1033) that would have allowed the Defense Department to provide a range of technical and operational support to Afghan counternarcotics authorities based on an element of the National Defense Authorization Act for Fiscal Year 1991 (P.L. 101- 510, Section 1004). The Senate version would have authorized "the use of U.S. bases of operation or training facilities to facilitate the conduct of counterdrug activities in Afghanistan" in response to the Defense Department's request "to provide assistance in all aspects of counterdrug activities in Afghanistan, including detection, interdiction, and related criminal justice activities."[93] This would have included transportation of personnel and supplies, maintenance and repair of equipment, the establishment and operation of bases and training facilities, and training for Afghan law enforcement personnel.

Redefining Eradication

Proponents of swift, widespread eradication argued that destroying a large portion of the 2004-2005 opium poppy crop was necessary in order to establish a credible deterrent before opium production in Afghanistan reaches an irreversible level. Critics of widespread, near-term eradication argued that eradication in the absence of existing alternative livelihood options for Afghan farmers would contribute to the likelihood that farmers would continue to cultivate opium poppy in the future by deepening opium based debt and driving up opium prices.[94] U.S. and Afghan authorities maintain that the Central Poppy Eradication Force and governor-led eradication programs were effective in deterring and reducing some opium poppy cultivation in 2005. However, given recurrent clashes between eradication forces and farmers, some observers and officials have expressed concern about the safety and effectiveness of current ground-based eradication efforts. During the 2006 season, "poppy elimination program" teams will be in place in key opium poppy growing provinces to monitor and direct early season, locally-executed eradication activities. This strategy is designed to minimize violent farmer resistance to central government forces and give farming families time to plant replacement cash crops.

Aerial Eradication. Policy makers are likely to engage in further debate concerning the option of aerial poppy eradication and its possible risks and rewards. Afghan and U.S. authorities discussed the introduction of aerial eradication to Afghanistan in late 2004, but decided against initiating a program in early 2005 due to financial, logistical, and political considerations. Afghan President Hamid Karzai has expressed his categorical opposition to the use of aerial eradication, citing public health and environmental safety concerns.[95] Proponents of aerial eradication argue that the large amount of rural land under poppy cultivation in Afghanistan and poor road infrastructure makes ground-based eradication inefficient and subjects eradication teams to unnecessary security threats. Critics of aerial eradication argue that the mixed-crop cultivation patterns common throughout Afghanistan will expose legitimate food crops to damage and warn that aerial spraying may produce widespread, possibly violent resistance by villagers with vivid memories of centrally directed Soviet military campaigns to destroy food crops and agricultural infrastructure. The Senate report on the FY2005 supplemental appropriations bill (H.R. 1268) specifies that "none of the funds recommended by the Committee may be available for aerial eradication programs within Afghanistan absent a formal request by the President of Afghanistan seeking such support."

Reports of unauthorized aerial spraying in eastern Nangarhar province in mid-November 2004 angered Afghan officials and led to an investigation by the Afghan Ministries of Agriculture and Health of claims that crops had been sprayed with herbicides by unidentified aircraft. The government investigation reportedly revealed that unidentified chemicals were present in soil samples, that non-narcotic crops had been destroyed, and that an increase in related illnesses in local villages had occurred. Afghan officials cited U.S. control of Afghan airspace in their subsequent demands for an explanation. U.S. and British officials have denied involvement in the spraying and assured Afghan authorities that they support President Karzai's position.[96] In early December 2004, then-U.S. Ambassador to Afghanistan Zalmay Khalilzad suggested that "some drug-associated people" may have sprayed the crops "in order to create the sort of distrust and problem between Afghanistan and some of its allies."[97] Observers noted that the vocal negative reaction of the Afghan population and government to an alleged isolated spraying incident illustrates the type of popular opposition that may accompany any future aerial eradication program.

Afghan government officials would have to approve any future aerial spraying operations undertaken by U.S. or coalition forces in Afghanistan. Any future aerial eradication in Afghanistan also would require specific funding and the introduction of airframes and military support aircraft that exceed current U.S. capabilities in the region. Aerial eradication programs, if employed in the future, could feature the use of chemical herbicide such as the glyphosate compound currently approved for use in Colombia. The use of *mycoherbicides*, or fungal herbicides, also has been discussed. Opium poppy-specific mycoherbicide has been developed with U.N., U.K., and U.S. support at the Institute of Genetics and Experimental

Biology, a former Soviet biological warfare facility in Tashkent, Uzbekistan.[98] Mycoherbicide tests continue, including efforts by USDA's Agricultural Research Service , although USDA officials and others have expressed various concerns about the use of mycoherbicides for counternarcotics purposes.[99]

Pending Legislation and Counternarcotics Funding

Several intelligence reform proposals in the 108th Congress sought to address the 9/11 Commission's recommendation on expanding the U.S. commitment to Afghanistan's security and stability, including U.S. counternarcotics efforts. Section 7104 of the Intelligence Reform and Terrorism Prevention Act of 2004 (P.L. 108 —458) states the sense of Congress that "the President should make the substantial reduction of illegal drug production and trafficking in Afghanistan a priority in the Global War on Terrorism" and calls on the Administration to provide a secure environment for counternarcotics personnel and to specifically target narcotics operations that support terrorist organizations. The act also required the submission of a joint Defense and State Department report within 120 days of enactment that described current progress toward the reduction of poppy cultivation and heroin production in Afghanistan and provided detail on the extent to which drug profits support terrorist groups and anti-government elements in and around Afghanistan.

In the 109th Congress, H.R. 1437, the "Afghan Poppy Eradication and Prosperity Act of 2005," would authorize $1 billion to support a two-year USAID-led cash-for-work and poppy eradication pilot program in Afghanistan. Under the program, Afghan laborers would receive $10 per day of work. As noted above, cash-for-work programs are currently being administered by USAID and British authorities in Afghanistan. The bill would require an annual report from USAID on progress toward poppy eradication and alternative livelihood creation. The bill has been referred to the House Committee on International Relations.

Counternarcotics Funding. Funding for U.S. counternarcotics operations in Afghanistan consists of program administration costs and financial and material assistance to Afghan counternarcotics authorities. Table 4 displays the funding appropriated for U.S. counternarcotics activities in Afghanistan and related regional programs from FY2002 through FY2006. Table 5 describes the Administration's planned use for the counternarcotics funding included in the FY2005 supplemental appropriation (P.L. 109-13), which provided $758.15 million of the $773.15 million in supplemental FY2005 counternarcotics funding originally requested by the Administration. Under the terms of P.L. 109-13, the Comptroller General must conduct an audit of the use of all Economic Support Fund and International Narcotics Control and Law Enforcement funds for bilateral counternarcotics and alternative livelihood programs in Afghanistan obligated and expended during FY2005. The General Accounting Office is currently conducting this audit. Requests for further funding for Department of Defense counternarcotics activities in Afghanistan will likely be made as part of future supplemental funding requests.

Table 4. U.S. Counternarcotics Funding for Afghanistan by Source, FY2002-FY2006
($ million)

	FY2002		FY2003		FY2004			FY2005		FY2006
	Appropriated Funds	P.L. 107-206	Appropriated Funds	P.L. 108-11	Appropriated Funds	P.L. 108-106	P.L. 107-38	Appropriated Funds	P.L. 109-13	Appropriated Funds
Department of State	$3.00[a]	$60.00	$3.00[a]	$25.00		$170.00[a]	$50.00[a]	$89.28	$260.00	$235.00
Department of Defense		-	($2.92)	-	-	$73.00	-	$15.40	$242.00	-
Drug Enforcement Agency[d]	($0.58)	-				($3.96)		($7.67)	$7.65	$17.60[e]
USAID[f]		$9.99	$14.29		$53.55			$95.69	$248.50	$90.50[g]
Annual Total	$73.57		$45.21			$350.51		$966.19		$343.10

Sources: U.S. Agency for International Development - Budget Justifications to the Congress, Department of State - Congressional Budget Justifications for Foreign Operations, Office of the Secretary of Defense - Defense Budget Materials, Office of Management and Budget, and Legislative Information System.

[a] $3 million funding for Southwest Asia Initiative counternarcotics programs in Pakistan partially designed to restrict the flow of Afghan opiates.

[b] Of the $170 million in supplemental funds, $110 million was channeled toward police training and judicial reform programs.

[c] Reprogrammed funds appropriated as part of $40 billion Emergency Response Fund established in the aftermath of the September 11th attacks.

[d] On May 8, 2002, Congress approved a reprogramming of 17 positions and $15,125,000 in Violent Crime Reduction Program prior year funds to support the Drug Enforcement Administration's 'Operation Containment,' which targets heroin trafficking in Southwest Asia. The figures for FY2002-FY2005 reflect annual expenditure of the reprogrammed obligated funds. (DEA response to CRS request, October 2004.)

[e] FY2006 funds include $7.72 million for Operation Containment, $4.3 million to support Foreign Advisory Support Teams (FAST) teams, and $5.58 million for DEA offices in Kabul and Dushanbe, Tajikistan. New funds were not appropriated for the creation of a DEA office in Dubai, United Arab Emirates authorized in House Report 109-272.

[f] USAID figures for FY2002-FY2005 reflect funds applied to USAID's "Agriculture" and "Agriculture and Alternative Livelihoods" programs (Program #306-001).

[g] USAID will shift activities currently funded through its "Agriculture and Alternative Livelihoods" program to a "Thriving Economy Led by the Private Sector" program (Program #306-YYY). Relevant funds include $90.5 million to "Develop and Expand Alternative Development."

Table 5. Planned Use of FY2005 Supplemental Appropriations, P.L. 109-13

($ million)

Agency	Amount	Proposed Purpose
Department of Defense (Drug Interdiction and Counter-Drug Activities)	$242	Funds for training, equipment, intelligence, infrastructure, and information operations related to the campaign against narcotics trafficking and narcotics-related terrorist activities in Afghanistan and the Central Asia area. Of this amount, $70 million restored funding to other DoD counternarcotics activities from which funds were used to finance counter-drug assistance to Afghanistan. P.L. 109-13 limited the provision of assistance to $34 million for the Afghan government and allows for the delivery of individual and crew-served weapons for counter-drug security forces. (Note: The Administration's original request was for $257 million.)
Department of State (International Narcotics Control and Law Enforcement Account)	$260	Funds to continue the expanded counternarcotics effort in Afghanistan begun in FY2005. Of the total amount requested, $95 million replenished funding advanced to start expanded crop eradication, establishment of a National Interdiction Unit, prosecution of drug traffickers, and public information programs. The remaining $165 million supported the Department of State's contribution to expanded efforts in eradication ($89 million), interdiction ($51 million), law enforcement ($22 million), and public information ($3 million).
United States Agency for International Development (Economic Support Fund)	$248.5	Funds to support alternative livelihoods programs. A portion ($138.5 million) of the amount replenished reconstruction and development aid accounts that had been drawn on previously to create alternative livelihood programs in late 2004 and early 2005. The balance ($110 million) is being used to expand alternative livelihood programs beyond pilot provinces.
Drug Enforcement Agency	$7.65	Funds to support and equip DEA's Foreign Advisory Support Teams (FAST) and to provide operational support for a 100-member Afghan Narcotics Interdiction Unit (NIU).
Total FY2005 Supplemental Appropriation	**$758.15**	

Source: P.L. 109-13 and Office of Management and Budget, Estimate #1: Emergency Supplemental — Ongoing Military Operations in the War on Terror; Reconstruction Activities in Afghanistan; Tsunami Relief and Reconstruction; and Other Purposes, February 14, 2005.

APPENDIX A

Cited Field Surveys

Jonathan Goodhand, "From Holy War to Opium War: A Case Study of the Opium Economy in North Eastern Afghanistan," Peacebuilding and Complex Emergencies Working Paper Series, Paper No. 5, University of Manchester, 1999.

Frank Kenefick, and Larry Morgan, "Opium in Afghanistan: People and Poppies —The Good Evil," Chemonics International Inc. for USAID, February 5, 2004.

Aga Kahn Foundation, "Badakhshan Province: Suggestions for an Area Development Based Counter-narcotics Strategy," April 2004.

David Mansfield, "Coping Strategies, Accumulated Wealth and Shifting Markets: The Story of Opium Poppy Cultivation in Badakhshan 2000-2003," Agha Khan Development Network, January 2004.

David Mansfield, "Alternative Development in Afghanistan: The Failure of Quid Pro Quo," International Conference on the Role of Alternative Development in Drug Control and Development Cooperation, January 2002.

Adam Pain, "The Impact of the Opium Poppy Economy on Household Livelihoods: Evidence from the Wakhan Corridor and Khustak Valley in Badakhshan," Aga Kahn Development Network, Badakhshan Programme, January 2004.

UNODC, "An Analysis of the Process of Expansion of Opium Cultivation to New Districts in Afghanistan," Strategic Study #1, June 1998.

UNODC, "The Dynamics of the Farmgate Opium Trade and the Coping Strategies of Opium Traders," Strategic Study #2, October 1998.

UNODC, "The Role of Opium as an Informal Credit," Preliminary Strategic Study #3, January 1999.

UNODC, "Access to Labour: The Role of Opium in the Livelihood Strategies of Itinerant Harvesters Working in Helmand Province, Afghanistan," Strategic Study #4, June 1999.

UNODC, "The Role of Women in Opium Poppy Cultivation in Afghanistan," Strategic Study #6, June 2000.

REFERENCES

[1]   United Nations Office on Drugs and Crime (UNODC)/Government of Afghanistan Counternarcotics Directorate (CND), Afghanistan Opium Survey 2004, Nov. 2004.

[2]   See Jonathan C. Randal, "Afghanistan's Promised War on Opium," *Washington Post*, Nov. 2, 1978, and Stuart Auerbach, "New Heroin Connection: Afghanistan and Pakistan Supply West With Opium," *Washington Post*, Oct. 11, 1979.

[3]   UNODC/Afghan Gov., Afghanistan Opium Survey 2004, Nov. 2004, pp. 105-7.

[4]   See Barnett Rubin, "Road to Ruin: Afghanistan's Booming Opium Industry," Center for International Cooperation, Oct. 7, 2004, and the World Bank Country Economic Report -Afghanistan: State Building, Sustaining Growth, and Reducing Poverty, Sept. 9, 2004.

[5]   Author interviews with U.S., U.N., and coalition officials, Kabul, Afghanistan, Jan. 2005.

[6]   In 1978, pro-Communist Afghan officials reportedly requested "a lot of assistance from abroad, especially economic help, to help replace farmers' incomes derived from opium poppy cultivation." Randal, Washington Post, Nov. 2, 1978.

[7]   Agreement on Provisional Arrangements in Afghanistan Pending the Re-establishment of Permanent Government Institutions [The Bonn Agreement], Dec. 5, 2001.

[8]   See Arthur Bonner, "Afghan Rebel's Victory Garden: Opium," *New York Times*, June 18, 1986, and Mary Thornton, "Sales of Opium Reportedly Fund Afghan Rebels," *Washington Post*, Dec. 17, 1983.

[9]   See James Rupert and Steve Coll, "U.S. Declines to Probe Afghan Drug Trade: Rebels, Pakistani Officers Implicated," *Washington Post*, May 13, 1990; Jim Lobe, "Drugs: U.S. Looks Other Way In Afghanistan and Pakistan," *Inter Press Service*, May 18, 1990; John F. Burns, "U.S. Cuts Off Arms to Afghan Faction," *New York Times*, Nov. 19, 1989; Kathy Evans, "Money is the Drug" *The Guardian* (UK), Nov. 11, 1989; and Lawrence Lifschultz, "Bush, Drugs and Pakistan: Inside the Kingdom of Heroin," *The Nation*, Nov. 14, 1988.

[10]   The Taliban government collected an agricultural tax (approximately 10%, paid in kind), known as *ushr,* and a traditional Islamic tithe known as *zakat* (variable percentages). The Taliban also taxed opium traders and transport syndicates involved in the transportation of opiates. UNODC, "The Opium Economy in Afghanistan," pp. 92, 127-8.

[11]   UNODC, "The Opium Economy in Afghanistan," p. 92.

[12]   In December 2001, then Assistant Secretary of State for International Narcotics and Law Enforcement Affairs Rand Beers stated that the Taliban had not banned opium cultivation "out of kindness, but because they wanted to regulate the market: They simply produced too much opium." Marc Kaufman, "Surge in Afghan Poppy Crop Is Forecast," *Washington Post*, Dec. 25, 2001. See **Table 1** and UNODC, Opium Economy in Afghanistan, p. 57.

[13]   The Bonn Agreement, Dec. 5, 2001.

[14]   Analysis in this report relating to the motives and methods of Afghan farmers, land owners, and traffickers is based on the findings of the UNODC's "Strategic Studies" series on Afghanistan's opium economy and a series of commissioned development reports by David Mansfield, the Aga Khan Foundation, Frank Kenefick and Larry Morgan, Adam Pain, and others. UNODC Strategic Studies reports are available at [http://www.unodc.org/ pakistan/en/publications.html]. Complete citations are provided in Appendix A.

[15]   David Mansfield, "The Economic Superiority of Illicit Drug Production: Myth and Reality," International Conference on Alternative Development in Drug Control and Cooperation, Aug. 2001.

[16]   See UNODC, "An Analysis of the Process of Expansion of Opium Poppy Cultivation to New Districts in Afghanistan," June 1998.

[17]   UNODC, "Afghanistan Opium Survey 2003," p. 8.

[18]   See UNODC, "The Opium Economy in Afghanistan," pp. 129-40, 165-8.

[19]   UNODC, "The Opium Economy in Afghanistan," pp. 139, 158.

[20]   "The involvement of Afghan groups/individuals is basically limited to the opium production, the trade of opium within Afghanistan, the transformation of some of the

opium into morphine and heroin, and to some extent, the trafficking of opiates to neighboring countries." UNODC, The Opium Economy in Afghanistan, p. 64.

[21] See Tamara Makarenko, "Bumper Afghan Narcotics Crop Indicates Resilience of Networks," *Jane's Intelligence Review*, May 1, 2002.

[22] Testimony of Robert B. Charles, Assistant Secretary of State for International Narcotics and Law Enforcement Affairs, House International Relations Committee, Sept. 23, 2004.

[23] See UNODC, "The Opium Economy in Afghanistan," p. 69, and Report of the Secretary-General on the Situation in Afghanistan and its Implications for International Peace and Security, Aug. 12, 2004.

[24] UNODC/CND, Afghanistan Opium Survey 2004, p. 66.

[25] The Afghan government's Central Eradication Force reportedly was "rocketed by furious villagers" during a 2004 eradication mission in Wardak province outside of Kabul. *Reuters*, Pressure on Karzai as Afghan Drug Problem Worsens, Oct. 5, 2004.

[26] See *Agence France Presse*, "Afghanistan Deploys 67 Million Dollars in War on Drugs," Apr. 11, 2002, and Anwar Iqbal, "War on Dug Begins in Afghanistan," *United Press International*, Apr. 10, 2002.

[27] Department of State, International Narcotics Control Strategy Report, Mar. 2005.

[28] *Agence France Presse*, "Curbing Rampant Afghan Opium Trade Will Take Karzai Years," Dec. 5, 2004.

[29] See *New York Times*, "7 Are Killed in a Clash of Afghan Militias," Feb. 9, 2004, and FBIS IAP20040707000101 - Afghanistan Briefing, July 5-7, 2004.

[30] See Victoria Burnett, "Outlook Uncertain: Can Afghanistan Take the Next Step to Building a State?" *Financial Times*, Aug. 19, 2004; Carol Harrington, "Ruthless Dostum a Rival for Karzai," *Toronto Star*, Sept. 20, 2004; and Jurgen Dahlkamp, Susanne Koelbl, and Georg Mascolo, (tr. Margot Bettauer Dembo), "Bundeswehr: Poppies, Rocks, Shards of Trouble," *Der Spiegel* [Germany], Nov. 10, 2003.

[31] Human Rights Watch, "The Rule of the Gun." Sept. 2004.

[32] Anne Barnard and Farah Stockman, "U.S. Weighs Role in Heroin War in Afghanistan," *Boston Globe*, Oct. 20, 2004.

[33] World Bank, State Building..., p. 87.

[34] International Monetary Fund, IMF Country Report No. 05/33 - Islamic State of Afghanistan: 2004 Article IV Consultation and Second Review, Feb. 2005.

[35] Author interviews with U.S. officials in Kabul, Afghanistan, Jan. 2005.

[36] Liz Sly, "Opium Cash Fuels Terror, Experts Say," *Chicago Tribune*, Feb. 9, 2004; John Fullerton, "Live and Let Live for Afghan Warlords, Drug Barons," *Reuters*, Feb. 5, 2002.

[37] See U.S. v. Bashir Noorzai, U.S. District Court, Southern District of New York, S1 05 Cr. 19, Apr. 25, 2005.

[38] See U.S. v. Baz Mohammed, U.S. District Court, Southern District of New York, S14 03 Cr. 486 [DC], Oct. 25, 2005.

[39] Tim McGirk, "Terrorism's Harvest," *Time Magazine* [Asia], Aug. 2, 2004.

[40] Haji Bashir reportedly described his time with U.S. forces in the following terms: "I spent my days and nights comfortably... I was like a guest, not a prisoner." *CBS Evening News*, "Newly Arrived US Army Soldiers Find it Difficult to Adjust...," Feb. 7, 2002.

[41] Steve Inskeep, "Afghanistan's Opium Trade," *National Public Radio*, Apr. 26, 2002.

[42] See Mark Corcoran, "America's Blind Eye," Australian Broadcasting Corporation, *Foreign Correspondent*, Apr. 10, 2002.

[43] Defense Department response to CRS inquiry, Nov. 12, 2004.

[44] Drug Enforcement Agency, "The Availability of Southwest Asian Heroin in the United States," May 1996.

[45] Drug Enforcement Agency, "Heroin Signature Program: 2002," Mar. 2004.

[46] In 1985, the DEA developed evidence against a wealthy Afghan national alleged to have been "involved in supplying Afghan rebels with weapons in exchange for heroin and hashish, portions of which were eventually distributed in Western Europe and the United States." See Select Committee on Narcotics Abuse and Control - Annual Report 1985, Dec. 19, 1986, p. 58; See U.S. v. Roeffen, et al. [U.S. District Court of New Jersey (Trenton), 86-00013-01] and U.S. v. Wali [860 F.2d 588 (3d Cir.1988)].

[47] Marcus W. Brauchli, "Pakistan's Wild Frontier Breeds Trouble — Drugs, Terrorism Could Overflow Into Other Regions," *Wall Street Journal*, June 3,1993; Kathy Gannon, "Pakistan Extradites Suspected Drug Dealers to U.S.," *Associated Press*, Oct. 16, 1993; Jeanne King, "U.S. Denies Bail to Alleged Pakistani Drug Baron," *Reuters*, Dec. 21, 1995; and Ron Synovitz, "U.S. Indicts 11 In Connection With Drug Ring," *RFE/RL*, Sep. 17, 2003.

[48] U.S. v. Afridi, et. al., [U.S. District Court of Maryland, (Baltimore), AW-03-0211].

[49] Testimony of DEA Administrator Karen Tandy before the House International Relations Committee, Feb. 12, 2004.

[50] James W. Crawley, "U.S. Warships Pinching Persian Gulf Drug Trade," *San Diego Union-Tribune*, February 9, 2004, and Tony Perry, "2 Convicted of Seeking Missiles for Al Qaeda Ally," *Los Angeles Times*, Mar. 4, 2004.

[51] Defense Department officials report that steps are taken to educate U.S. troops serving in Afghanistan about the dangers of narcotics use and to monitor and prevent drug use. Testimony of Lt. Gen. Walter L. Sharp, Director of Strategic Plans (J-5), Before the House International Relations Committee, Sept. 23, 2004.

[52] *Agence France Presse*, "Russia plans anti-drug centre in Kabul," Mar. 29, 2005.

[53] House of Commons (UK) - Foreign Affairs Committee, Seventh Report, July 21, 2004.

[54] For more information see Tamara Makarenko, "Crime, Terror and the Central Asian Drug Trade," Harvard Asia Quarterly, vol. 6, no. 3 (Summer 2002), and Integrated Regional Information Networks (IRIN) Report, "Central Asia: Regional Impact of the Afghan Heroin Trade ," U.N. Office for the Coordination of Humanitarian Affairs (OCHA), Aug. 2004. Available at [http://www.irinnews.org/webspecials/opium/regOvr.asp].

[55] UNODC, "The Opium Economy in Afghanistan," p. 33, 35.

[56] For more information, see the World Health Organization's Epidemiological Fact Sheets on HIV/AIDS at [http://www.who.int/GlobalAtlas/PDFFactory/HIV/ index.asp], and Julie Stachowiak and Chris Beyrer, HIV Follows Heroin Trafficking Routes," Open Society Institute - Central Eurasia Project, Available at [http://www.eurasianet.org/health.security/ presentations/hiv_trafficking.shtml].

[57] For more on Central Asian security and public health, including information on narcotics trafficking, organized crime, and terrorism see CRS Report RL30294, *Central Asia's Security: Issues and Implications for U.S. Interests*, and CRS Report RL30970,

Health in Russia and Other Soviet Successor States: Context and Issues for Congress, both by Jim Nichol.

[58] IRIN Report, "Tajikistan: Stemming the Heroin Tide," OCHA, Sept. 13, 2004. Available at [http://www.irinnews.org/webspecials/opium/regTaj.asp].

[59] *Agence France Presse*, "Tajiks to Take Over Patrolling Half of Tajik-Afghan Border From Russians," Oct. 1, 2004.

[60] See Rukhshona Najmiddinova, "Tajikistan Arrests Anti-Drug Agency Head," *Associated Press*, Aug. 6, 2004.

[61] *Moscow Interfax*, "Russia Says Around 9 Tonnes of Afghan Drugs Seized in International Operation," Nov. 13, 2005. FBIS Document CEP20051113029009.

[62] Ambassador Wendy Chamberlain, "Transcript: Hearing of the Subcommittee on Asia and the Pacific of the House International Relations Committee," Federal News Service, Mar. 20, 2003. See also, Ahmed Rashid, Taliban, Yale University Press, 2000, pp. 120-2, and Barnett Rubin, The Fragmentation of Afghanistan, Yale University Press, 2002, pp. 197-8. See also Rubin, Testimony Before the House Foreign Affairs Subcommittee on Europe and the Middle East and Asian and Pacific Affairs, Mar. 7, 1990.

[63] Jason Barnes, "The Desert Village that Feeds UK's Heroin Habit," *The Observer* (UK), Dec. 12, 1999.

[64] The Bonn Agreement, Dec. 5, 2001.

[65] Afghan Religious Scholars Urge End To Opium Economy, *Associated Press*, Aug. 3, 2004.

[66] Transitional Islamic State of Afghanistan, National Drug Control Strategy, May 18, 2003. Available at [http://www.cnd.gov.af/ndcs.html].

[67] Islamic Republic of Afghanistan, The 1384 (2005) Counter Narcotics Implementation Plan, Feb. 16, 2005. Available at [http://www.cnd.gov.af/ imp_plan.htm].

[68] Statement of James E. Stahlman, Assistant Operations Officer, U.S. Central Command, Committee on House Government Reform Subcommittee on Criminal Justice, Drug Policy, and Human Resources, May 10, 2005.

[69] *Agence France Presse*, "Afghanistan Launches Poppy Eradication Force," Feb. 2, 2005.

[70] David Shelby, "United States to Help Afghanistan Attack Narcotics Industry," *Washington File*, U.S. Department of State, Nov. 17, 2004.

[71] Ibid.

[72] "Afghan Religious Scholars Urge End To Opium Economy," *Associated Press*, Aug. 3, 2004.

[73] Interior Ministry spokesman Lutfullah Mashal. *Agence France Presse*, "Afghan Drugs Kingpin Seized by US was Untouchable in Afghanistan: Experts," Apr. 27, 2005.

[74] Author interview with U.S. officials, Kabul, Afghanistan, Jan. 2005 and Washington, D.C., May 2005.

[75] Sources: Author interviews with USAID officials, Kabul, Afghanistan, January 2005; and USAID Alternative Livelihoods Conference, Washington, D.C., May 2005.

[76] USAID has established a "Good Performer's Fund" to reward districts that end cultivation with high visibility infrastructure development projects.

[77] USAID, Alternative Livelihoods Update: Issue 3, Apr. 1-15, 2005; author consultation with USAID Afghanistan Desk Office, Jan. 2006.

[78] Author consultation with USAID Afghanistan Desk Office, Jan. 2006.

[79] DEA Administrator Karen P. Tandy, House Committee on Government Reform Subcommittee on Criminal Justice, Drug Policy and Human Resources, Feb. 26, 2004.

[80] Ibid.

[81] Statement of Michael Braun, Chief of Operations - Drug Enforcement Agency, Before the House Committee on International Relations, Mar. 17, 2005.

[82] Defense Department response to CRS inquiry, Nov. 12, 2004.

[83] Testimony of Thomas W. O'Connell, Assistant Secretary of Defense for Special Operations and Low-intensity Conflict Before House International Relations Committee, Feb. 12, 2004; and Defense Department response to CRS inquiry, Nov. 12, 2004.

[84] Statement of Lennard J. Wolfson, Assistant Deputy Director for Supply Reduction, Office of National Drug Control Policy, Committee on House Government Reform Subcommittee on Criminal Justice, Drug Policy, and Human Resources, May 10, 2005.

[85] Philip Webster, "4,000 Troops to be Sent to Troubled Afghan Province," *The Times* (London), Jan. 25, 2006.

[86] Author conversation with DEA official, Washington, D.C., May 2005.

[87] National Drug Control Strategy, Transitional Islamic State of Afghanistan, May 18, 2003.

[88] "Poppy cultivation is likely to continue until responsible governmental authority is established throughout the country and until rural poverty levels can be reduced via provision of alternative livelihoods and increased rural incomes... Drug processing and trafficking can be expected to continue until security is established and drug law enforcement capabilities can be increased. " State Department, INCSR, Mar. 2005.

[89] See Syed Saleem Shahzad, "U.S. Turns to Drug Baron to Rally Support," *Asia Times*, Dec. 4, 2001; Charles Clover and Peronet Despeignes, "Murder Undermines Karzai Government," *Financial Times*, July 8, 2002; Susan B. Glasser, "U.S. Backing Helps Warlord Solidify Power," *Washington Post*, Feb. 18, 2002; Ron Moreau and Sami Yousafzai, with Donatella Lorch, "Flowers of Destruction," *Newsweek*, July 14, 2003; Andrew North, "Warlord Tells Police Chief to Go," *BBC News*, July 12, 2004; Steven Graham, "Group: Warlords to Hinder Afghan Election," *Associated Press*, Sept. 28, 2004; and Anne Barnard and Farah Stockman, "U.S. Weighs Role in Heroin War in Afghanistan," *Boston Globe*, Oct. 20, 2004.

[90] Rubin, "Road to Ruin: Afghanistan's Booming Opium Industry," Oct. 7, 2004.

[91] Testimony of Mary-Beth Long, Deputy Assistant Secretary of Defense for Counternarcotics before the House Committee on International Relations, Mar. 17, 2005.

[92] "U.S. CENTCOM views narcotrafficking as a significant obstacle to the political and economic reconstruction of Afghanistan... Local terrorist and criminal leaders have a vested interest in using the profits from narcotics to oppose the central government and undermine the security and stability of Afghanistan." Major Gen. John Sattler, USMC, Dir. of Operations-US CENTCOM before the House Committee on Government Reform Subcommittee on Criminal Justice, Drug Policy, and Human Resources, Apr. 21, 2004.

[93] S.Rept. 109-69.

[94] Afghanistan's National Drug Control Strategy expects that farmers with a "legacy of debt" will find that their "situation will be exacerbated by eradication efforts." A

September 2004 British government report argues that "if not targeted properly, eradication can have the reverse effect and encourage farmers to cultivate more poppy to pay off increased debts." Response of the Secretary of State for Foreign and Commonwealth Affairs (UK) to the Seventh Report from the House of Commons Foreign Affairs Committee, Sep. 2004.

[95] Office of the Spokesperson to the President — Transitional Islamic State of Afghanistan, "About the Commitment by the Government of Afghanistan to the Fight Against Narcotics and Concerns About the Aerial Spraying of Poppy Fields."

[96] See David Brunnstrom, "Afghans Committed to Drug War But Against Spraying," *Reuters*, Nov. 19, 2004; and Stephen Graham, "Afghan Government Concerned at Spraying of Opium Crops by Mystery Aircraft," *Associated Press*, Nov. 30, 2004.

[97] Carlotta Gall, "Afghan Poppy Farmers Say Mystery Spraying Killed Crops," *New York Times*, Dec. 5, 2004, and *Reuters*, "U.S. Says Drug Lords May Have Sprayed Afghan Opium," Dec. 2, 2004.

[98] See Nicholas Rufford, "Secret Bio-weapon Can Wipe Out Afghan Heroin," *Sunday Times* (London), May 26, 2002; Antony Barnett, "UK in Secret Biological War on Drugs," *Observer* (London), Sept. 17, 2000; Juanita Darling, "Fungi May Be the Newest Recruits in War on Drugs Colombia," *Los Angeles Times*, Aug. 30, 2000.

[99] According to a USDA official, "The Department of Agriculture, as an agency, is opposed to the idea [of using mycoherbicides in Afghanistan]: The science is far from complete; There are real environmental and possible human health negative implications; There are very real image problems... the use of any agent like this would be portrayed as biological warfare." USDA response to CRS inquiry, Oct. 19, 2004.

In: Illegal Drugs and Governmental Policies
Editor: Lee V. Barton, pp. 137-142

ISBN 978-1-60021-351-9
© 2007 Nova Science Publishers, Inc.

Chapter 6

METHAMPHETAMINE: LEGISLATION AND ISSUES IN THE 109TH CONGRESS*

Celinda Franco

SUMMARY

Illicit methamphetamine (MA) production and use are longstanding and severe problems in some states. In recent years they have spread increasingly widely, emerging as an object of heightened federal concern. During the 109th Congress, over twenty-five bills have been introduced to address the MA problem. MA abuse has implications for public health, child welfare, crime and public safety, border security, and international relations. This report provides a brief overview of MA abuse, production, trafficking, and of the federal methamphetamine-specific programs, and legislation that is being actively considered by the 109th Congress.

BACKGROUND

Methamphetamine (MA), a drug of the amphetamine group, is a powerful and addictive central nervous system stimulant. Originally used as a nasal decongestant and bronchiodialator, MA has been marketed under the trade names Methedrine® and Desoxyn® since the 1940s. MA is currently used to treat medical conditions, including narcolepsy, attention deficit disorder/attention deficit/hyperactivity disorder (ADD/ADHD), and obesity.

Illicit MA production and use are longstanding and severe problems in some states, and there are indications that MA abuse may be rising.[1] While abuse of this drug may vary by region of the country, MA use has spread to every state, despite being more pervasive in the West and Midwest than in the Northeastern part of the country.[2] Methamphetamine can be administered orally, nasally, by injection, and, in the powder form that resembles granulated crystals, often referred to as "ice," by smoking.[3] MA can cause convulsions, stroke, cardiac arrhythmia, and hyperthermia. Chronic use can lead to irreversible brain and heart damage, psychotic behavior including paranoid ideation, visual and auditory hallucinations, and rages

---

* Excerpted from CRS Report RS22325, Updated November 17, 2005

and violence. Withdrawal from the drug can induce paranoia, depression, anxiety, and fatigue.[4]

The issue before the Congress is how to address the problem of illicit MA use and its production in clandestine labs. Among some options, Congress is considering legislation that would further regulate MA precursor chemicals, enhance penalties for drug trafficking, or increase funding for MA-specific state and local law enforcement programs.

SOURCES OF ILLICIT METHAMPHETAMINE

According to the Drug Enforcement Agency (DEA), most illicit MA available in the U.S. is produced in laboratories located in Mexico or California, that is then distributed across the country using existing drug trafficking routes. DEA estimates that between 65-80% of all MA consumed in the U.S. is smuggled into the country from Mexico.[5]

MA Precursor Chemicals. The precursor chemicals necessary for producing MA are ephedrine, pseudoephedrine, or phenylpropanolamine,[6] which are commonly found in over-the-counter (OTC) cold and sinus medicines that have legitimate uses, and are easily available in retail quantities from any drug store. These MA precursor chemicals are regulated (see below), yet the possibilities for criminal diversion exist and have been aggressively exploited by illicit MA producers.

Clandestine "Super" Laboratories. As noted above, most illicit MA available in the U.S. is produced in large clandestine laboratories in Mexico and California.[7] In these large labs, known as "super labs,"[8] MA is produced by persons linked to established drug trafficking organizations (DTOs). These super labs most often obtain the precursor chemicals they need to produce MA in wholesale quantities on the international market. According to DEA, much of the MA precursor chemical, pseudoephedrine, is either purchased by the DTOs from one of seven chemical companies in Europe, Asia, and the Far East and smuggled into Mexico and the U.S., or diverted from legitimate sources.

Small Clandestine Labs. The smallest of the domestic labs are those commonly referred to as "mom-and-pop" labs that can be set up in home kitchens, motel rooms, or other similar spaces, and produce MA with pseudoephedrine exclusively from retail stores. These small labs produce illicit MA using one of several relatively simple methods. The methods most commonly used are ones that use OTC cold medicines containing pseudoephedrine, and other ingredients including acetone, hydrochloric acid, sodium hydroxide, ether, anhydrous ammonia, cat litter, antifreeze, and drain cleaner.

CURRENT LAW

Methamphetamine is a Schedule II drug under the *Controlled Substances Act of 1970* (CSA).[9] Under the CSA (21 U.S.C. §801 et seq.), penalties for MA vary by the amount an individual is in possession of when arrested and can include a fine and a mandatory minimum sentence. The CSA has evolved over the years as the scope of the act was expanded to include regulation of chemicals used in the illicit production of a controlled substance.[10] Precursor chemicals used to produce MA were brought under CSA control by the *Comprehensive Methamphetamine Control Act of 1996* (MCA), which also increased penalties for the trafficking and manufacturing of MA and its precursor listed chemicals, and expanded the controls on products containing the licit chemicals ephedrine, pseudoephedrine, and phenylpropanolamine (PPA). The *Methamphetamine Penalty Enhancement Act of 1998* lowered certain quantity thresholds for mandatory minimum trafficking penalties. The *Methamphetamine Anti-Proliferation Act* (MAPA) of 2000 reduced the thresholds for single OTC purchases of pseudoephedrine and phenylpropanolamine products to 9 grams and required the use of "blister packs" for products of more than 3 grams of pseudoephedrine. MAPA also strengthened sentencing guidelines, provided training for federal and state law enforcement officers handling chemicals from clandestine MA labs, and expanded substance abuse prevention efforts.

FEDERAL PROGRAMS[11]

Many agencies and bureaus within DOJ are involved in addressing the issue of illicit MA. Chief among them is the Drug Enforcement Agency (DEA). Through collaborations with the Federal Bureau of Investigation (FBI), and numerous task forces, including the Organized Crime Drug Enforcement Task Force (OCDETF) and the High Intensity Drug Trafficking Areas (HIDTA), and collaborations with other federal, state and local law enforcement, DEA targets drug traffickers across the country and internationally to stem the flow of illegal drugs in the United States. According to DEA, the total amount of MA interdicted at the U.S. - Mexico border in 2002, had increased by over 17% since 1999.[12]

The "Meth Hot Spots" program under the Community Oriented Policing Services (COPS) program is a grant program that *specifically* provides funding for a broad range of initiatives designed to assist state and local law enforcement undertake anti-MA initiatives. For FY2006, the Meth Hot Spots program received appropriations of $63.6 million (H.Rept. 109-272). Between 1998 and mid-2004, the COPS program has provided over $350 million nationwide to address the MA problem.[13]

Additional DOJ grant programs provide assistance for a broad range of programs and initiatives which *can* include anti-MA efforts. **Table 1** provides DOJ funding for grants, *including Meth Hot Spots grants*, awarded to state and local programs related to anti-MA initiatives across the country. For the period FY2000 - FY2005, 470 grants were provided, totaling $263.8 million.

Table 1. DOJ Awards Relating to Methamphetamine Initiatives, FY2000 - FY2005

Fiscal Year	2000	2001	2002	2003	2004	2005
Total Grant Amount (in millions)	$12.6	$32.5	$52.5	$62.9	$55.0	$48.3
Total Number of Grants	23	44	118	101	97	87

Source: DOJ, Bureau of Justice Assistance, totals as of October 19, 2005.

LEGISLATION IN THE 109TH CONGRESS

Numerous bills have been introduced in the 109th Congress to curb MA use, trafficking, and production (see **Table 2**); two, S. 103 and H.R. 3889, have been reported from committees for consideration on the floors of the House and Senate. H.R. 3199, the *USA*

PATRIOT Improvement and Reauthorization Act of 2005, was passed by the House on July 21, 2005 and by the Senate on July 29, 2005. The conference report for H.R. 3199 was reported out of conference on November 9, 2005. It is anticipated that a compromise version of elements of both S. 103 and H.R. 3889 will be added to the conference report for H.R. 3199. The conference report for H.R. 3199 is expected to be voted on by the House and Senate by November 19, 2005.

S. 103, as amended and reported by the Senate Judiciary Committee on July 28, 2005, would limit the sale of pseudoephedrine to 7.5 grams in a 30-day period, except by prescription and sold by licensed pharmacist or pharmacy technician; establish a registry for purchasers of pseudoephedrine products; and permit limited sales of such products at airports. S. 103 would provide grants for drug endangered children, local grants for MA substance abuse treatment, and grants for MA research and training; authorize grants to states for establishing precursor monitoring programs; authorize appropriations of $15 million for COPS MA-training; permit the use of Meth Hot Spots grants for MA-related hiring, and authorize $5 million for hiring prosecutors to prosecute MA cases.

H.R. 3889, was introduced by Representative Souder on September 22, 2005, and reported by the House Judiciary Committee on November 11, 2005. The bill would reduce OTC purchases of pseudoephedrine from the current limit of 9 grams to only 3.6 grams; repeal the "blister pack" exemption; require the Attorney General to establish domestic production quotas for MA precursors and restrict their importation; require registered importers to file advance notice of their precursor customers with DOJ; and further regulate foreign imports of precursor chemicals. H.R. 3889 would require efforts to prevent smuggling of MA into the U.S. from Mexico; make it easier to convict MA "kingpins;"and give judges discretion in sentencing for crimes involving MA precursors. The bill would authorize $99 million annually for FY2006-FY2010 for the Meth Hot Spots program and $20 million annually in FY2006 and FY2007, for grants for programs that aid children living in a MA-lab home. H.R. 3889 would also give additional authority to the Department of Transportation (DOT) and the Environmental Protection Agency (EPA) to enforce environmental regulations against MA cooks and treat contaminated areas as hazardous waste sites. The bill was also marked up and reported by the House Committee on Energy and Commerce on November 16, 2005.

Table 2. Methamphetamine Legislation in the 109th Congress

Legislative Response	Bills Containing Relevant Provisions
Expand regulation of OTC medication	H.R. 314, H.R. 1056, H.R. 1083, H.R. 1350, H.R. 1378, H.R. 1446, H.R. 3324, H.R. 3513, H.R. 3568, H.R. 3889, S. 103, S. 430
Elimination of "blister pack" exemption	H.R. 1350, H.R. 1446, H.R. 3889
Adding pseudoephedrine to Schedule V or listed chemical	H.R. 314, S. 103, H.R. 1083, H.R. 1378, H.R. 3955,
Limit on amount of OTC purchase	H.R. 1056, H.R. 1446, H.R. 3889
Registry or 'behind-the-counter' sales	H.R. 314, S. 103, H.R. 3955
Training for retailers - MethWatch	H.R. 1056, H.R. 3513
Retail distributors of pseudoephedrine	H.R. 1056, H.R. 3955, H.R. 3889

Table 2. continued

Legislative Response	Bills Containing Relevant Provisions
Enhanced criminal penalties for MA or precursor chemicals	H.R. 1395, H.R. 1056, H.R. 3513, H.R. 3755, H.R. 3756, H.R. 3889
Import controls on MA and precursors	H.R. 1056, H.R. 3955, H.R. 3889
Precursor chemicals monitoring grants	H.R. 314, H.R. 1446, H.R. 3889, S. 103
MA Laboratory Remediation	H.R. 13, H.R. 314, H.R. 798, H.R. 3889,
Regulation of imports of precursor chemicals	H.R. 1446, H.R. 3889
Regulation/quotas for MA precursors	H.R. 1446, H.R. 2601, H.R. 3889
COPS Meth Hot Spots Grants	H.R. 314, S. 103, H.R. 1446, H.R. 3889*
COPS grants for hiring local prosecutors	H.R. 314, S. 103
Grants for services for drug-endangered children	H.R. 314, S. 103, H.R. 1395, H.R. 1446, H.R. 2335, H.R. 3889*
Grants for MA abuse treatment	H.R. 314, S. 103, H.R. 1446, H.R. 3513
Grants for research, training, technical assistance	H.R. 314, S. 103, H.R. 1446
U.S. Attorneys' hiring program	H.R. 314, S. 103, H.R. 1446
Research grants for pseudoephedrine alternatives	H.R. 1056
Reports on progress of anti-MA laws and regulations	H.R. 1056, H.R. 1446

*(as amended)

REFERENCES

[1] U.S. Department of Health and Human Services, Substance Abuse and Mental Health Services Administration, Office of Applied Statistics, *National Survey on Drug Use and Health Report*, September 16, 2005.

[2] National Institute of Justice, *Drug and Alcohol Use and Related Matters Among Arrestees, 2003,* 2004.

[3] U.S. Department of Justice, Drug Enforcement Agency, *Methamphetamine and Amphetamines*, Fact Sheet, available at [http://www.dea.gov/concern/ meth_factsheet.html], accessed on November 15, 2005.

[4] U.S. Executive Office of the President, Office of National Drug Control Policy, *Methamphetamine*, Fact Sheet available at [http://www.methresources.gov/], accessed on November 15, 2005.

[5] Ibid.

[6] For example, pseudoephedrine is an active ingredient in products like Sudafed, Actifed, NyQuil, and Claritin-D.

[7] U.S. DOJ, DEA, Methamphetamine Brief, accessed on November 15, 2005, available online at [http://www.usdoj.gov/dea/concern/meth_factsheet.html].

[8] A "super lab" is one that is capable of producing 10 pounds or more of MA per production cycle.

[9]   Drugs or other substances are classified under Schedule II after a finding that they (1) have a high potential for abuse, and (2) have a currently accepted medical use in treatment in the U.S. or a currently accepted medical use with severe dependence. Since 1971, all amphetamines, including all forms of MA, are classified under Schedule II.

[10]   For more information on regulation of pseudoephedrine in OTC medications see, CRS Report RS22177, *The Legal Regulation of Sales of Over-the-Counter Cold Medication*, by Jody Feder.

[11]   In addition to the programs and activities mentioned in this report, there are programs throughout the federal government that provide activities and services related to the prevention, education and treatment of MA, and to assisting localities with clandestine lab remediation. They are, however, beyond the scope of this report.

[12]   DEA Resources, For Law Enforcement Officers, Intelligence Reports, Federal-Wide Drug Seizures, available at [http://www.usdoj.gov/dea/].

[13]   U.S. Department of Justice, Office of Community Oriented Policing Services, *COPS Fact Sheet: Methamphetamine Initiative*, September 2004, available at [http://www.cops.usdoj.gov].

INDEX

A

academics, x, 59

acceptance, 75

access, 23, 26, 32, 42, 51, 71, 74, 83, 86, 88, 96, 105, 106, 120

accuracy, 46, 67

acetone, 43, 45, 138

acid, 138

addiction, 19, 61, 78, 87, 92, 107, 113

additives, 43, 44, 54, 55

ADHD, 137

adults, 77, 89, 96

advocacy, 83

affect, viii, 17, 25, 30, 31, 52, 72, 82, 85, 100, 109

Afghanistan, v, x, 18, 24, 27, 31, 32, 97, 98, 99, 100, 101, 102, 103, 104, 105, 106, 107, 108, 109, 111, 112, 113, 114, 115, 116, 117, 118, 119, 120, 121, 122, 123, 124, 125, 126, 127, 128, 129, 130, 131, 132, 133, 134, 135

Africa, 11, 60

age, 77, 78

agent, 11, 135

aggregates, 21

agriculture, 27, 52, 120

AIDS, 63, 64, 65, 69, 70, 74

Al Qaeda, x, 97, 107, 111, 112, 113, 123, 132

alcohol, 78, 81, 92, 93

alcohol use, 81

algae, 45

alternative, viii, ix, 3, 18, 20, 23, 24, 25, 27, 32, 35, 36, 37, 40, 41, 42, 43, 45, 48, 50, 51, 52, 65, 69, 83, 100, 104, 115, 116, 117, 118, 119, 120, 123, 124, 126, 134

alternatives, ix, x, 27, 36, 41, 43, 45, 51, 66, 97, 119, 141

altitude sickness, 38

ammonia, 43, 138

amphetamines, 13, 142

amphibia, 56

amphibians, 45, 56

animals, 25, 44, 45, 46

anorexia, 64, 69

antiemetics, 75

anxiety, 12, 74, 84, 138

appetite, 32, 38, 63, 65, 73, 74

argument, 26, 72, 81, 84, 88, 95

armed conflict, 48, 50, 122

armed forces, 30

arrest, vii, x, 1, 5, 11, 59, 62, 64, 66, 83, 84, 119

arthritis, 69, 92

Asia, 5, 6, 7, 11, 99, 112, 114, 127, 131, 132, 133, 134, 138

assessment, 11, 19, 46

assets, 4, 15, 18, 19, 27, 29, 105

attacks, 100, 108, 127

attention, viii, 2, 7, 17, 18, 29, 45, 93, 113, 114, 137

attitudes, 71

Attorney General, 140

Australia, 3, 12, 27

authority, viii, 17, 19, 24, 36, 40, 67, 85, 104, 108, 114, 122, 123, 134, 140

automobiles, 13, 28, 109

availability, vii, 17, 25, 47, 50, 92

awareness, 21, 118

Azerbaijan, 113

B

balance of payments, 20, 109

banking, 29

banks, 4, 29

barriers, 107

basic services, 42

behavior, 4, 72, 83, 137

beneficial effect, 76

benign, 45
biodiversity, 56
biological control, 24, 25, 26, 27, 45
birds, 45
birth, 88
black market, 64
blindness, 90
blood, 44
body, 73, 74, 93
Bolivia, viii, ix, 18, 21, 22, 23, 32, 35, 36, 37, 38, 39, 41, 42, 46, 47, 48, 49, 51, 52, 53, 54, 56, 57, 58
border control, 114
border security, xi, 114, 121, 137
brain, 74, 137
brain stem, 74
Brazil, 32, 36, 53
bribes, 15
Britain, 14
budding, 15
buildings, 42
Bulgaria, 12, 15
Burma, 31, 32
burn, 76
burning, 75

C

cabinet members, 109
California, 62, 63, 65, 66, 67, 68, 69, 71, 73, 74, 78, 81, 82, 83, 84, 85, 86, 88, 91, 92, 94, 95, 138
campaign strategies, 122
campaigns, 26, 98, 109, 116, 118, 121, 125
canals, 119
cancer, 64, 65, 66, 69, 70, 74, 76
candidates, 25, 109
cannabinoids, 65, 74, 76, 78, 87, 92, 93
cannabis, ix, x, 59, 60, 61, 62, 63, 64, 65, 66, 68, 69, 70, 71, 72, 74, 84, 88, 121
capsule, 64
carcinogen, 75
cardiac arrhythmia, 137
cardiovascular system, 72, 75
caregivers, 62, 65, 66, 67, 68, 69, 83, 84
Caribbean, 19, 31
cash crops, 27, 41, 122, 125
cash flow, 27
cast, 67
category a, 31
cation, viii, 18
Caucasus, 114, 120
CBS, 131
Central Asia, 106, 113, 114, 115, 120, 121, 132
central bank, 10

central nervous system, 137
channels, 29
chaos, 86
chemotherapy, 63, 64, 65, 74
children, 44, 140, 141
China, 3, 5, 11, 13, 32, 60
CIA, 11
civil war, 99, 104, 114
clinical trials, 65, 86
cocaine, vii, viii, ix, 11, 17, 19, 24, 30, 35, 36, 39, 40, 44, 45, 47, 81, 83, 89
coercion, 27
coffee, 38, 42
collaboration, 42
collateral, 106
Colombia, viii, ix, 14, 17, 20, 21, 22, 23, 25, 26, 29, 30, 31, 32, 33, 35, 36, 37, 38, 39, 40, 41, 42, 43, 44, 46, 47, 48, 49, 50, 51, 52, 53, 54, 55, 56, 57, 58, 125, 135
combustion, 76, 93
commitment, 27, 36, 49, 50, 98, 116, 126
communication, 92, 121
Communist Party, 5
community, 6, 7, 9, 10, 27, 42, 48, 50, 51, 98, 104, 107, 111, 115, 116
comparative advantage, 27
compatibility, 56
compensation, 27, 48, 49
compliance, 5, 27, 120
components, 6, 13, 18, 19, 20, 31, 32, 50, 64, 65
composition, 44, 106
compounds, 74
computer systems, 40
concentration, 30, 54, 55
concrete, 119
conduct, 48, 67, 82, 86, 117, 121, 124, 126
confidence, 13
conflict, 20, 21, 26, 30, 32, 44, 49, 50, 51, 108, 123
confrontation, 122
confusion, 81
congressional budget, 37, 42
consensus, 9
consent, 39
consolidation, 99, 106
conspiracy, 111
construction, 109, 119
consumer markets, 106
consumers, 25
consumption, vii, 17, 25, 86, 99, 107, 109, 112
control, vii, viii, 5, 9, 14, 17, 18, 19, 20, 21, 22, 23, 24, 25, 28, 30, 32, 36, 40, 44, 48, 50, 51, 61, 73, 74, 76, 81, 83, 88, 100, 101, 102, 104, 106, 108, 109, 114, 116, 125, 138

control group, 44

controlled studies, 72

Controlled Substances Act, ix, 59, 60, 61, 62, 63, 64, 66, 67, 71, 72, 77, 87, 90, 138

conversion, 24, 99

conversion rate, 99

corn, 48

corruption, x, 7, 9, 15, 23, 25, 28, 30, 97, 99, 107, 109, 113, 114, 122

costs, vii, 1, 3, 6, 8, 11, 54, 64, 82, 126

counsel, 61

Court of Appeals, 66, 67, 85, 86

coverage, 54

covering, 68

credit, 105, 106, 109, 119, 120

crime, vii, xi, 1, 2, 5, 7, 8, 9, 12, 18, 82, 115, 132, 137

criminal activity, vii, 1, 4, 6, 7, 8, 9, 11, 19

criminal behavior, 4

criminal justice system, 18

criminals, 114

criticism, 48, 56

crop production, vii, 1, 8, 51, 104, 119

crops, ix, 20, 24, 25, 26, 27, 35, 36, 38, 39, 40, 41, 42, 43, 44, 45, 46, 47, 48, 49, 50, 51, 52, 100, 106, 108, 111, 115, 117, 122, 125

crystals, 137

cultivation, viii, ix, x, 2, 6, 7, 8, 9, 14, 18, 20, 21, 22, 24, 25, 27, 32, 33, 35, 38, 39, 40, 41, 42, 45, 46, 47, 48, 49, 50, 67, 68, 69, 70, 97, 98, 99, 100, 101, 102, 104, 105, 106, 108, 109, 113, 114, 115, 116, 118, 119, 120, 121, 122, 125, 126, 130, 133, 134

currency, 4, 5, 9, 12, 14, 25, 120

current limit, 140

customers, 140

D

damage, 25, 43, 44, 125, 137

danger, 29, 75, 84, 107, 118

database, 54

death, 87, 108, 123

deaths, 49

debt, 105, 106, 118, 124, 134

debts, 135

decision makers, 113

decisions, 54, 123

decongestant, 137

defendants, ix, 59, 63

defense, 36, 63, 66, 71, 90, 91, 113, 121

deficit, 137

definition, 46

deforestation, 44

delivery, 65, 75, 93

demand, viii, 18, 19, 25, 29, 31, 50, 87, 99, 117, 118

democracy, viii, 30, 35, 36

denial, 91

density, 47

Department of Agriculture, 46, 135

Department of Defense, 5, 11, 28, 36, 112, 119, 121, 126

Department of Health and Human Services, 64, 77, 85, 141

Department of Justice, 60, 66, 81, 92, 119, 141, 142

depression, 92, 138

derivatives, 26, 61, 62, 89

desire, vii, 1, 9

destruction, 27, 45, 67, 108, 118, 121

detainees, 119

detection, 24, 39, 46, 121, 124

detention, vii, 1, 5

developing countries, 22, 26

developing nations, 27

development assistance, 40, 50, 52, 98, 122

dignity, 83

direct action, 100

direct costs, 26

directives, 121

disaster, 2

dislocation, viii, 17

disorder, 104, 137

displaced persons, 38, 50

displacement, 44, 50

dissenting opinion, 85

distress, 64

distribution, 4, 8, 19, 43, 66, 69, 84, 86, 91, 106

District of Columbia, 62, 71, 90

diversification, 120

diversity, 105

doctors, 64, 66, 68, 69, 71, 72, 77, 84, 87

domestic demand, 31, 50

Dominican Republic, 32

dosage, 76

draft, 81

drainage, 119

drought, 100, 105, 106

drug abuse, 18, 21, 51, 81, 86

drug addict, 78

drug addiction, 78

drug delivery, 65, 75, 76

drug education, 21

drug offense, 116, 119

drug therapy, 71

drug trafficking, vii, viii, x, 1, 2, 3, 4, 5, 7, 8, 9, 10, 11, 14, 18, 19, 26, 32, 33, 35, 36, 49, 97, 98, 104, 109, 116, 120, 121, 122, 123, 138

drug use, x, 7, 24, 25, 29, 31, 60, 61, 78, 81, 94, 115, 116, 118, 132

drugs, vii, x, 2, 4, 5, 6, 7, 8, 12, 13, 17, 18, 19, 20, 22, 23, 24, 25, 27, 28, 29, 30, 32, 39, 60, 61, 62, 65, 66, 73, 74, 76, 77, 78, 81, 83, 85, 86, 87, 88, 97, 104, 106, 112, 113, 114, 115, 118, 120, 121, 122, 139

dyspnea, 87

E

earnings, 19

earth, 4

East Asia, 3

economic assistance, 20, 22

economic competitiveness, 42

economic development, 27, 32, 50, 107

economic growth, 20, 26

economic resources, 24

ecosystem, 45

Ecuador, 22, 23, 32, 36, 37, 44, 48, 55, 57

Egypt, 11, 15

election, x, 18, 41, 49, 69, 97, 98, 116

embargo, 5

emergence, 114

emotion, 88

emotional responses, 74

emotions, 76

employees, 4, 123

employment, 20, 42

empowerment, 123

England, 69, 74, 87, 92, 93, 95

entrepreneurs, 42

environment, ix, 35, 43, 44, 45, 46, 126

environmental conditions, 99

environmental effects, 55

environmental factors, 99

environmental impact, 44

Environmental Protection Agency, 43, 47, 56, 140

environmental regulations, 140

EPA, 43, 44, 47, 54, 55, 140

epidemic, vii

epilepsy, 74

equality, 88

equipment, 14, 20, 21, 30, 31, 32, 36, 115, 116, 118, 121, 124

estimating, 7

ethics, 83

ethnic groups, 105

Eurasia, 132

Europe, viii, 5, 11, 14, 27, 35, 99, 112, 113, 114, 120, 133, 138

evidence, 3, 10, 14, 43, 44, 47, 61, 62, 63, 64, 65, 67, 72, 73, 75, 76, 78, 81, 84, 87, 92, 114, 119, 121, 132

excuse, 84

exercise, 19

expertise, 106

experts, 27, 64, 72, 73, 77, 86, 99, 105, 106, 109, 116

exports, 3, 6, 10, 21

F

failure, x, 52, 90, 97, 116

faith, 67

farmers, ix, 25, 27, 36, 40, 41, 42, 47, 49, 50, 51, 99, 100, 104, 105, 106, 108, 115, 116, 118, 119, 121, 122, 124, 130, 134

fatigue, 138

fatwa, 116

FBIS, 131, 133

FDA, 62, 63, 64, 74, 75, 85, 86, 87, 93, 95

fear, 25, 45, 46, 82, 83, 84, 100, 108, 109, 111, 114, 122

federal law, ix, 59, 60, 65, 68, 69, 75, 84, 91

federalism, 85

feet, 48

fertilizers, 106

Filipino, 12

finance, 6, 31

financial institutions, 19, 29, 32

financial support, 111, 120

financial system, 23

financing, 104

flora, 44

flora and fauna, 44

focusing, 25

food, vii, 1, 3, 8, 10, 13, 41, 44, 45, 46, 48, 49, 86, 125

foreign aid, 2, 3, 22, 26, 27, 50

foreign assistance, 2, 22, 31

foreign banks, 19

foreign exchange, 4, 6, 9, 12, 20

foreign intelligence, 111

foreign person, 21

foreign policy, vii, viii, 1, 7, 17, 29, 30, 31

forests, 44, 48

France, 10, 44, 131, 132, 133

freedom, 121

fruits, 42

fuel, 3, 39, 50, 100, 109

funding, vii, 20, 23, 25, 27, 33, 36, 37, 48, 50, 52, 78, 104, 111, 115, 121, 122, 125, 126, 127, 138, 139
funds, viii, 5, 12, 20, 21, 23, 32, 35, 36, 37, 62, 111, 125, 126, 127
fungus, 40, 46

G

Gallup Poll, 77
gangs, 9
GDP, x, 97, 100, 109
General Accounting Office, 94, 126
generation, 3, 50
Germany, 115, 131
glaucoma, 63, 65, 66, 69, 74
goals, vii, viii, 17, 31, 50, 88, 98, 107, 116, 118
gold, 4
governance, 30, 33, 36, 42, 87
government, vii, x, 1, 4, 5, 6, 7, 10, 11, 13, 15, 18, 19, 20, 21, 22, 24, 26, 27, 30, 31, 38, 40, 41, 42, 44, 45, 46, 48, 49, 50, 59, 61, 62, 63, 67, 72, 73, 74, 75, 77, 82, 83, 84, 85, 86, 87, 88, 90, 94, 97, 98, 99, 101, 102, 104, 105, 106, 108, 109, 113, 114, 115, 116, 118, 119, 120, 121, 122, 123, 125, 126, 130, 134, 135, 142
grants, 36, 115, 139, 140, 141
grasslands, 48
Greece, 60
gross domestic product, 3
groups, ix, x, 7, 8, 25, 26, 30, 31, 32, 35, 36, 44, 48, 50, 56, 57, 74, 93, 97, 99, 104, 105, 106, 107, 108, 109, 111, 113, 114, 115, 120, 122, 123, 126, 130
growth, 22, 25, 39, 49, 99, 106, 109, 112, 115, 118, 121
Guatemala, 31, 32
guidance, 121
guidelines, 139

H

hallucinations, 137
hands, 21, 107
hard currency, 3, 11
harm, x, 25, 44, 45, 48, 60, 66, 76, 78, 90, 91
harmful effects, 61, 76
harvesting, 106
Hawaii, 68, 70, 91
healing, 60

health, ix, 18, 25, 29, 35, 42, 43, 44, 45, 46, 48, 49, 50, 55, 62, 65, 69, 70, 73, 74, 75, 85, 88, 107, 112, 132, 135
health and environmental effects, ix, 35, 43, 44, 46
health care, 18, 51
health care costs, 18
health services, 42
heat, 76
herbicide, ix, 35, 39, 43, 44, 47, 48, 55, 125
heroin, vii, viii, ix, 1, 3, 4, 7, 8, 9, 11, 13, 15, 17, 19, 24, 35, 36, 47, 62, 75, 98, 99, 100, 104, 106, 107, 111, 112, 113, 114, 116, 120, 121, 126, 127, 131, 132
high school, 61
hiring, 140, 141
HIV, 66, 107, 113, 115, 132
HIV infection, 107, 113, 115
HIV/AIDS, 66, 132
host, 21, 23, 26, 27, 37
hostility, 45
House, ix, 11, 27, 59, 60, 61, 62, 63, 75, 88, 89, 110, 114, 126, 127, 131, 132, 133, 134, 135, 139, 140
human brain, 74
human rights, 30, 32
hyperactivity, 137
hyperthermia, 137
hypocrisy, 89

I

ideas, 23
identification, 46, 70, 83
identity, 54
ideology, 86, 88
illegal drug use, vii
imagery, 8, 14, 46
images, 46
IMF, 109, 131
immune system, 74
imperialism, 27
implementation, 23, 29, 31, 62, 116, 118, 123
imports, 3, 28, 109, 140, 141
imprisonment, 84
incarceration, 64, 118
incentives, 27, 50, 100
incidence, 18, 44
inclusion, 2
income, vii, ix, 1, 6, 8, 9, 13, 14, 24, 26, 27, 35, 42, 50, 51, 109, 115
India, 13, 32, 60
indication, 47, 86
indigenous, 38, 39, 41, 48, 49
industry, 19, 87

infection, 114
infectious disease, 64
influence, 25, 29, 36, 71, 82, 83, 88, 104, 108, 109
infrastructure, ix, 31, 36, 37, 41, 42, 50, 51, 109,
　　116, 118, 119, 120, 121, 124, 125, 133
initiation, 81
inmates, 18
insects, 25
insecurity, 27, 113, 122
instability, 30, 41, 49, 122
institution building, 37
institutions, 23, 29, 32, 115, 116, 117, 120
intelligence, viii, x, 5, 7, 8, 9, 11, 17, 28, 37, 97, 107,
　　111, 112, 113, 117, 121, 122, 124, 126
intelligence gathering, 107, 113
intensity, 134
intent, 3, 83, 86
interest, ix, 2, 22, 31, 35, 43, 50, 51, 113, 115, 122,
　　134
interference, 83, 85, 104
intermediaries, 38
International Monetary Fund, 131
international relations, xi, 137
international terrorism, 3, 29, 104
intervention, 20, 27, 87, 114
interview, 133
intoxication, 72
intraocular, 74
intraocular pressure, 74
investment, 109
Iran, 106, 112, 113, 114, 115
Iraq, 18
isolation, 51
Italy, 115

J

Jamaica, 19, 32
Japan, 3, 4, 5, 6, 8, 12, 13, 14, 27
jobs, 42
joints, 93
judges, 119, 140
judgment, 18
judicial branch, 66
Judiciary Committee, 82, 140
juries, ix, 59
jurisdiction, 119
justice, 10, 21, 23, 37, 42, 124
justification, 42, 113

K

Kazakhstan, 113, 114
knowledge, 15
Korea, vii, 1, 2, 3, 4, 5, 6, 7, 8, 9, 10, 11, 12, 13, 14,
　　15
Kyrgyzstan, 113, 114

L

labor, 11, 49, 106, 119
land, 13, 25, 28, 39, 40, 42, 45, 50, 51, 52, 99, 105,
　　106, 118, 120, 125, 130
land tenure, 42
language, 5, 10, 62
Laos, 32
Latin America, 21, 24, 30, 54, 56, 57, 58
law enforcement, 7, 8, 13, 18, 19, 20, 21, 22, 23, 24,
　　27, 28, 30, 32, 50, 66, 69, 70, 71, 81, 82, 83, 84,
　　94, 111, 115, 116, 117, 121, 124, 134, 138, 139
laws, ix, x, 4, 29, 41, 59, 60, 61, 62, 63, 65, 66, 67,
　　68, 69, 71, 72, 78, 81, 82, 84, 85, 86, 87, 88, 89,
　　92, 93, 94, 118, 119, 141
lead, x, 20, 44, 60, 77, 78, 93, 105, 113, 115, 122,
　　137
leadership, viii, 18, 115
legislation, xi, 31, 36, 43, 48, 50, 61, 77, 86, 116,
　　137, 138
lending, 106, 119
liability, 68, 83
licenses, 29, 66
likelihood, 48, 56, 124
links, x, 4, 19, 51, 97, 109, 112, 119, 123
loans, 32, 105, 106
local authorities, 122
local community, 118
local government, 51, 66, 67
location, 105
long distance, 49
loss of appetite, 65
Louisiana, 85, 95
loyalty, 6, 13
LSD, 62
lung cancer, 75

M

management, 51
manpower, 111
manufacturing, 2, 7, 62, 139
marijuana, vii, ix, x, 17, 19, 20, 39, 59, 60, 61, 62,
　　63, 64, 65, 66, 67, 68, 69, 70, 71, 72, 73, 74, 75,

76, 77, 78, 81, 82, 83, 84, 85, 86, 87, 88, 89, 90, 91, 92, 93, 94, 95
market, ix, 6, 13, 18, 19, 25, 28, 29, 36, 39, 41, 61, 73, 81, 83, 86, 105, 106, 114, 118, 119, 120, 130, 138
marketing, ix, 36, 38, 41, 51, 93
markets, 6, 7, 12, 25, 26, 27, 38, 42, 51, 99, 104, 107, 112, 119
marriage, 88
MAS, 49
measures, 18, 19, 25, 71, 82, 88, 94, 98, 115, 121, 122
media, 5, 7
Medicaid, 66
Medicare, 66
medication, 65, 75, 140
memory, 74
memory formation, 74
mentoring, 121
metals, 4
methodology, 46, 94
Mexico, 11, 19, 25, 32, 138, 139, 140
Miami, 57
Middle East, 10, 14, 60, 99, 106, 133
military, viii, xi, 4, 5, 6, 13, 15, 17, 18, 20, 25, 27, 28, 29, 30, 31, 32, 36, 37, 40, 48, 49, 98, 104, 105, 111, 112, 113, 114, 115, 117, 121, 122, 123, 124, 125
military aid, 29, 30
military spending, 5
militias, 108
minority, 73
missions, viii, 6, 35, 36, 39, 40, 48, 116, 117, 121, 124
mobility, 121
models, 94
momentum, 9, 52
money, 4, 19, 29, 109, 111, 112, 114
money laundering, 4, 19, 29, 111, 112, 114
monitoring, 140, 141
Montana, 70, 91
mood, 92
mood disorder, 92
morphine, 60, 77, 81, 87, 89, 106, 114, 120, 131
mortality, 45
Moscow, 11, 12, 133
motion, 66
motivation, 11, 83
motives, 105, 130
motor skills, 74
mountains, 45
movement, viii, x, 17, 29, 49, 60, 65, 82, 87, 88, 95, 104, 111, 114, 121

movement disorders, 65
MSNBC.com, 96
multiple sclerosis, 74, 75
muscle spasms, 66, 73
muscles, 93
Myanmar, 15

N

narcolepsy, 137
narcotic, 20, 24, 25, 26, 27, 104, 113, 121, 125
narcotics, vii, x, xi, 3, 4, 14, 17, 20, 21, 22, 23, 24, 25, 26, 27, 28, 29, 30, 31, 32, 97, 98, 99, 100, 104, 106, 107, 109, 110, 111, 113, 114, 115, 118, 119, 121, 122, 123, 124, 126, 129, 132, 134
National Institutes of Health, 91
national interests, 32
national parks, 43, 45
National Public Radio, 132
national security, 5, 28, 112
National Security Council, 117
natural enemies, 45
nausea, 63, 64, 65, 73, 75, 76
needs, vii, 1, 6, 7, 11, 71, 86, 105, 119
negative consequences, 51
negotiation, 29
nervous system, 74
network, 15, 28
networking, 107
NGOs, 42
Nigeria, 32
nodes, 26
North America, 45, 106
North Korea, v, vii, 1, 2, 3, 4, 5, 6, 7, 8, 9, 10, 11, 12, 13, 14, 15
nuclear program, 3, 11
nuclear weapons, 3, 14

O

OAS, 22, 43, 55
obesity, 137
observations, 46, 71, 94
offenders, 119
oil, 3, 27, 36, 42
oils, 93
opiates, 81, 106, 107, 111, 112, 113, 114, 115, 127, 130, 131
opinion polls, 71
organization, 12, 13, 30, 42, 105, 106, 111
Organization of American States, 22, 43, 57

organizations, x, 8, 9, 19, 22, 28, 36, 41, 42, 46, 51, 55, 72, 84, 88, 93, 94, 96, 97, 104, 107, 111, 120, 121, 138
orientation, 33
output, x, 6, 98, 99, 100, 104, 105, 118

P

Pacific, 31, 133
pain, 60, 65, 69, 73, 74, 75, 76, 77, 83, 87
paints, 9
Pakistan, 24, 32, 106, 109, 111, 112, 113, 114, 115, 127, 129, 130, 132
Panama, 32, 36, 53
Paraguay, 32
paranoia, 138
Parliament, 112
penalties, 27, 68, 69, 70, 84, 87, 93, 138, 141
Pentagon, 15
perceptions, 78
permit, ix, x, 26, 27, 59, 60, 64, 65, 66, 71, 76, 77, 85, 88, 93, 140
Persian Gulf, 132
personal relations, 36
personal relationship, 36
perspective, 123
Peru, viii, ix, 21, 22, 23, 25, 32, 35, 36, 37, 38, 39, 40, 41, 42, 46, 47, 48, 49, 51, 52, 54, 56, 57, 58
pesticide, 54, 55, 56
pests, 45
pharmaceuticals, 9, 15, 72, 74, 82, 93
Philippines, 6
planning, 78
plants, 24, 25, 43, 44, 45, 47, 67, 69, 70
police, 4, 5, 12, 13, 21, 25, 27, 30, 37, 48, 49, 65, 81, 82, 83, 108, 109, 115, 118, 119, 121, 123, 127
policy choice, 85
policy initiative, 118
policy makers, vii, 1, 7
political instability, viii, 17, 41, 107, 122
political leaders, 116
political legitimacy, 123
political opposition, 30
political parties, 94
politics, 86
poor, 6, 27, 51, 74, 75, 114, 125
popular vote, 86
population, 49, 68, 78, 90, 99, 104, 124, 125
portfolio, 2, 9
ports, 19
potassium, 45
poverty, 30, 50, 51
power, 3, 19, 21, 67, 85, 104, 108, 123

preference, 117
preparation, 76
pressure, 70, 104, 106
prevention, 23, 29, 51, 61, 116, 139, 142
prices, vii, 17, 19, 23, 25, 27, 40, 47, 52, 64, 100, 106, 107, 124
principle, 88
private investment, 120
private sector, 42, 51
private sector investment, 51
probability, 44
producers, 24, 26, 36, 45, 111, 138
production, vii, viii, x, xi, 1, 2, 3, 5, 6, 7, 8, 9, 11, 17, 18, 19, 20, 21, 22, 24, 25, 26, 27, 28, 30, 32, 38, 43, 44, 45, 47, 51, 97, 98, 99, 100, 102, 104, 106, 108, 109, 113, 114, 116, 118, 119, 121, 124, 126, 130, 137, 138, 139, 140, 141
production quota, 140
productivity, 18, 25, 56, 100
profitability, 105, 106
profits, vii, x, 1, 8, 18, 26, 29, 50, 87, 97, 100, 104, 106, 107, 109, 111, 126, 134
program, viii, 3, 6, 11, 14, 19, 20, 21, 22, 27, 32, 33, 35, 36, 40, 41, 42, 43, 45, 47, 48, 50, 52, 63, 69, 70, 78, 82, 88, 116, 119, 120, 122, 124, 125, 126, 127, 139, 140, 141
proliferation, 2, 3, 106
propaganda, 7
proposition, 73, 88
public awareness, 98, 117, 118
public education, 71
public health, xi, 70, 86, 107, 112, 113, 114, 115, 125, 132, 137
public opinion, 71, 72, 77, 83
public policy, 2, 28, 82
public safety, xi, 137
public support, 25, 83

Q

questioning, 2, 112
quotas, 141

R

range, x, 3, 6, 14, 15, 21, 22, 46, 60, 93, 97, 99, 113, 118, 124, 139
rape, 11
reality, 7
reasoning, 82
receptors, 74
recognition, 41, 74, 90

reconstruction, 98, 107, 134
recovery, x, 97
recreation, 81
reduction, 19, 24, 25, 26, 29, 32, 40, 46, 51, 53, 117, 120, 126
refining, 7, 26, 106
Registry, 140
regulation, 85, 86, 138, 140, 142
regulations, 141
regulators, 54
rehabilitation, 22, 42
rehabilitation program, 22
rejection, 64
relationship, ix, 15, 35, 43, 66, 67
relationships, 8, 99, 105, 106, 107, 111, 112
reliability, ix, 7, 10, 35, 43, 46
remittances, 10
remote sensing, 8
repair, 124
replacement, 122, 125
resistance, 86, 122, 125
resolution, x, 46, 60, 62
resources, 12, 18, 19, 21, 28, 31, 51, 52, 104, 124
respiratory, 65
responsibility, 85, 86, 109, 117, 123
restitution, 49
retail, 47, 92, 138
revenue, x, 5, 9, 97, 104, 106, 108, 109
rewards, 23, 125
rights, 85, 88
risk, 19, 30, 43, 44, 65, 84, 85, 86, 87, 122
risk assessment, 44
rubber, 42
rule of law, viii, 35, 36, 38, 42, 107, 123
rural areas, 49, 105, 120
rural poverty, 134
Russia, 5, 99, 107, 112, 113, 114, 120, 132, 133

S

safety, 55, 62, 64, 72, 73, 77, 78, 85, 86, 87, 90, 112, 125
sales, 9, 14, 19, 29, 140
sampling, 46
sanctions, 2, 20, 22, 26, 27, 29, 32, 64
satellite, 8, 46
scheduling, 86, 93
school, 42
Secretary of Defense, 127, 134
security, viii, x, 6, 17, 29, 31, 33, 49, 51, 97, 98, 107, 108, 109, 111, 112, 113, 114, 115, 116, 117, 119, 120, 121, 122, 123, 125, 126, 132, 134
seed, 120

seizure, 3, 120
self, 75, 82, 89, 114
Senate, 2, 11, 61, 62, 82, 89, 94, 124, 125, 139, 140
sensations, 87
sentencing, 63, 139, 140
September 11, 100, 127
series, viii, 4, 17, 115, 120, 130
services, 5, 6, 36, 106, 111, 113, 120, 141, 142
severity, 43
sex, 88
side effects, 87, 93
sign, 8, 40, 51, 70
Singapore, 12
sinus, 138
sites, 19, 48, 51, 52, 140
skills, 72
smoke, 65, 75, 76, 81, 93
smokers, 82
smoking, ix, x, 59, 65, 72, 75, 76, 81, 87, 93, 137
social development, 42
social fabric, 98
social welfare, 18
sodium, 138
sodium hydroxide, 138
soil, 9, 40, 45, 51, 125
South Korea, 3, 5, 6, 7, 8, 10, 12
Southeast Asia, 7, 8
Soviet Union, 113
spasticity, 63, 69, 73, 75
species, 4, 45, 46
spectrum, 65
speculation, 6, 7, 9, 14, 15, 104
speech, 66
speed, 48
spillover effects, 20
spinal cord, 74
stability, 21, 26, 27, 29, 30, 50, 98, 107, 109, 116, 121, 123, 124, 126, 134
standards, 62, 73, 77, 120
state control, 93
state laws, 71, 81, 87
states' rights, 85
statutes, 54, 68
stigma, 26
stimulant, 38, 137
stomach, 38
storage, 119, 121
strategic planning, 37
strategies, 31, 41, 98
street drugs, 61
stress, 7, 26, 29
stroke, 137
structural barriers, 105

students, 61
subsistence, 26, 51
substance abuse, 139, 140
substitutes, 25, 74
substitution, 41, 46, 52
suicide, 111
sulfuric acid, 43, 45
summer, 89
supervision, 62, 64, 70, 76
suppliers, 47, 71
supply, viii, 9, 13, 17, 18, 19, 20, 21, 24, 25, 28, 31,
    35, 36, 39, 40, 45, 50, 64, 70, 99, 100, 104, 105,
    121
suppression, 20
Supreme Court, 66, 67, 71, 73, 84, 85, 89, 91, 92, 95
surfactant, 39, 43, 44, 55
surplus, 25
surveillance, 46
survival, 10, 104
susceptibility, 45
suspects, 4, 119
sustainability, ix, 35, 42, 43, 47, 50, 52
sustainable development, 41
symptomatic treatment, 72
symptoms, x, 59, 69, 70, 72, 74, 87, 92
syndrome, 25
systems, viii, 17, 21, 28, 37, 42, 65, 72, 75, 76, 86,
    93, 106, 119, 120

T

Taiwan, 4, 8
Tajikistan, 113, 114, 127, 133
Taliban, x, 24, 97, 100, 101, 102, 104, 105, 107, 111,
    112, 113, 120, 123, 130, 133
targets, 117, 119, 122, 124, 127, 139
technical assistance, 20, 22, 29, 42
technician, 140
technology, 6, 14, 117
telephone, 69
temperature, 48, 76
tendons, 93
terminally ill, 75
terrorism, vii, 1, 7, 29, 31, 98, 111, 115, 124, 132
terrorist organization, 113, 126
Thailand, 6, 14, 15, 32
therapeutic benefits, 73, 74
therapy, 76, 87
threat, vii, viii, x, 17, 22, 26, 28, 51, 70, 84, 97, 112,
    116, 118, 123
threats, 98, 107, 114, 125
threshold, 2
thresholds, 139

time, ix, 6, 9, 13, 14, 23, 36, 45, 49, 50, 59, 62, 63,
    64, 70, 76, 99, 112, 122, 125, 131
tin, 74
tobacco, 65, 93
total costs, 18
toxic effect, 25
toxicity, 44, 45, 55, 93
tracking, 8, 29
trade, vii, x, xi, 1, 3, 4, 5, 7, 9, 10, 14, 19, 23, 25, 26,
    29, 30, 32, 43, 48, 50, 64, 97, 98, 99, 104, 105,
    106, 107, 109, 110, 111, 112, 113, 114, 115, 116,
    118, 122, 123, 124, 130, 137
trade deficit, 10
trade union, 25
trading, 5, 8, 12, 15, 28
tradition, 38, 83
traffic, 3, 4, 26, 83, 87, 113, 115
traffic stops, 83
training, 21, 23, 28, 29, 30, 36, 42, 73, 114, 115, 117,
    118, 119, 121, 124, 127, 139, 140, 141
training programs, 21, 121
transactions, 29
transformation, 130
transport, 28, 109, 130
transportation, ix, 22, 26, 36, 41, 42, 45, 51, 104,
    108, 111, 119, 124, 130
trauma, 75
treaties, 5, 29
trees, 48
trend, 21, 40, 94, 99, 105, 114
trial, 10, 66, 67, 87, 90
Turkey, 112, 113
Turkmenistan, 113, 114

U

UK, 130, 132, 133, 135
uniform, 86
unions, 49
United Kingdom, 44, 105, 112, 113, 115, 116
United Nations, 14, 19, 23, 29, 38, 39, 46, 99, 100,
    104, 115, 129
United States, vii, viii, ix, x, 1, 2, 3, 5, 7, 13, 17, 18,
    19, 20, 21, 22, 23, 24, 25, 26, 27, 28, 29, 30, 31,
    35, 36, 39, 40, 41, 42, 43, 44, 46, 47, 48, 51, 52,
    60, 61, 62, 64, 65, 72, 73, 74, 77, 84, 85, 87, 89,
    91, 93, 97, 98, 99, 105, 107, 111, 112, 114, 115,
    116, 120, 123, 132, 133, 139
uranium, 6
USSR, 14
Uzbekistan, 113, 114, 126

V

validity, 88
vapor, 76
variable, 130
variables, 50
vegetation, 43
Venezuela, 32, 36
vessels, 3, 4, 31
Vietnam, 32
violence, 21, 30, 33, 51, 104, 108, 113, 138
violent crime, 18, 32, 61
voice, 61
vomiting, 63, 64, 74
voters, ix, 59, 60, 67, 68, 69, 70, 71, 83
voting, 72
vulnerability, 21, 111

W

wages, 109
war, x, 21, 28, 60, 66, 81, 83, 98, 104
War on Terror, 126, 128
warlords, 99, 100, 123

water, 39, 42, 43, 44, 45, 56, 105, 106, 119
wealth, viii, 17, 92
weapons, vii, 1, 6, 7, 111, 112, 120, 123, 132
weapons of mass destruction, vii, 1, 6, 7
weight loss, 63, 64
welfare, xi, 85, 137
well-being, 18
Western Europe, 99, 107, 112, 113, 132
wheat, 3, 27, 119
White House, ix, 18, 30, 35, 53
wholesale, 19, 138
wildlife, 44
wind, 48
withdrawal, 104
women, 44
wood, 42
workers, 25, 26, 44
workplace, 18
World Bank, 107, 108, 109, 129, 131
World Health Organization, 132
writing, 68, 88, 120

Y

yield, 6, 9, 19, 99, 100